CLEP

College Level Examination Program

THE FIVE GENERAL EXAMINATIONS

by David R. Turner, M.S. in Ed.

arco 219 Park Avenue South
New York, N.Y. 10003

Fourth Edition (B-3443)

Published by ARCO PUBLISHING COMPANY, INC.
219 Park Avenue South, New York, N.Y. 10003

Library of Congress Cataloging in Publication Data

Turner, David Reuben, 1915-
    C. L. E. P., college level examination program.

    1. Universities and colleges--Examinations.
2. Universities and colleges--Entrance requirements.
3. Advanced placement programs (Education)
I. Title   II. Title: College level examination
program.

LB2367.T75   1978   378.1'66'4   78-11953

ISBN 0-668-04146-3 (Library Edition)
ISBN 0-668-04150-1 (Paper Edition)

Printed in the United States of America

CONTENTS

HOW TO USE THIS INDEX
Slightly bend the right-hand edge
of the book. This will expose
the corresponding Parts
which match the index, below.

...continued on next page

PART

1

2

3

4

5

6

CONTENTS continued

PART SIX: SOCIAL SCIENCES-HISTORY

PART

1
2
3
4
5
6

ACKNOWLEDGEMENT

We would like to acknowledge the assistance
of the following authors who contributed
questions for the Verisimilar Examinations
included in this book:

Roger Gaess, B.A.,M.A.
K. Heavil, B.A., M.A.
Ronald S. Horning, B.A., M.A.
Sherry Manasse, A.B., M.A.
Ralph Sperry, B.A.
Sol J. Barer, B.S., M.S., Ph.D.
Ellen Colwell, B.A., M.S.
Robert Kern Curtis, A.B., Ph.L., M.S.
Judy Plano, B.S., M.A.T.
Robert Menschel, B.A.
Julie Hanson, B.A.
Martin McDonough, B.A., M.A.

WHAT CLEP WILL DO FOR YOU

To get the greatest help from this book, please understand that it has been carefully organized. You must, therefore, plan to use it accordingly. Study this concise, readable book earnestly and your way will be clear. You will progress directly to your goal. You will not be led off into blind alleys and useless fields of study.

COLLEGE WITHOUT TEARS

This book is for people who have attained the college level of education in nontraditional ways. It is for those who have gained their education outside the classroom. It tells about examinations that help you show what you know. These examinations give you the opportunity to

1) have your educational attainment validated, thereby establishing the fact that you possess college-level skills and knowledge,
2) attain college credit for the knowledge you have attained outside the classroom and help you progress toward a degree,
3) avoid classroom attendance in subjects you already know and obtain advanced placement in a college curriculum,
4) qualify for jobs in industry that require college training as a prerequisite for employment or advancement,
5) demonstrate for your own satisfaction the college-level ability that you have gained.

If you want to take the CLEP exams but are reluctant for fear they may be too difficult, don't sell yourself short. The exams are not easy, but this book defines their difficulty and shows how to get ready. So read on . . .this book is for you. You will find out all about the CLEP General Examinations. You will learn:

1) how to register for the examinations;
2) where and when they are given;
3) how to interpret your scores and use the results to your best advantage;
4) how to prepare for the exams with hundreds of questions and answers typical of those found on the actual tests.

CAN YOU PREPARE FOR CLEP?

We believe, most certainly, that you *can* with the aid of this "self-tutor!"

It's not a "pony." It's not a complete college education. It's not a "crib sheet." It's no *How To Succeed On Tests Without Really Trying.* There's nothing in it that will give you a higher score than you really deserve. It's just a top quality course which you can readily review in less than twenty hours . . .a digest of material which you might have written yourself after many hundred hours of laborious digging.

To prepare for your test, you must motivate yourself . . .get into the right frame of mind for learning from your "self-tutor." You'll have to urge *yourself* to learn and that's the only way people ever learn. Your efforts to score high on the test will be greatly aided by the fact that you will have to do this job on your own . . .perhaps without a teacher. Psychologists have demonstrated that studies undertaken for a clear goal . . .which you initiate yourself and actively pursue . . .are the most successful. You, yourself, want to pass this test. That's why you bought this book and embarked on this program. Nobody forced you to do it, and there may be nobody to lead you through the course. Your self-activity is going to be the key to your success in the forthcoming weeks.

Used correctly, your "self-tutor" will show you what to expect and will give you a speedy brush-up on the subjects peculiar to your exam. Some of these are subjects not taught in schools at all. Even if your study time is very limited, you will:

- become familiar with the type of examination it is;
- improve your general examination-taking skill;
- improve your skill in analyzing and answering questions involving reasoning, judgment, comparison, and evaluation;
- improve your speed and skill in reading and understanding what you read—an important part of your ability to learn and an important part of most tests;
- prepare yourself in the particular fields which measure your learning.

This book will tell you exactly what to study by presenting in full every type of question you will get on the actual exam. You'll do better merely by familiarizing yourself with them.

This book will help you find your weaknesses and find them fast. Once you know where you're weak, you can get right to work (before the exam,) and concentrate on those soft spots. This is the kind of selective study which yields maximum results for every hour spent.

This book will give you the *feel* of the exam. Almost all our sample and practice questions are taken from actual previous exams. Since previous exams are not always available for inspection by the public, these sample test questions are quite important for you. The day you take your exam you'll see how closely this book follows the format of the real exam.

This book will give you confidence *now*, while you are preparing for the exam. It will build your self-confidence as you proceed. It will beat those dreaded before-test jitters that have hurt so many other test-takers.

This book stresses the modern, multiple-choice type of question because that's the kind you'll undoubtedly get on your exam. In answering these questions you will add to your knowledge by learning the correct answers, naturally. However, you will not be satisfied with merely the correct choice for each question. You will want to find out why the other choices are incorrect. This will jog your memory...help you remember much you thought you had forgotten. You'll be preparing and enriching yourself for the exam to come.

Of course, the great advantage in all this lies in narrowing your study to just those fields in which you're most likely to be quizzed. Answer enough questions in those fields and the chances are very good that you'll meet a few of them again on the actual test. After all, the number of questions an examiner can draw upon in these fields is rather limited. Examiners frequently employ the same questions on different tests for this very reason.

Arco Publishing Company has been involved with trends and methods in testing ever since the firm was founded in 1937. We have *specialized* in books that prepare people for exams. Based on this experience it is our modest boast that you probably have in your hands the best book that could be prepared to help *you* score high. Now, if you'll take a little advice on using it properly, we can assure you that you will do well.

To write this book we carefully analyzed every detail surrounding the forthcoming examination...

- official and unofficial announcements concerning the examination;
- all the available previous examinations;
- many related examinations;
- technical literature that explains and forecasts the examination.

As a result of all this (which you, happily, have not had to do) we've been able to create the "climate" of your test, and to give you a fairly accurate picture of what's involved.

PART ONE

What CLEP is All About.

How You Can Make It Help You.

LET'S TALK ABOUT CLEP

Anyone may take the CLEP examinations to gain college credit without attending formal college classes. If you possess college-level knowledge gained through study or experience and wish to earn credit for what you know, these exams can be important for you. If you are attending college for the first time you may be able to gain a whole year's credit, thus saving time as well as tuition. If you are already attending college, you may be able to meet your general education requirements through CLEP examinations. If you are unable to attend college full-time, CLEP can provide you with a flexible way of progressing at your own speed toward a college degree. The information in this chapter is summarized from various official announcements. We urge you to study it carefully because it is written to help you achieve the best possible score on your examination.

Do you have know-how that was gained from other than accredited college training? Have you read widely, or had life experiences that qualify you for jobs you can't get because you don't have the college credits? Or are you disqualified for advanced placement in college because you don't have the course credits from an accredited institution? If so, you are among the large number of people for whom the College-Level Examination Program is geared.

The College-Level Examination Program (C.L.E.P.) offers you an opportunity to show a college admissions officer, or a prospective employer, or just yourself, what you know in a variety of subject areas. Some employers in business, industry, professional groups, and government use the results of this test when they want to assess a potential employee's educational level, regardless of the credits listed on his resume. Many college admissions officers use the results of the test to determine where to place college applicants in their traditional four-year programs.

C.L.E.P. (College-Level Examination Program) is given by the College Entrance Examination Board, a nonprofit membership organization, which for many years has offered testing and guidance services to schools and colleges and to students who progress from high school to college in the usual way. However, for those who have gained their education through correspondence courses, television courses, home-study courses via records or tape cassettes, on-the-job training, and experience, no widely recognized evaluation test has been available until C.L.E.P.

The C.L.E.P. examinations may be taken by anyone who so desires if he but fulfills the formalities described in this chapter and pay the fees. However, there is no charge to military personnel on active duty.

THE CLEP EXAMINATION: GENERAL AND SUBJECT

The College-Level Examination Program (CLEP) consists of examinations that you may take for college credit or to demonstrate college-level competency. The program comprises two types of examinations: the *General Examinations* and the *Subject Examinations*.

The *Subject Examinations* test knowledge of a specific topic and are similar to the final examination in a particular undergraduate course.

The *General Examinations* are broader in scope and cover material you might be expected to know after two years' study in a basic liberal arts curriculum. They do not measure specialized knowledge of a particular discipline, nor are they based on a particular curriculum or course of study. They measure broad-based ability that can be acquired in a number of ways, through personal reading, employment, television, radio, adult classes, or advanced high school work.

EXTERNAL DEGREE PROGRAMS

A new trend in American higher education is the expansion of external degree programs. The traditional way of obtaining a college degree is to attend formal classes on campus for a period of about four years. Colleges that offer external degree programs allow independent study, have individualized curriculums with time schedules to suit the learner's needs, use new instructional methods, and have examinations to satisfy some of the degree requirements. In some cases, degrees are awarded on the basis of examination only.

CLEP Tests are used extensively in external degree programs. This kind of program is being developed in a number of states and at a variety of institutions. If you wish to learn on your own and would like to investigate an example of such a program, you may write Regents External Degrees, 99 Washington Avenue, Albany, New York 12210 or Thomas A. Edison College, Box 1293, Trenton, New Jersey 08625.

The New York State Board of Regents offers the following External Degrees: Associate in Arts, Bachelor of Science in Business Administration, and Associate in Applied Science in Nursing. The State of New Jersey offers a similar program administered through the Thomas A. Edison College. No classroom attendance is required and persons outside the states are eligible for admission to the programs.

Before you go to the time and expense of preparing and taking the General Examinations, determine your purpose for taking the tests. If your goal is to gain information about your college-level abilities for your own use, go right ahead. However, if you wish to submit the scores to a college or institution for possible advanced placement or college credit, make certain that that college or institution will award credit based on scores earned. To obtain a list of participating institutions, write to the office named at the end of this chapter for the "Bulletin Of Information For Candidates." Finally, if you wish to submit the scores to a prospective employer as evidence of your capabilities, check with that company or organization to determine whether it accepts C.L.E.P. scores.

THE FIVE GENERAL EXAMINATIONS

The General Examinations cover material that is known in colleges as the "general education" requirement. This is what many colleges expect students to complete during their freshman and sophomore years regardless of their special interests or college major. The General Examinations may demonstrate you have acquired this basic college education.

There are five General Examinations: English Composition, Humanities, Mathematics, Natural Sciences, and Social Sciences-History. Each General Examination consists of about 90 to 150 multiple-choice questions and takes 90 minutes. You may elect to take one or all of them, depending on your special needs and goals.

Each Examination measures certain broad-based intellectual experiences in the major fields of knowledge that individuals can be expected to have had by the end of two years of college-level study, whether in or out of college. These abilities can be acquired through personal reading, employment, television, radio, adult classes, or advanced high-school work. The Examinations do not measure the specialized knowledge of a particular discipline, nor are they based on a particular curriculum or course of study.

I. THE GENERAL EXAMINATION IN ENGLISH COMPOSITION

The English Composition Examination tests your ability to understand and use standard English, the kind of language used in most textbooks and formal writing. This exam has seven kinds of multiple-choice questions:

1. Sentence Correction. Substitute words or phrases for the underlined portion of a sentence without changing the original meaning.

2. Sentence Completion. Select the word or words which will produce the best possible sentence when inserted in the blank spaces of the original sentence.

3. Construction Shift. Rephrase a given sentence in accordance with specific directions that follow the sentence.
4. Clarity of Expression. Choose the one way of phrasing a particular thought that produces the clearest and most concise sentence.
5. Reading Between the Lines. Based upon your reading of a brief statement, you are to pinpoint the underlying assumptions, draw a conclusion or make a judgment about the information provided.
6. Relationships Between Sentences. Determine the way in which two sentences are related or the method of their organization.
7. Logic and Organization. Correct a brief paragraph in terms of organization, grammatical structure and word choice.

II. THE GENERAL EXAMINATION IN THE HUMANITIES

The Humanities Examination covers the knowledge of literature, art, music, and philosophy that you might acquire by reading widely, attending concerts, movies, plays and by visiting galleries. The questions provide a way to show understanding as well as factual knowledge of the Humanities.

III. THE GENERAL EXAMINATION IN MATHEMATICS

The Mathematics Examination covers the knowledge of math that you might need for such college courses as business, economics, social science, and psychology. It does not include the mathematics that a person majoring in math would be expected to know. About half the questions deal with topics that require reasoning and a knowledge of basic arithmetic, algebra, geometry and logic. The other half contains questions on more advanced topics.

IV. THE GENERAL EXAMINATION IN NATURAL SCIENCES

The Natural Science Examination tests your ability to reason and to understand scientific principles, problems and processes. If you read and understand scientific articles in magazines and newspapers, you could answer many of the questions correctly. The questions deal with biology, physical science and general science. They stress understanding as well as knowledge.

V. THE GENERAL EXAMINATION IN SOCIAL SCIENCES—HISTORY

The Social Sciences-History Examination contains multiple-choice questions on history, government, economics, and sociology, and general social science. Many of the questions in this exam call for a knowledge of facts and others ask for interpretation. If you read widely, watch films, educational television and have an interest in world politics, you would have an advantage in answering these questions.

TYPE AND AUTHORSHIP OF QUESTIONS

Each of the five General Examinations is comprised of multiple-choice questions. They are written by committees of outstanding scholars and teachers from universities throughout the country. Questions are refined by specialists at Educational Testing Service, and by consultants. These people determine the scope of the exams; define the content and the skills to be measured; select types of questions; and review test results.

After an exam is first administered, score reports of the students sampled are used to establish norms against which you can be compared. The exams are standardized by statistical analysis and are released only when their validity and reliability have been established. It takes between 18 and 30 months to develop a new exam.

BACKGROUND FOR TAKING THE EXAMS

The best way to learn about the Examinations is to study this book carefully and to send for the ETS booklets. In reviewing the sample questions, try to ascertain whether the material is at all familiar. Do not be discouraged if one or two topics seem outside your experience. Have you studied, worked, or read in the areas described? What kinds of informal educational experiences above the high school level have you had which might help you handle the topics discussed?

Though there are five General Examinations, you are not expected to have equal facility in all. In fact, you do not have to take all five tests. If you feel that your mastery of mathematics is limited, you might omit the exam. However, before you omit an exam, find out exactly what's required or recommended by the institution, college, or organization that will be receiving your tests' results; and make certain that you take the tests that you need.

Since the General Examinations are not based on the content of particular courses, no specific educational background is required in preparation for them. Obviously, two years of Liberal Arts study in a college or university would be a highly desirable way of preparing. Alternately, a series of credit or noncredit college courses would be another. However, many less formal educational experiences at the college level can be valuable as preparation for the exams. Independent study, diversified reading, correspondence courses, and kindred activities will help. Do not lose sight of the fact that perceptive, interested, and intelligent individuals can draw heavily on the experiences of living and working.

It is unlikely that you can prepare for most of the questions by cramming, inasmuch as the material covered by the Examinations is very broad in scope. Attempts to shortcut the necessary learning experiences would likely have little effect on your test score. The idea behind each exam is to evaluate your ability to think about facts, to use facts, and to interpret materials related to those facts.

Now let us summarize the comprehensive nature of the General Examinations.

• They emphasize ability to comprehend the written word; ability to recognize relationships; ability to understand and apply basic concepts and principles.

• Each General Examination covers material that could reasonably be included in a basic liberal arts course of study to meet the "general education" requirement.

• They sample widely the content of the major disciplines with which each is concerned.

• The factual materials on the examinations can be found in many non-conventional learning situations, as well as in the different courses customarily offered in colleges and universities.

• No attempt is made to measure the outcomes of specialized courses that individuals might pursue when majoring in a particular field.

• The Examination questions encompass a wide range of difficulty, both in the amount of understanding needed and in the skills and abilities tested.

• It is not necessary to answer all the questions on an exam in order to demonstrate college-level ability.

A FEW DETAILS ABOUT TAKING THE GENERAL EXAMINATIONS

The CLEP Examinations are sponsored by the College Entrance Examination Board. The Board employs the services of Educational Testing Service (ETS) to develop and administer the exams. ETS is a non-profit corporation specializing in test development and educational research. The College Board with the support of the Carnegie Corporation of New York has developed the CLEP program to aid students who wish to gain college credit for achievement outside the classroom. CLEP is designed for those entering college as well as those already in a college program.

Over 1,400 colleges in the United States now offer credit on the basis of CLEP scores. If you are taking the exams for credit, you should write or visit the school you wish to attend. Inquire about its policy in regard to CLEP. Credit is given only through the colleges and not by CLEP itself.

HOW TO REGISTER FOR THE EXAMINATIONS

The first thing you should do if you are considering the possibility of utilizing your life experiences to obtain college credit is to write for the *CLEP Registration Guide* and the *CLEP General and Subject Examinations booklet.*

A combined Registration and Admission Form is available from Educational Testing Service. This completed form must be sent with your test fee to the test center you select no later than three weeks before the test is scheduled. Be sure to send your completed form and fee to the test center, not to the College Board. The Registration Form calls for many detailed answers. The Bulletin in which you find it contains several pages of helpful explanation. Study these directions and make sure you fill out the form accordingly.

If you wish to obtain college credit for participating in the CLEP program, it is important that you contact your college guidance department to learn what regulations govern the use of the tests at your school. College credit is awarded only by the colleges and universities that participate in the program. Although the tests are devised and administered by the College Entrance Examination Board, the Board is not a college and does not give college credit. Colleges have their own policies regarding CLEP scores and it is your responsibility to find out what they are.

ADDRESSES OF INTEREST

For additional information or to arrange for a special administration of the test in regard to the General Examinations, write to Program Director, College-Level Examination Program, Box 592, Princeton, New Jersey 08540. You should ask for the following free booklets:

CLEP General and Subject Examinations: Descriptions and Sample Questions,

CLEP Registration Guide,

CLEP Score Interpretation Guide,

CLEP Test Centers and Other Participating Institutions.

Write to College Entrance Examinations Board, Box 592, Princeton, New Jersey 08540, or Box 1025, Berkeley, California 94701, for your copy of BULLETIN OF INFORMATION FOR CANDIDATES AND/OR A DESCRIPTION OF THE SUBJECT EXAMINATION.

If you are in the Armed Forces, CLEP Examinations are available to you at no charge through your education officer or by writing to U. S. Armed Forces Institute (USAFI), Madison, Wisconsin 53713.

TAKING THE GENERAL EXAMINATIONS

The exams are given throughout the United States in approximately 500 locations. When you register you may ask to take your exams in the most convenient location. Shortly before you take the test, you will receive an admission ticket that will state the exact address of your test site. Ordinarily the Examinations are held during the third week of each month. The day of the week that tests are administered at each site is listed in the ETS booklet, *CLEP Test Centers and Other Participating Institutions*. There is a regional test center in Washington, D.C. that offers CLEP tests on any weekday during the year. An additional fee of $5 is charged at this test center.

If you live more than 100 miles from one of the listed test centers, the College Board may be able to arrange a special test location that is nearer your home. If you require special arrangements, you must fill out a Registration-Admission Form and pay an extra fee. Arrangements for a special testing center take about five weeks. If you live outside the United States, you may request a special administration of the CLEP exams. You must list at least three cities where you could be tested. This request must be made at least four months before the testing date.

Each Examination requires about 1½ hours of testing time and contains about 100 questions. You may register for one or more Examinations on a given testing date. Ordinarily the Examinations are scheduled for three hours in the morning and two hours in the afternoon. No matter which Examination you take, you must arrive at the start of the test session. Late arrivals will usually not be admitted, as they may disturb those who have begun testing.

Can I Repeat the Tests? You may retake CLEP Examinations if you request permission at least four weeks in advance. Unless you request this permission, your scores will be cancelled and your fees forfeited. The General Examinations may be repeated three months after you were last tested. You must wait six months to repeat one of the Subject Examinations. No test may be repeated more than once in a twelve month period. When you request permission to repeat a CLEP test, it is important to indicate when and where you last took the test. ETS will mail you an authorization to repeat the test.

Who Receives The Test Scores? You alone determine who receives your scores. If you take the optional essay tests, they are sent to the institution you designate for grading. Educational Testing Service keeps your scores on file for five years and will, during this period, send them to any institution you designate.

What If I Do Not Want My Tests Scored? If you do not want your test scored, tell the test supervisor before leaving the testing room, or write to CEEB, Princeton, NJ 08540, Attention: Resolution Section. You must write within two days after the testing date. You will receive no refund. If at a later time you wish to repeat the test, you may do so by following the procedures for repeating tests. If, after registering for an exam, you decide not to take it, you may cancel your registration and obtain a refund. Fill out the appropriate space on the bottom of your Admission Form, sign your name, and send the form to the test center where you would go. Your request must be sent no later than two days before the testing date. You will receive a refund check about eight weeks later for one-half your testing fee.

What Happens to the Test Results? Educational Testing Service will notify you and the institutions you have designated about four weeks after you have taken the tests. Along with your test results you will receive a booklet explaining them. Test results are kept on file for five years. Along with your score report you will receive a request form that you can use to have test results forwarded to any institution during this five-year period.

WHAT YOUR CLEP SCORES MEAN

Let us say that you have registered for the tests, paid your fees, filled out all the forms necessary, appeared at the test center and blackened your answers on the answer sheets. At some later time, you will get the results of your test in terms of scores. How will you, or the institutions you designate to receive the scores, interpret the scores? What do they really mean? With your scores you will receive a booklet called "What Your Scores Mean." It will explain the scores for you.

There are no passing or failing scores on the General Examinations. Your scores merely tell you how you rate in relation to others who have taken the Examinations before you. CLEP scores are used to measure the relative standing of one student with a group of students; or of one student with another.

When the Examinations were first developed, sample exams were given to full-time undergraduate students near the termination of their sophomore year. The exams of these students were scored by counting the number of correct answers and subtracting a percentage of wrong answers as a correction for guessing. Scaled scores were then assigned to their exams. The average score was arbitrarily assigned the number 500 and the scores gained by two-thirds of the group were given numbers between 400 and 600. The results you obtain on the General Examinations are converted to this scale, which goes from a low of 200 to a high of 800.

Each General Examination (except English Composition) yields a basic score and two subscores. The Humanities Examination has a subscore for Fine Arts and one for Literature; the Mathematics Exam has a subscore for Basic Skills and one for Course Content; Natural Sciences yields a subscore for Biological Science and one for Physical Science; Social Sciences-History has a subscore for Social Science and one for History.

Institutions using the test results establish their own score levels for awarding credit. You should ask what those score levels are so you can assess your performance. Query the institution for which you are taking the tests. If you wish to obtain college credit for participating in the CLEP program, it is important that you contact your college guidance department to learn what regulations govern the use of the tests at your school. College credit is awarded only by the colleges and universities that participate in the program. Although the tests are devised and administered by the College Entrance Examination Board, the Board is not a college and does not give college credit. Colleges have their own policies regarding CLEP scores and it is your responsibility to find out what they are.

HINTS FOR SCORING HIGH ON CLEP

It's really quite simple. Do things right . . . right from the beginning. Make successful methods a habit by practicing them on all the exercises in this book. Before you're finished you will have invested a good deal of time. Make sure you get the largest dividends from this investment.

1.   *Be Confident.* It is important to know that you are not expected to answer every question correctly on the CLEP Examinations. The questions have a range of difficulty and differentiate between several levels of skill. It's quite possible that an ''A'' student might answer no more than 60% of the questions correctly.

2.   *Skip Hard Questions and Go Back Later.* There is a time limit for each exam. You will not be expected to finish each exam. Even though you do not finish each one, you may still perform well in terms of your final score. However, it is important that you use your time well and pace yourself in order to answer as many questions as possible.

It is a good idea to make a mark on the question sheet next to all questions you cannot answer easily, and to go back to those questions later. First answer the questions you are sure about. Do not panic if you cannot answer a question. Go on and answer the questions you know. Usually the easier questions are presented at the beginning of the exam and the questions become gradually more difficult. However, all questions on this exam have equal weight in determining your score. No one question will receive more credit than any other regardless of difficulty. If you do skip ahead on the exam, be sure to skip ahead also on your answer sheet. A good technique is periodically to check the number of the question on the answer sheet with the number of the question on the test. You should do this every time you decide to skip a question. If you fail to skip over the corresponding answer blank for that question, all of your following answers will be wrong.

3.   *Guess If You Are Nearly Sure.* Guessing is probably worthwhile if you have an intuition as to the correct answer or if you can eliminate one or more of the wrong options, and can thus make an ''educated'' guess. However, if you are entirely at a loss as to the correct answer, it may be best not to guess. A correction is made for guessing when the exam is scored. A

percentage of wrong answers is subtracted from the number of right answers. Therefore, it is sometimes better to omit an answer than to guess.

4. *Mark the Answer Sheet Clearly.* When you take the General or the Subject Examinations, you will mark your answers to the multiple-choice questions on a separate answer sheet that will be given to you at the test center. If you have not worked with an answer sheet before, it is in your best interest to become familiar with the procedures involved. Remember, knowing the correct answer is not enough! If you do not mark the sheet correctly, so that it can be machine scored, you will not get credit for your answers!

In addition to marking answers on the separate answer sheet, you will also be asked to give your name and other information, including your social security number. (Remember, you *must* have your social security number for identification purposes.)

Read the directions carefully and follow them exactly. When you print your name in the boxes provided, write only one letter in each box. If your name is longer than the number of boxes provided, omit the letters that do not fit. Remember, you are writing for a machine; it does not have judgment. It can only record the pencil marks you make on the answer sheet.

Use the answer sheet to record all your answers to questions on both the General and the Subject Examinations. Each question, or item, has five answer choices labeled (A), (B), (C), (D), (E). You will be asked to choose the letter for the alternative that best answers each question. Then you will be asked to mark your answer by blackening the appropriate space on your answer sheet. Be sure that each space you choose and blacken with your pencil is *completely* blackened. If you change your mind about an answer, or mark the wrong space in error, you must erase the wrong answer. Erase as thoroughly and neatly as possible. The machine will "read" your answers in terms of spaces blackened. Make sure that only one answer is clearly blackened.

5. *Read Each Question Carefully.* The questions on the General Examinations are not designed to trick you through misleading or ambiguous alternative choices. On the other hand, they are not all direct questions of factual information. Some are designed to elicit responses that reveal your ability to reason, or to interpret a fact or idea. It's up to you to read each question carefully so you know what is being asked. The exam authors have tried to make the questions clear. Do not go too far astray in looking for hidden meanings.

6. *Materials and Conduct At The Test Center.* You need to bring with you to the test center your Admission Form, your social security card and several No. 2 pencils. Arrive on time as you may not be admitted after testing has begun. Instructions for taking the tests will be read to you by the test supervisor and time will be called when the test is over. If you have ques-

tions, you may ask them of the supervisor. Do not give or receive assistance while taking the exams. If you do, you will be asked to turn in all test materials and told to leave the room. You will not be permitted to return and your tests will not be scored. The College Board also reserves the right to cancel your score at any time if there is any reason to question its accuracy. However, before exercising its right to cancel a score, the Board will offer the student a chance to take the test again at no additional fee.

THE GIST OF TEST STRATEGY

- APPROACH THE TEST CONFIDENTLY. TAKE IT CALMLY.

- REMEMBER TO REVIEW, THE WEEK BEFORE THE TEST.

- DON'T "CRAM." BE CAREFUL OF YOUR DIET AND SLEEP .. ESPECIALLY AS THE TEST DRAWS NIGH.

- CHOOSE A GOOD SEAT. GET COMFORTABLE AND RELAX.

- BRING THE COMPLETE KIT OF "TOOLS" YOU'LL NEED.

- READ ALL DIRECTIONS CAREFULLY. TWICE IF NECESSARY. PAY PARTICULAR ATTENTION TO THE SCORING PLAN.

- START RIGHT IN, IF POSSIBLE. STAY WITH IT. USE EVERY SECOND EFFECTIVELY.

- DO THE EASY QUESTIONS FIRST; POSTPONE HARDER QUESTIONS UNTIL LATER.

- DETERMINE THE PATTERN OF THE TEST QUESTIONS. IF IT'S HARD-EASY ETC., ANSWER ACCORDINGLY.

- ARRIVE ON TIME . . . AND READY.

- LISTEN CAREFULLY TO ALL DIRECTIONS.

- APPORTION YOUR TIME INTELLIGENTLY WITH AN "EXAM BUDGET."

- LOOK OVER THE WHOLE TEST BEFORE ANSWERING ANY QUESTIONS.

- GET ALL THE HELP YOU CAN FROM "CUE" WORDS.

- REPHRASE DIFFICULT QUESTIONS FOR YOURSELF. WATCH OUT FOR "SPOILERS."

- THINK! AVOID HURRIED ANSWERS. GUESS INTELLIGENTLY.

- READ EACH QUESTION CAREFULLY. MAKE SURE YOU UNDERSTAND EACH ONE BEFORE YOU ANSWER. RE-READ, IF NECESSARY.

- WATCH YOUR WATCH AND "EXAM BUDGET," BUT DO A LITTLE BALANCING OF THE TIME YOU DEVOTE TO EACH QUESTION.

- REFRESH YOURSELF WITH A FEW, WELL-CHOSEN REST PAUSES DURING THE TEST.

- USE CONTROLLED ASSOCIATION TO SEE THE RELATION OF ONE QUESTION TO ANOTHER AND WITH AS MANY IMPORTANT IDEAS AS YOU CAN DEVELOP.

- NOW THAT YOU'RE A "COOL" TEST-TAKER, STAY CALM AND CONFIDENT THROUGHOUT THE TEST. DON'T LET ANYTHING THROW YOU.

- EDIT, CHECK, PROOFREAD YOUR ANSWERS. BE A "BITTER ENDER." STAY WORKING UNTIL THEY MAKE YOU GO.

STUDYING AND USING THIS BOOK

Even though this course of study has been carefully planned to help you get in shape by the day your test comes, you'll have to do a little planning on your own to be successful. And you'll also need a few pointers proven effective for many other good students.

SURVEY AND SCHEDULE YOUR WORK

Regular mental workouts are as important as regular physical workouts in achieving maximum personal efficiency. They are absolutely essential in getting top test scores, so you'll want to plan a test-preparing schedule that fits in with your usual program. Use the Schedule on the next page. Make it out for yourself so that it really works with the actual time you have at your disposal.

There are five basic steps in scheduling this book for yourself and in studying each assignment that you schedule:

1. SCAN - the entire job at hand.
2. QUESTION - before reading.
3. READ - to find the answers to the questions you have formulated.
4. RECITE - to see how well you have learned the answers to your questions.
5. REVIEW - to check up on how well you have learned, to learn it again, and to fix it firmly in your mind.

Scan

Make a survey of this whole book before scheduling. Do this by reading our introductory statements and the table of contents. Then leaf through the entire book, paying attention to main headings, sub-headings, summaries, and topic sentences. When you have this bird's eye view of the whole, the parts take on added meaning, and you'll see how they hang together.

Question

As you scan, questions will come to your mind. Write them into the book. Later on you'll be finding the answers. For example, in scanning this book you would naturally change the headline STUDYING AND USING THIS BOOK into *What don't I know about studying? What are my good study habits? How can I improve them? How should I go about reading and using this book?* Practice the habit of formulating and writing such questions into the text.

Read

Now, by reviewing your questions you should be able to work out your schedule easily. Stick to it. And apply these five steps to each assignment you give yourself in the schedule. Your reading of each assignment should be directed to finding answers to the questions you have formulated and will continue to formulate. You'll discover that reading with a purpose will make it easier to *remember* the answers to your questions.

Recite

After you have read your assignment and found the answers to your questions, close the book and recite to yourself. For example, if your question here was "What are the five basic steps in attacking an assignment?" then your answer to yourself would be scan, question, read, recite, and review. Thus, you check up on yourself and "fix" the information in your mind. You have now seen it, read it, said it, and heard it. The more senses you use, the more you learn.

Review

Even if you recall your answers well, review them in order to "overlearn." "Overlearning" gives you a big advantage by reducing the chances of forgetting. Definitely provide time in your schedule for review. It's the clincher in getting ahead of the crowd. You'll find that "overlearning" won't take much time with this book because the text portions have been written as concisely and briefly as possible. You may be tempted to stop work when you have once gone over the work before you. This is wrong because of the ease with which memory impressions are bound to fade. Decide for yourself what is important and plan to review and overlearn those portions. Overlearning rather than last minute cramming is the best way to study.

Your Time is Limited—
Schedule Your Study

1. SCOPE OF EXAMINATION

SUBJECT SCHEDULE

Test Subjects	No. of Questions	Percentage of Total (Weight)
Total:		100 percent

2. YOUR KNOWLEDGE OF SUBJECT

Test Subjects	Poor	Fair	Good	Very Good	Excellent

3. DIVIDING YOUR STUDY TIME

Test Subjects	Total Hours	Hours Per Week
Total:		

Total number of weeks for study ....

Hours per week ....

Total number of hours ....

The SUBJECT SCHEDULE is divided into three parts: 1. Scope of Examination; 2. Your Knowledge of Subject; and 3. Dividing Your Study Time. To use your schedule, put down in part 1 all the subjects you will face on your test, the number of questions in each subject, and the "weight," or percentage, given to each subject in the total make-up of the test.

In part 2, again fill in all the test subjects and, with a check mark, rate yourself *honestly* as to your knowledge of each subject.

At the top of part 3, put down the number of weeks you will be able to devote to your studying. Determine the number of hours you will study each week and multiply that figure by the number of weeks to give you the total hours of study.

Again fill in the subjects. Then, take the weight given to each test subject (in part 1) and average it against your knowledge of that subject (as checked in part 2) to arrive at the number of hours you should allow for study of that subject out of your total study hours. In Chapter 2, under the heading "10. Total Time Allowed For Each Subject," you will find a more detailed explanation of how to divide your study time.

After you have fixed the total number of hours to be devoted to each subject, divide them by the number of weeks of study to arrive at the total weekly hours you will study each subject.

STUDY TIMETABLE
PRELIMINARY

Key Letters	Study Subjects
A	
B	
C	
D	
E	
F	

Key Letters	Study Subjects
G	
H	
I	
J	
K	
L	

Mon.

Tues.

Wed.

Thur.

Fri.

Sat.

Sun.

HOW TO USE THE STUDY TIMETABLE

At right is a sample timetable filled in for a whole week to show you how a typical schedule might be arranged. The letters *A, B, C,* etc., are keyed to your study subjects so that, for example, *A* might stand for Vocabulary, *B* for Numerical Relations, and so forth. You will note that each day is divided into nine possible study hours and each hour, in turn, is divided into four 15-minute periods.

Sample timetable:

Mon. 7AM | 12 PM | 7PM | 8PM | 9PM — BB AA BBCC CCEE GG

Tues. 12 PM | 7PM | 8PM | 9PM — FF AABB DDDD GG

Wed. 7AM | 12PM | 7PM — CC BB BBBB

Thur. 12 PM | 7PM | 8PM | 9PM | 10PM — A AA BBEEE FFHH

Fri. 7AM | 7PM | 8PM — AA FFFEE CC

Sat. 10AM | 11AM | 12PM | 3PM | 4PM — DDD AAAA BBB FF

Sun. 1PM | 2PM | 3PM | 4PM | 8PM — DDD CCCC AAHHH BB

STUDY TIMETABLE

FINAL

Key Letters	Study Subjects
A	
B	
C	
D	
E	
F	

Key Letters	Study Subjects
G	
H	
I	
J	
K	
L	

Mon.																								

Tues.																								

Wed.																								

Thur.																								

Fri.																								

Sat.																								

Sun.																								

A SCHEME FOR CHARTING YOUR PROGRESS

DIRECTIONS: Track your progress and rate yourself by listing each chapter in which you answered practice questions. List the title of each such chapter once only . . . the first time you work it. Then record the number of questions you answered in that chapter. Do this in the second column. Do it each time you answer questions in that chapter. In the third column, get the total of your correct answers. At the proper time derive your scores for the different chapters. Compare those scores critically. Devote futher study time to your weak spots, the subjects that fall below 75%.

1. Chapter Title	2. Number of Questions Answered in Chapter	3. Your Correct Answers	4. Your Scores. Compare them.
	Total:	Total:	$\dfrac{\text{NO. CORRECT}}{\text{NO. OF QUESTIONS}}$ .....%
	Total:	Total:	$\dfrac{\text{NO. CORRECT}}{\text{NO. OF QUESTIONS}}$ .....%
	Total:	Total:	$\dfrac{\text{NO. CORRECT}}{\text{NO. OF QUESTIONS}}$ .....%
	Total:	Total:	$\dfrac{\text{NO. CORRECT}}{\text{NO. OF QUESTIONS}}$ .....%
	Total:	Total:	$\dfrac{\text{NO. CORRECT}}{\text{NO. OF QUESTIONS}}$ .....%
	Total:	Total:	$\dfrac{\text{NO. CORRECT}}{\text{NO. OF QUESTIONS}}$ .....%
	Total:	Total:	$\dfrac{\text{NO. CORRECT} \div}{\text{NO. OF QUESTIONS}}$ .....%
	Total:	Total:	$\dfrac{\text{NO. CORRECT} \div}{\text{NO. OF QUESTIONS}}$ .....%
	Total:	Total:	$\dfrac{\text{NO. CORRECT} \div}{\text{NO. OF QUESTIONS}}$ .....%
	Total:	Total:	$\dfrac{\text{NO. CORRECT} \div}{\text{NO. OF QUESTIONS}}$ .....%

2

PART TWO

English Composition

A Verisimilar General Examination English Usage for Test-Takers

THE GENERAL EXAMINATION IN ENGLISH COMPOSITION

This chapter offers you a bird's-eye view of the General Examination in English Composition. The "mini-exam" contains good samples of the various types of questions you may expect to encounter. The sample questions show you the subjects that will be included, the different types of questions, and the levels of difficulty you may expect. For more intensive practice with English Composition questions, we urge you to consult CLEP: THE GENERAL EXAMINATION IN ENGLISH COMPOSITION which is available from Arco Publishing Company, 219 Park Avenue South, New York, New York 10003.

The General Examination in English Composition was completely revised in 1978 in order to make it a more accurate measure of those skills the college freshman is expected to acquire in an introductory course in English Composition. The new General Examination in English Composition is available in two different editions. One edition consists of two forty-five minute multiple-choice sections. The other edition consists of one forty-five minute multiple-choice section and one forty-five minute essay section. The all multiple-choice exam is offered at each monthly administration. The edition with the essay is given twice a year—spring and fall.

Both editions of the General Examination in English Composition are designed to measure your understanding of and ability to use the conventions of "Standard Written English." Standard Written English is the language used in most college textbooks, and it is the language that you will be expected to use in compositions, essays, and term papers throughout your college career. The questions on Standard Written English do not ask you to cite specific rules of grammar, but rather to demonstrate your ability to apply those rules in the context of specific sentences.

No matter which edition of the English Composition Exam you take, the first half of the exam will be devoted to objective questions dealing primarily with logical and structural relationships within the sentence. This section includes questions in each of the following categories:

1. Sentence Correction. Substitute words or phrases for the underlined portion of a sentence without changing the original meaning.

33

2. Sentence Completion. Select the word or words which will produce the best possible sentence when inserted in the blank spaces of the original sentence.

3. Construction Shift. Rephrase a given sentence in accordance with specific directions that follow the sentence.

4. Clarity of Expression. Choose the one way of phrasing a particular thought that produces the clearest and most concise sentence.

The second half of the all multiple-choice examination consists of questions dealing with the logical arrangement of ideas, the use of evidence, and the adaptation of language to purpose and audience. These skills are tested by questions that fall into the following categories:

1. Reading Between the Lines. Based upon your reading of a brief statement, you are to pinpoint the underlying assumptions, draw a conclusion or make a judgment about the information provided.

2. Relationships Between Sentences. Determine the way in which two sentences are related or the method of their organization.

3. Logic and Organization. Correct a brief paragraph in terms of organization, grammatical structure and word choice.

The second half of the combination Objective-Essay Exam consists of planning and writing an essay on a single topic. You will have forty-five minutes in which to complete your essay. In that time you are expected to present a point of view, develop an argument logically, and provide evidence from reading or personal experience in support of your stand. Your essay will be centrally scored by English faculty members selected from institutions throughout the country. These faculty members will be trained to score the essays "holistically." (The holistic method of scoring assumes that the whole of a piece of writing is more than a series of factors to be isolated and scored independently.)

The essay section and the multiple-choice section of the Combination exam will be given equal weight in determining the composite score. Score reports will indicate whether you took the all multiple-choice or the essay and multiple-choice edition of the English Composition Exam.

A MINI-EXAM IN ENGLISH COMPOSITION

Time allowed for the entire Examination: 16 Minutes.

PART I. THE SENTENCE

DIRECTIONS: Each question consists of a sentence with all or part of the sentence underlined. Following the sentence are five alternative ways of phrasing the underlined part of the original sentence. You are to select the one phrasing that has the same or nearly the same meaning as the original and, at the same time, follows the requirements of standard written English. In making your selection, keep in mind not only meaning, but also grammar, word choice, sentence structure and punctuation. Mark your answer sheet for the letter of the phrasing you think makes the clearest and most effective sentence.

Correct and explanatory answers are provided at the end of the exam.

1. It is not necessary for you to go; but you may if you wish.

    (A) You don't need to go, not unless you want to.
    (B) There is no need for you to go unless it's what you want.
    (C) There is no necessity for your going unless you want to.
    (D) You need not go unless you want to.
    (E) It is unnecessary for you to go unless that's what you want to do.

2. Our not having arrived on time meant that we missed the first half of the program.

    (A) Due to being late,
    (B) Our lateness was the cause that
    (C) Because we were late,
    (D) The fact that we did not arrive on time meant that
    (E) Lateness was the reason why

3. The young man had shining black hair, a slender build and an ambition to become a champion swimmer.

    (A) The slender, black-haired young man was ambitious
    (B) He was a young man with shining black hair, a slender build and an ambition
    (C) The slender man was young, had shining black hair, and an ambition
    (D) Young and slender, the black-haired man had an ambition
    (E) He was young and black-haired and slender and his ambition was

DIRECTIONS: For each of the following questions, select the choice which best answers the question or completes the statement.

4. When tickets went on sale for the rock concert, _____ lined up at the box office.

    (A) a great lot of young people
    (B) scads of youths
    (C) huge amounts of young persons
    (D) almost every young person in town
    (E) everybody and his brother

5. The irate director scheduled a rehearsal for 9 o'clock and _____ being late.

    (A) warned of the actors
    (B) urged caution on the part of the actors
    (C) cautioned the actors against
    (D) stressed the dire consequences for the actors in
    (E) admonished the actors

6. My attorney _____ remain silent.

    (A) said it would be better for me to
    (B) counseled me to
    (C) advised me that I should
    (D) said I'd be better off to
    (E) pointed out that I had better

DIRECTIONS: For each question in this test you are given a sentence to rephrase or "rewrite" according to the directions that follow it. If you wish, you may mentally rephrase the sentence and make notes in your test book before you decide on an answer.

Below each sentence and its directions are listed choices of words and phrases lettered from A to E for your "rewritten" sentence. The word or phrase you select should be the one that, if used in the sentence, would make your "rewritten" sentence best comply with the requirements of standard written English. When you have thought out a good sentence, choose the letter for the word or phrase that you need for that sentence and blacken that letter on your answer sheet.

If the sentence you thought out does not include any of the five choices given, try to rephrase your sentence, since there are different correct sentences to be obtained, given the original sentence and the directions. Remember, make only those changes required by the directions. Your "rewritten" sentence must comply with the requirements of standard written English and should convey, as far as possible, the original meaning of the sentence.

7. There is a bank on which the wild thyme grows.
    Change There is a bank to I know a bank.

    (A) whereon
    (B) in which
    (C) whereby
    (D) from which
    (E) by which

8. It is more rewarding to make friends than it is to be antisocial.
   Begin with *Making friends*.

   (A) than to be antisocial
   (B) than being antisocial
   (C) than to be like an antisocial person
   (D) than it is to be antisocial
   (E) than antisocial

9. These codes of behavior were important not only to those who hoped for acceptance by high society, but also to those who aspired for nothing more elegant than Mr. Smith's cookouts.
   Substitute *both* for *not only*.

   (A) also
   (B) as well as
   (C) but
   (D) too
   (E) and

DIRECTIONS: Each of the following questions consists of five different ways in which the same thought may be phrased. You are to choose the one phrasing that makes the intended meaning clear. The correct answer is the one that avoids ambiguity, that does not leave the actual meaning open to questions, or that does not leave you guessing about what is intended. The answer must also be grammatically correct and logical in its sequence.

10. (A) Jane could barely remember her grandmother since she was only three when she died.

    (B) Jane, whose grandmother died when she was only three, could scarcely remember that sweet old lady.

    (C) Because she was only three when her grandmother died, Jane retained few memories of that sweet old lady.

    (D) When her grandmother died Jane was so young that she could barely remember her.

    (E) Being only three when her grandmother died, Jane's memory of her was dim.

11. (A) Peter likes football better than his brother.
    (B) Better than his brother, Peter likes football.
    (C) Peter plays football which he likes better than his brother.
    (D) The game of football is better liked by Peter than his brother is.
    (E) Peter likes playing football better than his brother does.

12. (A) The shingle house which was white, and the shutters and roof which were green, blended beautifully with the handsome white birch trees that lined the winding driveway.

   (B) The white shingle house, with green shutters and roof, blended beautifully with the handsome white birch trees that lined the winding driveway.

   (C) The white shingle house at the end of the winding driveway had green shutters and a green roof, which blended beautifully with the handsome white birch trees along the driveway.

   (D) Green shuttered and green roofed, the house which was white shingled blended beautifully with the handsome white birch trees lining the winding driveway.

   (E) The green and white house, which was at the end of the winding driveway, blended beautifully with the handsome white birch trees that lined it.

END OF PART

Go on to the following Test in the next Part of this Examination, just as you would be expected to do on the actual exam. If you have any available time use it to make sure that you have marked your Answer Sheet properly for this Part. Correct Answers for all Parts of this Exam follow the last question. Derive your scores only after completing the entire Exam.

PART II. LOGIC IN READING AND WRITING

DIRECTIONS: For each question in this test, read carefully the stem and the five lettered choices that follow. Choose the answer which you consider correct or most nearly correct. Mark the answer sheet for the letter you have chosen: A, B, C, D, or E.

Questions 1 and 2

"There is nothing so stimulating as a good game of backgammon. The boredom and restlessness of a rainy Saturday afternoon disappear as soon as you start to play this absorbing game."

1. The speaker assumes that all people
    (A) get bored and restless when it rains
    (B) are restless on Saturday afternoons
    (C) play backgammon equally well
    (D) can be stimulated in the same way
    (E) like playing games

2. What conclusion about backgammon must we accept if we accept the speaker's statement?
    (A) Every game of backgammon will have the same effect on the player.
    (B) No one should play backgammon unless he is bored and restless.
    (C) Backgammon is a rainy-day activity.
    (D) One should play backgammon only with experts.
    (E) Backgammon is not so absorbing on sunny days.

3. Which of the following statements is an expression of fact rather than one of opinion?
    (A) "Lake Geneva is the most attractive resort in Europe," said the scientist.
    (B) "The gas shortage is nothing but a conspiracy among the oil companies," stated the cab driver.
    (C) "My hospital gives the finest quality of health care," asserted the surgeon.
    (D) "An overloaded circuit can cause the wires to burn up," said the electrician.
    (E) "The white men have pillaged our land unjustly," stated the Indian chief.

DIRECTIONS: In this group of questions, two or more sentences are followed by a question or statement about them. Read each group of sentences, then choose the best answer to the question or the best completion of the statement. On your answer sheet, blacken the space under the letter (A, B, C, D, or E) of your answer choice.

4. Words are the tools of the writer.
   The composer works with sounds.

   What is happening in the sentences?

   (A) A comparison is made in terms of words and music.
   (B) A conclusion is drawn on the basis of difficulty.
   (C) A recommendation is made on the basis of artistic achievement.
   (D) A comparison is made in terms of writing and composing.
   (E) A relationship is drawn between literature and music.

5. "Everybody talks about the weather, but no one does anything about it."
   Meteorologists are working on ways to increase precipitation, dispel fog and suppress lightning.

   What does the second sentence do?

   (A) It gives a definition of the concept.
   (B) It presents an exception.
   (C) It draws a conclusion.
   (D) It provides an example.
   (E) It makes a comparison.

DIRECTIONS: This test consists of brief passages in which each sentence is numbered. Following each passage are questions which refer to the numbered sentences in the passage. Answer each question by choosing the best alternative (A,B,C,D, or E) and blacken the space corresponding to your choice on the Answer Sheet provided.

[1]It is not easy to write in a familiar style. [2]Many people mistake a familiar for a vulgar style. [3]Suppose that to write without formality is to write at random. [4]On the contradiction, there is nothing that requires more precision, and if I may say so, purity of expression, than the style I am speaking of. [5]It utterly rejects all meaningless. [6]It does not take the first word that offers itself, but takes the best word in common use. [7]It does not throw words together in any pleasing combination we please, but uses the true idioms of the language. [8]To write in a genuine familiar style is written as anyone would speak in everyday conversation. [9]The familiar style demonstrates a thorough commandment of the English language as it is spoken. [10]Studies are for delight, for ornament and for ability.

6. What should be done with sentence 3?

   (A) It should be left as it is.
   (B) It should be joined to the beginning of sentence 4.
   (C) It should be joined to the end of sentence 2 with *and*.
   (D) It should be made into two sentences.
   (E) The phrase *without formality* should be changed to *informally*.

7. In sentence 4, the word *contradiction* should be

   (A) left as it is
   (B) changed to *contrary*
   (C) changed to *contract*
   (D) changed to *detraction*
   (E) changed to *contradicting*

8. The meaning of sentence 5 would be clearest if

   (A) the sentence were left as it is
   (B) the sentence began with *Nevertheless it*
   (C) the part after *all* were omitted
   (D) the sentence began with *Regardless it*
   (E) *pretensions* were added to the end of the sentence

9. Sentence 7 would be best if

   (A) left as it is
   (B) the part after *idioms* were omitted
   (C) it were made into two sentences
   (D) *true* were omitted
   (E) *pleasing* were omitted

10. The word *written* in sentence 8 should be

    (A) left as it is
    (B) changed to *wrote*
    (C) changed to *had written*
    (D) changed to *to write*
    (E) changed to *composition*

11. In sentence 9 *commandment* should be

    (A) left as it is
    (B) changed to *command*
    (C) changed to *commanding*
    (D) changed to *commandeer*
    (E) changed to *commanded*

12. What should be done with sentence 10?

    (A) It should be left as it is.
    (B) It should be moved to the beginning of the passage.
    (C) It should begin a new paragraph.
    (D) It should be omitted entirely.
    (E) It should follow sentence 5.

END OF EXAMINATION

ANSWER SHEET FOR THIS MINI-EXAM

Consolidate your key answers here just as you would do on the actual exam. Using this type of Answer Sheet will provide valuable practice. Tear it out along the indicated lines and mark it up correctly. Use a No. 2 (medium) pencil. Make only ONE mark for each answer. Additional and stray marks may be counted as mistakes. In making corrections erase errors COMPLETELY. Make glossy black marks.

PART I. THE SENTENCE

```
    A B C D E      A B C D E      A B C D E      A B C D E      A B C D E      A B C D E      A B C D E      A B C D E
 1 [ ][ ][ ][ ][ ]  2 [ ][ ][ ][ ][ ]  3 [ ][ ][ ][ ][ ]  4 [ ][ ][ ][ ][ ]  5 [ ][ ][ ][ ][ ]  6 [ ][ ][ ][ ][ ]  7 [ ][ ][ ][ ][ ]  8 [ ][ ][ ][ ][ ]

                    A B C D E      A B C D E      A B C D E      A B C D E
                 9 [ ][ ][ ][ ][ ] 10 [ ][ ][ ][ ][ ] 11 [ ][ ][ ][ ][ ] 12 [ ][ ][ ][ ][ ]
```

PART II. LOGIC IN READING AND WRITING

```
    A B C D E      A B C D E      A B C D E      A B C D E      A B C D E      A B C D E      A B C D E      A B C D E
 1 [ ][ ][ ][ ][ ]  2 [ ][ ][ ][ ][ ]  3 [ ][ ][ ][ ][ ]  4 [ ][ ][ ][ ][ ]  5 [ ][ ][ ][ ][ ]  6 [ ][ ][ ][ ][ ]  7 [ ][ ][ ][ ][ ]  8 [ ][ ][ ][ ][ ]

                    A B C D E      A B C D E      A B C D E      A B C D E
                 9 [ ][ ][ ][ ][ ] 10 [ ][ ][ ][ ][ ] 11 [ ][ ][ ][ ][ ] 12 [ ][ ][ ][ ][ ]
```

CORRECT ANSWERS FOR THIS MINI-EXAM

PART I. THE SENTENCE

1.D	3.A	5.C	7.A	9.E	11.E
2.C	4.D	6.B	8.B	10.C	12.B

1. **(D)** This is the most concise expression of the original thought.

2. **(C)** This sentence is grammatically correct and conveys the same meaning as the original sentence.

3. **(A)** Even though the original series is parallel in grammatical construction, the items in the series are not parallel in idea. Sentence (A) solves this problem most effectively.

4. **(D)** All of the other choices contain colloquialisms which are inappropriate in standard written English.

5. **(C)** This is the only phrase which will produce a correct and effective sentence when inserted in the blank.

6. **(B)** While (A), (C) and (E) would all produce a sentence that is correct, choice (B) produces the most concise sentence.

7. **(A)** The revised sentence is—I know a bank *whereon* the wild thyme grows.

8. **(B)** The revised sentence is—Making friends is more rewarding *than being antisocial.*

9. **(E)** The revised sentence is—These codes of behavior were important both to those who hoped for acceptance by high society *and* to those who aspired for nothing more elegant than Mr. Smith's cookouts.

10. **(C)** This sentence resolves both problems of reference by making it clear that *Jane* was *three years old* and by removing the ambiguity of having two forms of the same pronoun (*she, her*) refer to two different antecedents.

11. **(E)** This is the only sentence that makes it clear that the boys are being compared in terms of how much they like playing football.

12. **(B)** This sentence provides the best description of the scene because all of the many modifiers attach themselves to the right nouns.

PART II. LOGIC IN READING AND WRITING

1.D	3.D	5.C	7.B	9.E	11.B
2.A	4.D	6.C	8.E	10.D	12.D

1. **(D)** The speaker assumes that all people will react to backgammon in the same way that he does.

2. **(A)** The game can be stimulating or not depending upon the ability and interest of the players.

3. **(D)** The electrician is the only person speaking in his own area of expertise on a topic which does not arouse an emotionally defensive reaction. All of the other respondents are either speaking on emotional topics or areas outside their own field of expertise.

4. **(D)** The second sentence provides three examples of the practical application of geometry.

5. **(C)** The conclusion that prices will come down is based on the fact that favorable weather conditions have produced a good crop.

6. **(C)** *Sentence relationship.* Sentence 3 as it stands is an imperative statement that does not fit into the grammatical structure of the paragraph. When joined to the end of sentence 2 with "and" it is well integrated into the paragraph.

7. **(B)** *Diction.* "Contradiction," which is defined as the assertion of the opposite of, should be "contrary," which is defined as quite different. "On the contrary" is a figure of speech.

8. **(E)** *Clarification.* "Meaningless" is an adjective without a noun to modify. The addition of the noun, "pretensions," reveals the full meaning of the sentence.

9. **(E)** *Diction.* "We please" and the gerund, "pleasing," both convey essentially the same meaning. The omission of "pleasing" prevents sentence 7 from being verbose.

10. **(D)** *Diction.* "Written" is the past participle of the verb to write. It must be changed to the infinitive "to write" to be grammatically correct.

11. **(B)** *Diction.* "Commandment" is a noun defined as an order or direction. "Command," a noun implying possession of authority or control over, most accurately completes the meaning of sentence 9.

12. **(D)** *Ordering.* Sentence 10, whose subject is "studies" rather than "a familiar style of writing," does not belong in the passage.

ENGLISH COMPOSITION FIRST VERISIMILAR EXAMINATION

This Examination is very much like the one you'll take. It was constructed by professionals who utilized all the latest information available. They derived a series of Tests which neatly cover all the subjects you are likely to encounter on the actual examination. Stick to business; follow all instructions closely; and score yourself objectively. If you do poorly . . . review. If necessary, take this Examination again for comparison.

Time allowed for the entire Examination: 1½ Hours

In order to create the climate of the actual exam, that's exactly what you should allow yourself . . . no more, no less. Use a watch to keep a record of your time, since it might suit your convenience to try this practice exam in several short takes.

In constructing this Examination we tried to visualize the questions you are *likely* to face on your actual exam. We included those subjects on which they are *probably* going to test you.

Although copies of past exams are not released, we were able to piece together a fairly complete picture of the forthcoming exam.

A principal source of information was our analysis of official announcements going back several years.

Critical comparison of these announcements, particularly the sample questions, revealed the testing trend; foretold the important subjects, and those that are likely to recur.

In making up the Tests we predict for your exam, great care was exercised to prepare questions having just the difficulty level you'll encounter on your exam. Not easier; not harder, but just what you may expect.

The various subjects expected on your exam are represented by separate Tests. Each Test has just about the number of questions you may find on the actual exam. And each Test is timed accordingly.

The questions on each Test are represented exactly on the special Answer Sheet provided. Mark your answers on this sheet. It's just about the way you'll have to do it on the real exam.

As a result you have an Examination which simulates the real one closely enough to provide you with important training.

Proceed through the entire exam without pausing after each Test. Remember that you are taking this Exam under actual battle conditions, and therefore you do not stop until told to do so by the proctor.

Certainly you should not lose time by trying to mark each Test as you complete it. You'll be able to score yourself fairly when time is up for the entire Exam.

Correct answers for all the questions in all the Tests of the Exam appear at the end of the Exam.

ANALYSIS AND TIMETABLE: VERISIMILAR EXAMINATION I.			
This table is both an analysis of the exam that follows and a priceless preview of the actual test. Look it over carefully and use it well. Since it lists both subjects and times, it points up not only what to study, but also how much time to spend on each topic. Making the most of your study time adds valuable points to your examination score.			
SUBJECT TESTED	*Time Allowed*	*SUBJECT TESTED*	*Time Allowed*
THE SENTENCE			
Sentence Correction	15 Minutes	Construction Shift	12 Minutes
Sentence Completion	10 Minutes	Clarity of Expression	8 Minutes
LOGIC IN READING AND WRITING			
Reading Between the Lines	15 Minutes	Logic and Organization	15 Minutes
Relationships Between Sentences	15 Minutes	Total Time for this General Examination	90 Minutes

ANSWER SHEET FOR VERISIMILAR EXAMINATION I.

TEST I. SENTENCE CORRECTION

TEST II. SENTENCE COMPLETION

TEST III. CONSTRUCTION SHIFT

TEST IV. CLARITY OF EXPRESSION

TEST V. READING BETWEEN THE LINES

TEST VI. RELATIONSHIPS BETWEEN SENTENCES

TEST VII. LOGIC AND ORGANIZATION

SCORE YOURSELF

Compare your answers to the Correct Key Answers at the end of the Examination. To determine your score, count the number of correct answers in each test. Then count the number of incorrect answers. Subtract ¼ of the number of incorrect answers from the number of correct answers. Plot the resulting figure on the graph below by blackening the bar under each test to the point of your score. Plan your study to strengthen the weaknesses indicated on your scoring graph.

EXAM I ENGLISH COMPOSITION	Very Poor	Poor	Average	Good	Excellent
SENTENCE CORRECTION 22 Questions	1-3	4-8	9-15	16-19	20-22
SENTENCE COMPLETION 15 Questions	1-2	3-6	7-10	11-13	14-15
CONSTRUCTION SHIFT 17 Questions	1-2	3-7	8-12	13-15	16-17
CLARITY OF EXPRESSION 10 Questions	1-2	3-4	5-7	8-9	10
READING BETWEEN THE LINES 20 Questions	1-3	4-8	9-14	15-17	18-20
RELATIONSHIPS BETWEEN SENTENCES 20 Questions	1-3	4-8	9-14	15-17	18-20
LOGIC AND ORGANIZATION 24 Questions	1-4	5-9	10-16	17-21	22-24

PART I. THE SENTENCE

TEST I. SENTENCE CORRECTION

TIME: 15 Minutes. 22 Questions.

DIRECTIONS: A sentence is given, of which one part is underlined. Following the sentence are five choices. The first (A) choice simply repeats the underlined part. Then you have four additional choices which suggest other ways to express the underlined part of the original sentence. If you think that the underlined part is correct as it stands, write the answer A. If you believe that the underlined part is incorrect, select from the other choices (B or C or D or E) whichever you think is correct. Grammar, sentence structure, word usage, and punctuation are to be considered in your decision. The original meaning of the sentence must be retained. Explanations of the key points behind these questions appear with the answers at the end of this exam.

1. Society does not *submerge itself under nature* but rather takes control of nature and utilizes its power.

    (A) submerge itself under nature
    (B) submit over itself to nature
    (C) submit itself to nature
    (D) submerge itself under the presence of nature
    (E) submerge itself to the presence of nature

2. We were amazed to see the *amount of people waiting in line to see Santa Claus*.

    (A) amount of people waiting in line to see Santa Claus.
    (B) number of people waiting in line to see Santa Claus.
    (C) amount of persons waiting in line to see Santa Claus.
    (D) amount of people waiting to see Santa Claus.
    (E) amount of people waiting in line to Santa Claus.

3. The ebullient chairman *was neither in favor of or opposed to the plan*.

    (A) was neither in favor of or opposed to the plan.
    (B) was not in favor of or opposed to the plan.
    (C) was neither in favor of the plan or opposed to it.
    (D) was neither in favor of the plan or opposed to the plan.
    (E) was neither in favor of nor opposed to the plan.

4. He will probably continue *to go astray among* his shallow and nebulous ideals.

    (A) to go astray among
    (B) to wander askance and astray among
    (C) to go askance amonst
    (D) to wander askance amongst
    (E) to wander askance and astray between

5. Of the two candidates, I think *he is the best suited.*
   - (A) he is the best suited.
   - (B) that he is the best suited.
   - (C) he is suited best.
   - (D) he is the better suited.
   - (E) he's the best suited.

6. Every pupil in the whole class understood the assignment *except I* and that is why I feel so stupid.
   - (A) except I
   - (B) excepting I
   - (C) outside of me
   - (D) excepting me
   - (E) except me

7. Geronimo, American Indian chief of the Apache tribe, lived to *the age of eighty years old.*
   - (A) the age of eighty years old.
   - (B) the old and ripe age of eighty.
   - (C) the ripe old age of eighty years old.
   - (D) be eighty years old.
   - (E) be a ripe and eighty years old.

8. European film distributors originated the art of "dubbing"—*the substitution of lip-synchronized translations* in foreign languages for the original soundtrack voices.
   - (A) —the substitution of lip-synchronized translations
   - (B) ; the substitution of lip-synchronized translations
   - (C) —the substitutions of translations synchronized by the lips
   - (D) , the lip-synchronized substitution of translations
   - (E) . The substitution of lip-synchronized translations

9. At dawn in the morning of the fiftieth day at sea, *a glimpse of the islands was caught.*
   - (A) a glimpse of the islands was caught.
   - (B) a glimpse of the islands were caught.
   - (C) we caught a glimpse of the islands.
   - (D) the islands were caught a glimpse of.
   - (E) we caught a glimpse of the islands's view.

10. *Finally and at long last* the old dog opened both eyes and sniffed the morning air.
    - (A) Finally and at long last
    - (B) Finally
    - (C) But at long last
    - (D) So finally
    - (E) Yet at long last

11. Sitting around the bonfire on the beach, *mystery stories were told by each of us.*
    - (A) mystery stories were told by each of us.
    - (B) mystery stories were told by all of us.
    - (C) each of us told mystery stories.
    - (D) stories of mystery were told by each of us.
    - (E) there were told mystery stories by each of us.

12. "When my husband *will come home*, I'll tell him you called," the housewife sighed into the phone.

    (A) will come home,

    (B) will come home

    (C) will have come home,

    (D) comes home,

    (E) has come home,

13. The pseudonym of Emily Bronte, *the author of Wuthering Heights*, was Ellis Bell.

    (A) , the author of *Wuthering Heights,*

    (B) , the authoress of *Wuthering Heights,*

    (C) (she happens to have written *Wuthering Heights*)

    (D) (she happens to be the authoress of *Wuthering Heights*)

    (E) (she wrote *Wuthering Heights* all by herself)

14. *After he graduated school,* he joined the army.

    (A) After he graduated school,

    (B) After he was graduated from school,

    (C) When he graduated school,

    (D) After hc graduated school

    (E) As he was graduated from school,

15. This book has been *laying here for weeks*.

    (A) laying here for weeks.

    (B) laying here weeks.

    (C) laying down here for weeks.

    (D) lieing here for weeks.

    (E) lying here for weeks.

16. Successful revolution from *the utmost first to the utmost last* is a movement calling for the iron unity of all members.

    (A) the utmost first to the utmost last

    (B) the very first to the very last

    (C) the utmost

    (D) first to last

    (E) the first to the last

17. Inspecting her son's report card, *his mother noted* that he had made good grades in Latin and history.

    (A) his mother noted

    (B) it was noted by his mother

    (C) his mother had noted

    (D) a notation was made by his mother

    (E) Robert's mother noted

18. The loud noise of subway trains and trolley cars *frighten people from the country*.

    (A) frighten people from the country.

    (B) frighten country people.

    (C) frighten persons from the country.

    (D) frightens country people.

    (E) frighten people who come from the country.

19. George Washington Carver was *an American botanicalist* around the turn of the eighteenth century.

    (A) an American botanicalist
    (B) a American botanicalist
    (C) an American botanist
    (D) a botanicalist in America
    (E) a botanist of the United States of America

20. I think they, *as a rule, are much more conniving than us.*

    (A) as a rule, are much more conniving than us.
    (B) as a rule are much more conniving than us.
    (C) as a rule, are much more conniving than we.
    (D) as a rule; are much more conniving than us.
    (E) are, as a rule, much more conniving than us.

21. The old man told *Mary and I* many stories about his childhood in the hills of Scotland.

    (A) Mary and I   (D) I and Mary
    (B) Mary and me   (E) Mary together with me
    (C) me and Mary

22. The soldiers who left Valley Forge with General Washington *sure enough had won* a spiritual victory.

    (A) sure enough had won   (D) had won
    (B) sure had won   (E) will have won
    (C) sure must have won

END OF TEST

Go on to do the following Test in this Examination, just as you would be expected to do on the actual exam.

TEST II. SENTENCE COMPLETION

TIME: 10 Minutes. 15 Questions.

DIRECTIONS: Each of the completion questions in this test consists of an incomplete sentence. Each sentence is followed by a series of lettered words, one of which best completes the sentence. Select the word that best completes the meaning of each sentence, and mark the letter of that word opposite that sentence.

1. An _____ study should reveal the influence of environment on man.
   (A) ecumenical   (B) endemic
   (C) ecological   (D) epiigraphic
   (E) incidental

2. The researcher in the field of _____ was interested in race improvement.
   (A) euthenics   (B) euthanasia
   (C) euphuism   (D) euphonics
   (E) philology

3. _____ concerns itself with _____ of plants.
   (A) etiology . . . eating
   (B) ethnology . . . drying
   (C) etiolation . . . blanching
   (D) epistemology . . . collecting
   (E) cardiology . . . sitting

4. Through a _____ circumstance, we unexpectedly found ourselves on the same steamer with Uncle Harry.
   (A) fortuitous   (B) fetid
   (C) friable   (D) lambent
   (E) habitual

5. I had a terrible night caused by an _____ during my sleep.
   (A) epilogue   (B) insipidity
   (C) insouciance   (D) optimum
   (E) incubus

6. The Romans depended on the _____ for the _____ of their homes.
   (A) lares . . . protection
   (B) caries . . . painting
   (C) aborigines . . . blessing
   (D) mores . . . erection
   (E) resilience . . . insolvency

7. In the study of grammatical forms, the _____ is very helpful.
   (A) syllogism   (B) mattock
   (C) paradigm   (D) pimpernel
   (E) palladium

8. The _____ method is used to _____ admission.
   (A) plutonic . . . offer
   (B) Socratic . . . elicit
   (C) sardonic . . . bar
   (D) Hippocratic . . . prepare
   (E) refrigerant . . . desist

9. They had a wonderful view of the bay through the _____.
   (A) nadir   (B) behemoth
   (C) oriel   (D) fiat
   (E) pastorate

10. There is no reason to insult and _____ the man simply because you do not agree with him.
    (A) depict   (B) enervate
    (C) defame   (D) distort
    (E) enhance

11. Almost every citizen of a large city suffers from the _____ of organized crime.
    (A) debility   (B) tenuousness
    (C) depredations   (D) fortuitousness
    (E) depletion

12. He failed the examination because none of his answers was _____ to the questions asked.
    (A) pertinent   (B) omniscient
    (C) referential   (D) implacable
    (E) elusive

13. The new champion, accompanied by his
    _____, took over the country club
    dining room.
    (A) traumas   (B) reveries
    (C) entourage   (D) sobriquet
    (E) pasquinade

14. Her feeling of _____ was so _____
    that all the other patients were soon smiling
    or laughing.
    (A) contrition . . . repulsive
    (B) embolism . . . catastrophic
    (C) melancholia . . . cataclysmic
    (D) ebullience . . . contagious
    (E) rehabilitation . . . paranoiac

15. His _____ was so great that he
    became the _____ of all our disputes
    about art and music.
    (A) euphony . . . censor
    (B) irascibility . . . canister
    (C) contumely . . . reimburser
    (D) erudition . . . arbiter
    (E) pomposity . . . idolater

END OF TEST

*Go on to do the following Test in this Examination, just as you would
be expected to do on the actual exam.*

TEST III. CONSTRUCTION SHIFT

TIME: 12 Minutes. 17 Questions.

DIRECTIONS: *For each question in this test you are given a sentence to rephrase or "rewrite" according to the directions that follow it. If you wish, you may mentally rephrase the sentence and make notes in your test book before you decide on an answer.*

Below each sentence and its directions are listed choices of words and phrases lettered from A to E for your "rewritten" sentence. The word or phrase you select should be the one that, if used in the sentence, would make your "rewritten" sentence best comply with the requirements of standard written English. When you have thought out a good sentence, choose the letter for the word or phrase that you need for that sentence and blacken that letter on your answer sheet.

If the sentence you thought out does not include any of the five choices given, try to rephrase your sentence, since there are different correct sentences to be obtained, given the original sentence and the directions. Remember, make only those changes required by the directions. Your "rewritten" sentence must comply with the requirements of standard written English and should convey, as far as possible, the original meaning of the sentence.

1. Take those apples even though they are a bit green.

   Change *even though they* to *which.*

   (A) nevertheless
   (B) let's hope
   (C) we realize
   (D) consequently
   (E) it seems

2. Perhaps by noon we shall have shot five rabbits.

   Begin the sentence with *When noon arrives.*

   (A) we may shoot
   (B) we might have shot
   (C) it is our expectation to shoot
   (D) it is estimated that we will have shot
   (E) we shot

3. Jerry was running in the rain and he tripped on a stick.

   Begin with *Running in the rain,*

   (A) Jerry tripped on a stick.
   (B) a stick tripped Jerry.
   (C) a stick caused Jerry to trip.
   (D) a stick made Jerry trip.
   (E) Jerry was tripped on a stick.

4. He wrote all kinds of plays including plays that were comedies, histories, and tragedies.

   Change *all kinds of plays* to *several kinds of plays.*

   (A) . They were comedies,
   (B) . They are comedies,
   (C) , comedies
   (D) : comedies
   (E) ; comedies

5. Help was asked of Tom and me by my father.

   Begin with *My father asked.*

   (A) Tom and me to help.
   (B) Me and Tom to help.
   (C) Tom and I to help.
   (D) I and Tom to help.
   (E) help from Tom and me.

6. Was she really the one whom you saw last night?

   Begin with *Was it really.*

   (A) she which
   (B) she who
   (C) her who
   (D) her whom
   (E) she whom

7. It displeases my parents when Richard and I stay out late every night.

   Begin with *My parents don't approve.*

   (A) of me and Richard staying out
   (B) of Richard and me staying out
   (C) of Richard's and my staying out
   (D) when Richard and me stay out
   (E) about Richard and me staying out

8. That man is a famous man in England as well as Russia.

   Begin with *He is.*

   (A) not only of fame in England but also in Russia.
   (B) also famous in England as well as in Russia.
   (C) famous not only in England but also in Russia.
   (D) not only famous in England but also in Russia.
   (E) of a famous reputation in England as well as in Russia.

9. He likes swimming and he also likes playing tennis.

   Change *swimming* to *to swim.*

   (A) and playing tennis.
   (B) and he likes playing tennis.
   (C) and he likes to play tennis.
   (D) and to play tennis.
   (E) also to play tennis.

10. My whole family was invited by them to the cookout; my father, my mother, my sister and I were invited.

    Begin with *They invited.*

    (A) cookout, my mother, my father, my sister and me.
    (B) cookout, my mother, my father, my sister and I.
    (C) cookout—my mother, my father, my sister and I.
    (D) cookout—my mother, my father, my sister and me.
    (E) cookout including my mother, my father, my sister and I.

11. The search for the lost ring was abandoned as we had been raking the beach for hours.

    Change *as* to *after.*

    (A) raking the beach
    (B) the beach had been raked
    (C) having the beach raked
    (D) the time that the beach was raked
    (E) we had raked the beach

12. Her brother at no time has been dependable and he never will be dependable.

    Begin with *Her brother has never.*

    (A) been dependable and he never will be.
    (B) tried to be dependable and never will be.
    (C) been dependable and never will be.
    (D) shown dependability and never will be.
    (E) at any time been dependable and never will be.

13. That book is interesting; it is full of stories of adventure.

Change the semicolon to *because*.

(A) it is filled with
(B) there is in it
(C) it is stuffed with
(D) we find in it
(E) it has many

14. That he was bitterly disappointed was clearly indicated by his tone.

Begin with *His tone*.

(A) clearly implied
(B) clearly inferred
(C) clearly remarked
(D) implied a clear inference
(E) clearly implied and inferred

15. At this time kick your feet in the water in the way that Gregory just did.

Begin with *Now*.

(A) like Gregory just done.
(B) just like Gregory did.
(C) like Gregory just did.
(D) just as Gregory did.
(E) as Gregory just did.

16. Carson's sells merchandise of equal quality while having a lower price.

Change *while* to *and*.

(A) prices its merchandise lower.
(B) sells at a lower price.
(C) is having a lower price.
(D) has a lower price.
(E) its prices are lower.

17. The reason Frank is going to Arizona is explained by the fact that he is in need of a climate which is dry.

Change *is explained by the fact that* to *is that*.

(A) he must have a climate which is dry.
(B) a dry climate is what he needs.
(C) a climate which is dry is what he needs.
(D) the climate is dry.
(E) he needs a dry climate.

END OF TEST

TEST IV. CLARITY OF EXPRESSION

TIME: 8 Minutes. 10 Questions.

DIRECTIONS: Each of the following questions consists of five different ways in which the same thought may be phrased. You are to choose the one phrasing that makes the intended meaning clear. The correct answer is the one that avoids ambiguity, that does not leave the actual meaning open to questions, or that does not leave you guessing about what is intended. The answer must also be grammatically correct and logical in its sequence.

Correct and explanatory answers are provided at the end of the exam. After you have completed the entire exam, read the explanations carefully. They'll reinforce your strengths and pinpoint your weaknesses so that you know just what to study to raise your score.

1. (A) The supervisor told Mr. Johnson that he thought his work was improving.
   (B) Mr. Johnson was told by his supervisor that his work was improving.
   (C) The supervisor told Mr. Johnson that his work was improving he thought.
   (D) The supervisor complimented Mr. Johnson on the improvement in the quality of his work.
   (E) The supervisor thought his work was improving and he told Mr. Johnson so.

2. (A) When you have finished the book and written your report, please return it to the library.
   (B) After you finish the book and write your report, please return it to the library.
   (C) When you have finished the book and written your report, please return the book to the library.
   (D) After finishing the book and writing your report, it must be returned to the library.
   (E) When you have read the book and written your report, you should return it to the library.

3. (A) Cruising rapidly up the muddy river, the captain suddenly spotted a huge log swirling directly in front of the boat.
   (B) While cruising rapidly up the muddy river, a huge log was suddenly spotted swirling directly in front of the boat.
   (C) While the boat was cruising rapidly up the muddy river, the captain suddenly spotted a huge log swirling directly ahead.
   (D) While cruising rapidly up the muddy river, the captain suddenly came upon a huge log swirling directly in front of him.
   (E) The captain suddenly spotted a huge log swirling directly ahead while cruising up the muddy river.

4. (A) I have enjoyed the study of the Spanish language not only because of its beauty and the opportunity it offers to understand the Hispanic culture, but also because of its usefulness in business associations.
   (B) I have enjoyed studying Spanish not only because of its beauty and the opportunity to understand the Hispanic culture, but also because of its usefulness in business associations.
   (C) I have enjoyed the study of the Spanish language not only because of its beauty and the opportunity it offers to understand the Hispanic culture, but also to make use of it in business associations.
   (D) I have enjoyed studying Spanish not only because it is beautiful and it affords an opportunity to understand the Spanish people, but also to use it in business associations.
   (E) I have enjoyed the study of the Spanish language not only because of its beauty and the opportunity it offers to understand the Hispanic culture, but because of its usefulness in business associations.

5. (A) After failing four tests in a row, the instructor summoned me to his office for a conference.
   (B) Failing four tests in a row, the instructor and I scheduled a conference in his office.
   (C) Since I flunked four tests in a row, the instructor had summoned me for a conference to his office.
   (D) Because of failing four tests in a row, the instructor summoned me to his office for a conference.
   (E) After I had failed four tests in a row, the instructor summoned me to his office for a conference.

6. (A) If anyone wants to volunteer for the job, they should raise their hand.
   (B) Anyone who wants to volunteer for the job should raise their hand.
   (C) If anyone wants to volunteer for the job, he or she should raise their hand.

(D) If anyone wants to volunteer for the job, he should raise his hand.

(E) Any person wishing to volunteer for the job should raise their hand.

7. (A) Bob and Jim gathered their fishing gear and their bikes, heading for the lake the day after school closed for the summer.

(B) The day after school closed for the summer, Bob and Jim gathered their fishing gear, jumped on their bikes and headed for the lake.

(C) Gathering their fishing gear and jumping on their bikes, Bob and Jim headed for the lake the day after school closed for the summer.

(D) The day after school closed for the summer, Bob and Jim jumped on their bikes with their fishing gear and headed for the lake.

(E) Bob and Jim headed for the lake with their bikes and fishing gear the day after school closed for the summer.

8. (A) Because he was using a new lightweight racquet, Eric was able to defeat John in their tennis match.

(B) Eric attributed the fact that he was able to defeat John at tennis to his new lightweight racquet.

(C) That Eric was able to defeat John at tennis was primarily due to his new lightweight racquet.

(D) Eric won the match against John primarily because of his new lightweight racquet.

(E) John lost the tennis match to Eric primarily because he was using his new lightweight racquet.

9. (A) Although the doctor operated at once, it was not a success and the patient died.

(B) Although the doctor operated at once, it was unsuccessful and the patient died.

(C) Although the doctor operated at once, it could not save the patient's life.

(D) In spite of the speed with which the doctor operated, it was not a success and the patient died.

(E) Although the doctor performed the operation at once, it was not a success and the patient died.

10. (A) The investigator followed the suspect all the way from San Francisco to Los Angeles where he finally saw him meet a confederate.

(B) The investigator followed the suspect from San Francisco to Los Angeles before he saw him meet a confederate.

(C) The investigator had to follow the suspect all the way from San Francisco to Los Angeles before he saw him meet a confederate.

(D) The investigator followed the suspect all the way from San Francisco to Los Angeles and there finally saw him meet a confederate.

(E) The investigator followed the suspect all the way from San Francisco to Los Angeles and then he saw him meet a confederate.

END OF PART

PART II. LOGIC IN READING AND WRITING

TEST V. READING BETWEEN THE LINES

TIME: 15 Minutes. 20 Questions.

DIRECTIONS: This test of reading comprehension consists of a number of different passages. Several questions are based on each passage. The questions consist of incomplete statements about the passage. Each incomplete statement is followed by five choices lettered (A) (B) (C) (D) (E). Mark your answer sheet with the letter of the choice which best completes the statement, and which best conveys the meaning of the passage.

Questions 1 to 5

Society everywhere is in conspiracy against the manhood of every one of its members. Society is a joint-stock company, in which the members agree for the better securing of his bread to each shareholder, to surrender the liberty and culture of the eater. The virtue in most request is conformity. Self-reliance is its aversion. It loves not realities and creators, but names and customs.

1. According to the passage, the practice of adhering, at all times, to the status quo is

    (A)   praiseworthy
    (B)   characteristic of inadequate people
    (C)   a matter of democratic choice
    (D)   reserved only for the intelligent
    (E)   not practical

2. The second sentence of the paragraph uses which of the following rhetorical devices?

    (A) Circumlocution   (D) Simile
    (B) Inversion   (E) Alliteration
    (C) Metaphor

3. Society, so the selection implies,

    (A)   does not encourage an individual to be creative
    (B)   wants its members to be self-starters
    (C)   can thrive only under democratic rule
    (D)   encourages investments in stocks and bonds
    (E)   will not improve unless the quality of its leaders improves

4. You may infer that the author

   (A) was a philosopher-humorist
   (B) was a leader of oyster pirates, a deck hand on a North Pacific sealer, a mill worker hobo, and a college student for a time
   (C) achieved a reputation as a clever business entrepreneur
   (D) was a vivid personality who led a strenuous life and became president of the United States
   (E) was an intelligent, energetic non-conformist

5. The attitude of the writer is

   (A) sardonic and destructive
   (B) petulant and forbidding
   (C) maudlin and merciful
   (D) critical and constructive
   (E) reflective and passive

6. Was Mussolini sincere?

   The question above suffers from

   (A) a false analogy
   (B) alliteration
   (C) an undefined abstraction
   (D) synergism
   (E) inversion

7. Representative democracy will not work because if a quarterback has to poll the team before every play, he will never score a point.

   The statement above suffers from

   (A) parallelism
   (B) an omitted conclusion
   (C) the fallacy of seeing a cause where there is none shown
   (D) a synedoche
   (E) a false analogy

Questions 8 to 9

   At times I sit at my narrow window and gaze down upon the courtyard below. I muse upon the eighty years of my life. And wish profoundly, oh so profoundly, that I had it all to do over again.

8. The sentences above are written in the

   (A) second person plural
   (B) third person singular
   (C) second person singular
   (D) first person singular
   (E) third person plural

9. The mood of the speaker in the sentences above is one of

   (A) boredom
   (B) regret
   (C) anger
   (D) celebration
   (E) fear

10. My ancestors are New England Puritans; therefore I am naturally opposed to liberal Democrats.

    The statement above is an example of which of the following logical fallacies?

    (A) Non-sequitur
    (B) Unsupported sampling
    (C) Faulty comparison
    (D) Unsupported generalization
    (E) Vague abstraction

11. "This little car is the best, the greatest, the most fantastic economy car on the market. I cannot begin to describe to you the praise, the cries of delight, the veritable enthusiasm that its buyers have expressed to me," the salesman spluttered.
    "Try more information and less pitch next time, fella," the woman said and walked away.

    The customer criticizes the salesman because his remarks are too

    (A) detailed and circumstantial
    (B) exact and specific
    (C) verbose and unspecific
    (D) general and philosophical
    (E) impolite and disrespectful

12. He ran down the avenue, making a noise like ten horses at a gallop.

    Which of the following rhetorical devices are employed in the sentence above?

    (A) Parallelism and metaphor
    (B) Hyperbole and simile
    (C) Alliteration and metaphor
    (D) Hyperbole and onomatopoeia
    (E) Analogy and paralepsis

13. Every investigation by my parents into the moral decency of my friends inevitably becomes a witch hunt.

    The statement above suffers from

    (A) unsupported generalization
    (B) insufficient sampling
    (C) name calling
    (D) vague abstraction
    (E) an omitted conclusion

14. The liberalization of education has produced a generation of college graduates who can neither read nor write.

    The statement above suffers from

    (A) name calling
    (B) unsupported generalization
    (C) faulty comparison
    (D) alliteration
    (E) synergism

Questions 15 to 20

"I have considered the structure of all volant animals, and find the folding continuity of the bat's wings most easily accomodated to the human form. Upon this model I shall begin my task tomorrow, and in a year expect to tower into the air beyond the malice or pursuit of man. But I will work only on this condition, that the art shall not be divulged, and that you shall not require me to make wings for any but ourselves."

"Why," said Rasselas, "should you envy others so great an advantage? All skill ought to be exerted for universal good; every man has owed much to others, and ought to repay the kindness that he has received."

15. The word "volant," in the context of the preceding paragraph, means

(A) crawling   (D) ferocious
(B) violent   (E) flying
(C) carnivorous

16. The point of view of Rasselas is one that encourages

(A) helping others   (D) artistic pursuits
(B) military victory   (E) protecting ones property
(C) intellectual pursuits

17. Rasselas' tone of voice is

(A) childlike and pure   (D) malicious and cunning
(B) philosophically parental   (E) bewildered
(C) lighthearted

18. The person to whom Rasselas is speaking is

(A) a tailor   (D) an artist
(B) a gambler   (E) a biologist
(C) a bat

19. The attitude of the person giving his point of view is one of

(A) optimism   (D) innocence
(B) sprightliness   (E) sarcasm
(C) distrust

20. The conversation is probably being held

(A) in private   (D) in a movie theater
(B) at a cocktail party   (E) in an airplane
(C) with many friends present

END OF TEST

TEST VI. RELATIONSHIPS BETWEEN SENTENCES

TIME: 15 Minutes. 20 Questions.

DIRECTIONS: In this group of questions, two or more sentences are followed by a question or statement about them. Read each group of sentences, then choose the best answer to the question or the best completion of the statement. On your answer sheet, blacken the space under the letter (A, B, C, D, or E) of your answer choice.

Correct and explanatory answers are provided at the end of the exam. After you have completed the entire exam, read the explanations carefully. They'll reinforce your strengths and pinpoint your weaknesses so that you know just what to study to raise your score.

1. David is very well organized.
    The top of his desk can best be described as chaotic.

    What does the second sentence do?
    (A) It gives a definition of the concept.
    (B) It presents an exception.
    (C) It draws a conclusion.
    (D) It provides an example.
    (E) It makes a comparison.

2. The elementary school is just around the corner from our house.
    The high school is two miles away on the other side of town.

    The objects in the sentences are organized according to
    (A) how large they are   (D) what they look like
    (B) when they are seen   (E) where they are
    (C) how they are used

3. I'll have a hot dog and french fries for lunch.
    The tuna salad is more nutritious and it has fewer calories.

    What is happening in the sentences?
    (A) A comparison is made in terms of taste and quantity.
    (B) A recommendation is made on the basis of nutritive value.
    (C) A conclusion is drawn on the basis of taste.
    (D) A comparison is made in terms of calories and cost.
    (E) A relationship is drawn between quantity and quality.

4. The crystal goblets are beautiful but not very practical.
   The plastic glasses are practical but unaesthetic.

   What does the second sentence do?
   (A) It gives a definition of the concept.
   (B) It presents an exception.
   (C) It draws a conclusion.
   (D) It provides an example.
   (E) It makes a comparison.

5. Tuition costs at private colleges are very high.
   Enrollment at state universities is on the rise.

   What does the second sentence do?
   (A) It gives a cause.   (D) It makes a generalization.
   (B) It gives an example.   (E) It gives an effect.
   (C) It makes an exception.

6. There are more male architects than female architects.
   Men are better at building than women are.

   What does the second sentence do?
   (A) It gives a cause.
   (B) It gives an example.
   (C) It makes an exception.
   (D) It makes a generalization.
   (E) It confirms the first statement.

7. Mary is excellent at spelling.
   She reads a few pages from her dictionary every night before going to sleep.

   What does the second sentence do?
   (A) It gives a cause.
   (B) It gives an example.
   (C) It makes an exception.
   (D) It makes a generalization.
   (E) It confirms the first statement.

8. A plane leaves New York at 1 PM and arrives in Toronto before 2 PM.
   A car leaves New York right after breakfast and arrives in Toronto in time for dinner.

   What is happening in the sentences?
   (A) A comparison is made in terms of speed and cost.
   (B) A recommendation is made on the basis of time.
   (C) A conclusion is drawn on the basis of speed.
   (D) A comparison is made in terms of time and method of transportation.
   (E) A relationship is drawn between air travel and time.

9. Bob is very responsible.
   When he is asked to do a job, he does it immediately.

   What does the second sentence do?

   (A) It gives a cause.
   (B) It gives an example.
   (C) It makes an exception.
   (D) It makes a generalization.
   (E) It makes a comparison.

10. My apartment is on the second floor next door to the laundry room.
    My friend lives on the fourth floor across from the elevator.

    The objects in the sentences are organized according to

    (A) how old they are
    (B) when they are seen
    (C) how they are used
    (D) how they look
    (E) where they are

11. The tenor sang beautifully but his girth was inconsistent with his role as
    the handsome rake.
    All opera singers are too fat for the roles they play.

    What does the second sentence do?

    (A) It gives a cause.
    (B) It gives an example.
    (C) It makes an exception.
    (D) It makes a generalization.
    (E) It confirms the first statement.

12. Jules Verne has been called the father of modern science fiction.
    In his tales of adventure and romance, he predicted many scientific
    achievements of the 20th century.

    What does the second sentence do?

    (A) It gives a definition of the concept.
    (B) It presents an exception.
    (C) It draws a conclusion.
    (D) It provides an example.
    (E) It makes a comparison.

13. The Civil War seems remote and lifeless in the pages of my history
    book.
    When reading *The Red Badge of Courage* I can picture the soldiers in
    combat and hear the sound of their gunfire.

    What is happening in these sentences?

    (A) A comparison is being made in terms of past and present.
    (B) A recommendation is made on the basis of history.
    (C) A conclusion is drawn on the basis of fact.
    (D) A comparison is made in terms of historical fact and historical
        fiction.
    (E) A relationship is drawn between literature and life.

14. Geometry has many practical applications in daily life.
Bridges, skyscrapers and homes are based upon geometric principles.

What does the second sentence do?

(A) It gives a definition of the concept.
(B) It presents an exception.
(C) It draws a conclusion.
(D) It provides an example.
(E) It makes a comparison.

15. Favorable weather conditions resulted in an excellent vegetable crop this year.
Prices are sure to come down.

What is happening in the sentences?

(A) A conclusion is drawn on the basis of opinion.
(B) A recommendation is made on the basis of weather conditions.
(C) A conclusion is drawn on the basis of fact.
(D) A comparison is made in terms of food prices and weather conditions.
(E) A relationship is drawn between growing conditions and crop size.

16. I prefer comedies to tragedies.
"King Lear" is my favorite play.

What does the second sentence do?

(A) It gives a definition of the concept.
(B) It presents an exception.
(C) It draws a conclusion.
(D) It provides an example.
(E) It makes a comparison.

17. Jim was only two when his brother Jack was born.
Jack was in kindergarten when Jane came into the world.

The objects in the sentences are organized according to

(A) how old they are
(B) what sex they are
(C) how they look
(D) how they are related
(E) where they live

18. Idioms can only be interpreted as a unit.
The separate words that make up expressions such as *all in all* or *right of way* do not mean a thing when analyzed word by word.

What does the second sentence do?

(A) It gives a definition of the concept.
(B) It presents an exception.
(C) It draws a conclusion.
(D) It provides an example.
(E) It makes a comparison.

19. Mathematicians of old performed their calculations by moving the beads on an abacus.

    Today mathematical equations are solved by pushing buttons on a calculator.

    What is happening in the sentences?

    (A) A comparison is made in terms of science and mathematics.
    (B) A recommendation is made on the basis of speed.
    (C) A conclusion is drawn on the basis of accuracy.
    (D) A comparison is made in terms of past and present.
    (E) A relationship is drawn between speed and accuracy.

20. Home heating costs have tripled in the last decade.
    The home insulation business is booming.

    What does the second sentence do?

    (A) It gives a cause.
    (B) It gives an example.
    (C) It gives an effect.
    (D) It makes a generalization.
    (E) It confirms the first statement.

END OF TEST

*Go on to do the following Test in this Examination, just as you would
be expected to do on the actual exam.*

TEST VII. LOGIC AND ORGANIZATION

TIME: 15 Minutes. 24 Questions.

DIRECTIONS: This test consists of brief passages in which each sentence is numbered. Following each passage are questions which refer to the numbered sentences in the passage. Answer each question by choosing the best alternative (A,B,C,D, or E) and blacken the space corresponding to your choice on the Answer Sheet provided.

Questions 1 to 8

[1]When television is good, nothing—not the theater, not the magazines or newspapers—nothing is inferior. [2]But when television is bad, nothing is worse. [3]I invite you to sit down in front of your television set when your station goes on the air and stay there without a book, magazine, newspaper, or anything else to distract you. [4]Keep your eyes glued to that set until the station signs off. [5]There are many people in this great country, and radio stations must serve all of us. [6]I can assure you that you will observe a vast wasteland. [7]They are game shows, violence, audience participation shows and formula comedies about totally unbelievable families. [8]Followed by blood and thunder, mayhem, more violence, sadism, murder, Western badmen, Western goodmen, private eyes, gangsters, still more violence, and cartoons. [9]And, endlessly, there are commercials that scream and cajole and offend without end. [10]True, you will see a few things you will enjoy. [11]And most of all, there is boredom. [12]But they will be very, very few. [13]And if you think I exaggerate and overstate the matter, try it.

1. The word *inferior* in sentence 1 should be

   (A) left as it is
   (B) changed to *worse*
   (C) changed to *the best*
   (D) changed to *anterior*
   (E) changed to *better*

2. What should be done with sentence 5?

   (A) It should be left as it is.
   (B) It should follow sentence 1.
   (C) It should be omitted entirely.
   (D) It should be made into two separate sentences.
   (E) It should follow sentence 8.

3. The word *wasteland* in sentence 6 should be

   (A) left as it is
   (B) changed to *baseball park*
   (C) changed to *ocean*
   (D) changed to *alley*
   (E) changed to *football field*

4. The meaning of sentence 7 would be clearest if

(A) left as it is
(B) the phrase *They are* is changed to *You will see*
(C) the phrase *They are* is changed to *They will see*
(D) the word *totally* is omitted
(E) everything after *comedies* is omitted

5. What should be done with sentence 8?

(A) It should be left as is.
(B) It should be joined to sentence 7.
(C) It should be divided into 2 sentences.
(D) It should begin with *Thus*.
(E) It should end with *therefore*.

6. Sentence 9 would be most improved if

(A) *and offend* were omitted
(B) *without end* were omitted
(C) *and advertisements* were added after *commercials*
(D) *ceaselessly* were substituted for *endlessly*
(E) *cajole* were changed to *cavort*

7. Sentence 11 is best placed

(A) after sentence 6
(B) after sentence 13
(C) after sentence 9
(D) after sentence 5
(E) after sentence 12

8. Sentence 13 would be best if the phrase *exaggerate and overstate the matter* were

(A) left as it is
(B) changed to *exaggerate and understate the matter*
(C) changed to *magnify and overstate*
(D) changed to *multiply the matter*
(E) changed to *exaggerate*

Questions 9 to 16

[1]With increasing prosperity, West European youth is having a fling that is creating distinctive consumer and cultural patterns. [2]The increasing emergence in Europe of that phenomenon well known in America as the "youth market." [3]This is a market in which enterprising businesses cater to the demands of teenagers and older youths. [4]The Norwegians have simply adopted the English word "teenager." [5]In the United States, the market is large, successful, wide-ranging and well established. [6]Moreover, in Western Europe, the youth market may appropriately be said to be in its diapers. [7]In some countries, such as Britain, West Germany and France, it is more advanced than in the others. [8]Some manifestations of the market, chiefly sociological, have been recorded. [9]But they are only just beginning to be the subject of organized consumer research and promotion.

9. In sentence 1, *having a fling* is best
    (A) left as it is
    (B) changed to *making an ascent*
    (C) changed to *throwing a party*
    (D) changed to *racing with time*
    (E) changed to *having a flight*

10. The meaning of sentence 2 would be clearest if the sentence is
    (A) left as it is
    (B) begun with *The hope will be*
    (C) ended with *and often grandparents*
    (D) begun with *The result has been*
    (E) ended with *and that is all*

11. What should be done with sentence 4?
    (A) It should be left as it is.
    (B) It should be made into two separate sentences.
    (C) It should be the topic sentence of the second paragraph.
    (D) The word *simply* should be omitted.
    (E) It should be omitted entirely.

12. Sentence 5 would be most improved if
    (A) it were left as it is
    (B) *In the United States* were omitted
    (C) *large, successful* were omitted
    (D) the entire sentence were joined to the end of sentence 4
    (E) the entire sentence were joined to the end of sentence 3 with *and*

13. Sentence 6 should begin
    (A) the way it begins now
    (B) with *Western Europe*
    (C) with *Outside of Western Europe*
    (D) with *In Western Europe*
    (E) with *In Western Europe, therefore*

14. The word *diapers* in sentence 6 should be
    (A) left as it is
    (B) changed to *infancy*
    (C) changed to *winter*
    (D) changed to *insanity*
    (E) changed to *prison*

15. Sentence 7 is best placed
    (A) where it is now
    (B) after sentence 3
    (C) before sentence 3
    (D) after sentence 9
    (E) after sentence 8

16. If the passage is to be divided into three paragraphs, the third paragraph should begin with
    (A) sentence 6
    (B) sentence 8
    (C) sentence 4
    (D) sentence 2
    (E) sentence 7

Questions 17 to 24

[1]A Polish proverb claims that fish, to taste right, should swim three times. [2]To taste right it should swim in water, in butter and in wine. [3]The early efforts of scientists in the food industry were directed at improving the preparation, preservation and distribution. [4]Our memories of certain food-stuffs eaten during the Second World War suggest that, although these might have been nutritious. [5]They certainly did not taste good nor were they particularly appealing in appearance or smell. [6]With regard to touch, systems of classification are of little value because of the extraordinary sensitivity of the skin. [7]This neglect of the sensory appeal of foods is happily becoming a thing of the past. [8]A book grew out of this course. [9]Indeed, in 1957, the University of California considered the subject of such main importance to set up a course in the analysis of foods by sensory methods. [10]The authors hope that it will be useful to food technologists in industry. [11]They also hope to help others researching the problem of the sensory evaluation of foods according to sight, taste and smell.

17. Sentence 2 would be best if

    (A) it were left as it is
    (B) the part after *swim* were joined with sentence 1
    (C) the part after *swim* were omitted
    (D) the part after *swim* were joined to sentence 1 with *since*
    (E) it were made into two sentences, the new one beginning after *swim*

18. Sentence 3 would be most improved if

    (A) it began with *At that time*
    (B) it ended with *of fish in butter and wine*
    (C) it ended with *of nutritious food*
    (D) the part after *preparation* were omitted
    (E) the word *preservation* were omitted

19. What should be done with sentence 4?

    (A) It should be left as it is.
    (B) It should be joined to sentence 3 with *since*.
    (C) It should be joined to sentence 2 with *and*.
    (D) It should begin with *Thus*.
    (E) It should be joined to sentence 5.

20. What should be done with sentence 6?

    (A) It should be left as it is.
    (B) It should follow sentence 3.
    (C) It should be made into two separate sentences.
    (D) It should be made into three separate sentences.
    (E) It should be omitted entirely.

21. Sentence 8 is best placed

    (A) after sentence 6
    (B) after sentence 3
    (C) after sentence 9

    (D) after sentence 11
    (E) after sentence 12

22. In sentence 9, *such main* is best

    (A) left as it is
    (B) changed to *charitable*
    (C) changed to *sufficient*

    (D) changed to *insufficient*
    (E) changed to *such suffering*

23. What should be done with sentence 11?

    (A) It should be left as it is.
    (B) It should begin with *Thus*.
    (C) The part after *foods* should be omitted.
    (D) It should end with *forever*.
    (E) The part after *sight* should be omitted.

24. If the passage is to be divided into two paragraphs, the second paragraph should begin with

    (A) sentence 7
    (B) sentence 6
    (C) sentence 11

    (D) sentence 5
    (E) sentence 3

END OF EXAMINATION

If you finish before the allotted time is up, check your work on this test only. Do not go back to earlier tests. When time runs out, compare your answers for this test and all the other tests in the examination with the correct key answers that follow.

CORRECT ANSWERS FOR VERISIMILAR EXAMINATION I.

TEST I. SENTENCE CORRECTION

1.C	4.A	7.D	10.B	13.A	16.D	19.C	21.B
2.B	5.D	8.A	11.C	14.B	17.A	20.C	22.D
3.E	6.E	9.C	12.D	15.E	18.D		

TEST I. EXPLANATORY ANSWERS

1. **(C)** *Under* is redundant when used with *submerge*.

2. **(B)** The word *amount* refers to *quantity thought of as a unit*. The word *number* refers to *quantity thought of as a collection of individual things*.

3. **(E)** Always use *neither* with *nor* and *either* with *or*.

4. **(A)** This sentence is correct.

5. **(D)** Use the comparative degree, *better*, when comparing two things or persons; use the superlative degree, *best*, when comparing more than two.

6. **(E)** The objective case, *me*, is correct because the object of a preposition (in this case, *except*) is in the objective case.

7. **(D)** *Age* and *years old* are synonyms and unnecessarily repetitive. Either one, but not both, may be used in this sentence.

8. **(A)** This sentence is correct.

9. **(C)** The introductory phrase requires a personal subject to modify.

10. **(B)** *Finally* and *at long last* are synonyms.

11. **(C)** Phrase and clause modifiers should be placed as close as possible to the words they modify. In the sentence in question, *each of us*, not *mystery stories*, was sitting around the campfire.

12. **(D)** The present tense is used to express future time in a subordinate clause beginning with *if*, *when*, *after*, *before*, *until*, and *as soon as*.

13. **(A)** According to *Webster's New Collegiate Dictionary*, an author is *one who writes* and is not *gender-dependent*. Commas are used to set off a nonrestrictive adjective modifier.

14. **(B)** The verb *graduate* means to receive an academic degree or diploma, which must be granted *from* some person or institution.

15. **(E)** The verb *lie* means *to assume a lying position* or *to be in a lying position*, as the book is. It is differentiated from the verb *lay*, which must always have an object; and it is conjugated *lie, lying, lay, lain*.

16. **(D)** *Utmost*, which means of the greatest or highest degree, is incorrectly used in the original sentence.

17. **(A)** This sentence is correct.

18. **(D)** The singular subject (*noise*) requires a singular verb (*frightens*). *Country people* is more concise than *people from the country*.

19. **(C)** The correct word for one who makes a study of plants is *botanist*.

20. **(C)** If the word following *than* introduces a clause, that word must be in the nominative case. This rule is true even if part of the clause is understood. In this sentence, *we* is the subject of the clause *than we are conniving*.

21. **(B)** The personal pronoun *I* should be *me*, since it serves as an object of the verb *told*.

22. **(D)** *Had won* is more concise than any other alternative.

TEST II. SENTENCE COMPLETION

1.C	3.C	5.E	7.C	9.C	11.C	13.C	15.D
2.A	4.A	6.A	8.B	10.C	12.A	14.D	

TEST III. CONSTRUCTION SHIFT

1.C	4.D	6.E	8.C	10.D	12.C	14.A	16.D
2.D	5.A	7.C	9.D	11.E	13.E	15.E	17.E
3.A							

TEST III. EXPLANATORY ANSWERS

1. **(C)** Take those apples *which we realize* are a bit green. This is the only choice that has the same connotation as the *even though* of the original sentence.

2. **(D)** *When noon arrives, it is estimated that we will have shot* five rabbits. *Perhaps* indicates an estimate.

3. **(A)** *Running in the rain, Jerry tripped on a stick.* The introductory phrase must modify *Jerry*.

4. **(D)** He wrote *several kinds of plays: comedies*, histories, and tragedies. A colon is used after an expression that formally introduces a list.

5. **(A)** *My father asked Tom and me to help. Me* is required since it is an object of the verb *ask*.

6. **(E)** *Was it really she whom* you saw last night? *She* is in the nominative case because it follows the verb *to be. Whom* is the object of the verb *saw*.

7. **(C)** *My parents don't approve of Richard's and my staying out* late every night. A noun or pronoun immediately preceding a gerund (staying) must be in the possessive case.

8. **(C)** *He is famous not only in England but also in Russia.* The correlative conjunctions *not only* and *but also* must each be followed by the same part of speech.

9. **(D)** He likes to *swim and to play tennis.* Repeat the preposition before the second of two connected elements.

10. **(D)** *They invited* my whole family to the cookout—*my mother, my father, my sister and me.* All of the people listed are objects of the verb invited; hence, the last person is *me* (not *I*).

11. **(E)** The search for the lost ring was abandoned *after we had raked the beach* for hours. The past perfect (had raked) is necessary to indicate an action in the past that preceded another action in the past.

12. **(C)** *Her brother has never been dependable and never will be.* This is the most concise, and therefore the most effective, way to word this sentence.

13. **(E)** That book is interesting *because it has many* stories of adventure. As explained above, the more concise the sentence, the better.

14. **(A)** *His tone clearly implied* that he was bitterly disappointed. The speaker *implies*; the listener *infers*.

15. **(E)** *Now* kick your feet in the water *as Gregory just did.* The conjunction *as* can replace *in the way that* with no change in meaning.

16. **(D)** Carson's sells merchandise of equal quality *and has a lower price. And* is used to join words or ideas of the same grammatical construction. Therefore, Carson's *sells merchandise* and *has a lower price.*

17. **(E)** The reason Frank is going to Arizona *is that he needs a dry climate.* The introductory clause must be followed by *he*, which it modifies.

TEST IV. CLARITY OF EXPRESSION

1. D	3. C	5. E	7. B	9. E
2. C	4. A	6. D	8. A	10. D

TEST IV. EXPLANATORY ANSWERS

1. **(D)** Different forms of the same pronoun (*he, his*) cannot be used to refer to different antecedents. This is the only sentence in which *his* clearly and unambiguously refers only to Mr. Johnson.

2. **(C)** The pronoun *it* could refer to either the report or the book. Sentence C is the only one that eliminates this ambiguity.

3. **(C)** This is the only sentence that makes it clear that the *boat* is doing the *cruising* and the *captain* is the one who *spotted* the log.

4. **(A)** The correlative conjunctions *not only—but also* work in pairs to connect sentence elements of equal rank. Each member of the pair of correlative conjunctions must be followed by the same part of speech.

5. **(E)** This is the only sentence in which it is clear that *I* failed the tests. *Flunked* is a colloquialism.

6. **(D)** *Anyone* is singular and requires a singular pronoun. By convention, *he* may be used to mean *he* or *she*.

7. **(B)** This is the only sentence in which the events occur in logical sequence with no misplaced modifiers to confuse the reader.

8. **(A)** This is the only sentence in which it is clear that the new light-weight racquet belongs to *Eric*.

9. **(E)** The antecedent of the pronoun *it* should be a specific word that is stated in the sentence, not merely implied. In this sentence *it* refers to the *operation*.

10. **(D)** A single pronoun cannot refer to two different antecedents. In sentences A, B, C, and E, the pronoun *he* could refer to either the *investigator* or the *suspect*.

TEST V. READING BETWEEN THE LINES

1.B	4.E	7.E	10.A	13.C	15.E	17.B	19.C
2.C	5.D	8.D	11.C	14.B	16.A	18.D	20.A
3.A	6.C	9.B	12.B				

TEST V. EXPLANATORY ANSWERS

1. **(B)** The first sentence of the paragraph states that society destroys the "manhood" of its members, or in other words, makes them "inadequate." The third sentence states that one of the major ways that it does this is to require "conformity" which is to uphold "the status quo."

2. **(C)** A "metaphor" is an implied comparison between two or more unlike things. "Society" is compared to a "stock company."

3. **(A)** Society encourages its members to surrender their "liberty and culture," to conform. In other words, it discourages individual creativity.

4. **(E)** The author, in criticizing conformity, in speaking up for the values of liberty and culture, reveals himself as intelligent and a non-conformist.

5. **(D)** The author criticizes society and at the same time points out the constructive, higher values of human life.

6. **(C)** An "abstraction" is a word that stands for a quality found in a number of different objects, people or events; therefore, it usually requires some clarification.

7. **(E)** A "false analogy" occurs when the rule that is true in one set of circumstances is not necessarily true in another set of circumstances.

8. **(D)** "I" indicates the first person singular. "At times I sit at my window..."

9. **(B)** The speaker regrets her life and wishes that she "had it all to do over again."

10. **(A)** "Non-sequitur" means "it does not follow"; it is an amusing illogicality because it usually expresses, beneath its apparent incongruity, an imaginative, associative, or personal truth.

11. **(C)** "Verbose" is defined as "using too many words." "Best ... greatest ... most fantastic" are verbose when used together.

12. **(B)** "Hyperbole" is exaggeration. He did not really run "like ten horses at a gallop." The use of "like" also indicates the presence of a simile, which is a direct comparison between two or more unlike things, normally introduced by like or as.

13. **(C)** "Name calling" is a common unfairness in controversy which places in an unflattering category that which the writer dislikes or opposes. "Witch hunt" is a just such a name.

14. **(B)** Without further proof to back up this statement, it must be classified as an unsupported generalization.

15. **(E)** The subject under study is that of flying. A second clue as to the meaning of "volant" is the mention of a flying animal, the bat.

16. **(A)** Rasselas states that he believes that "all skill ought to be exerted for universal good," in other words, that one should use his skill for the good of all, not just to help himself.

17. **(B)** Rasselas' use of the modals "should" and "ought" gives his speech a tone of obligation that is generally associated with moral duty.

18. **(D)** The man identifies himself when he asks that his "art shall not be divulged."

19. **(C)** The artist "distrusts" the rest of the human race. He does not want his marvelous discovery to be made available for public use.

20. **(A)** Since the artist wants only Rasselas to know about his discovery, the conversation is most likely being held "in private."

TEST VI. RELATIONSHIPS BETWEEN SENTENCES

1.B	4.E	7.A	10.E	13.D	15.C	17.A	19.D
2.E	5.E	8.D	11.D	14.D	16.B	18.D	20.C
3.B	6.D	9.B	12.A				

TEST VI. EXPLANATORY ANSWERS

1. **(B)** Chaotic, which means in a state of confusion is the opposite of organized; therefore, the condition of David's desk provides an exception to his otherwise well-organized nature.

2. **(E)** The elementary school and the high school are described in terms of their distances from the house.

3. **(B)** The nutritive value of the tuna salad is what makes it a better choice.

4. **(E)** The second sentence compares plastic glasses to crystal goblets in terms of beauty and practicality.

5. **(E)** Greater numbers of students enrolling in less costly state universities is one effect of the higher cost of private colleges.

6. **(D)** From the fact that there are more male architects than female architects, the second sentence makes the invalid generalization that men are better at building things than women are.

7. **(A)** Studying the dictionary is likely to have a beneficial effect on one's spelling ability.

8. **(D)** The comparison relates the time it takes to get from New York to Toronto to the method of transportation (plane *vs.* car).

9. **(B)** That he does his job promptly is an example of how responsible Bob is.

10. **(E)** The apartments are described in terms of where they are in the building.

11. **(D)** The second sentence makes a generalization about all opera singers based upon observation of some opera singers.

12. **(A)** Science fiction is highly imaginative or fantastic writing involving some actual or projected scientific phenomenon.

13. **(D)** The comparison is made between reading history as a series of cut and dry facts and the kind of historical fiction that makes the past come alive.

14. **(D)** The second sentence provides three examples of the practical application of geometry.

15. **(C)** The conclusion that prices will come down is based on the fact that favorable weather conditions have produced a good crop.

16. **(B)** "King Lear" is one of Shakespeare's best known tragedies; therefore, the second sentence provides an exception to, but does not negate, the first sentence.

17. **(A)** Jim, Jack and Jane are related to each other in terms of age.

18. **(D)** *All in all* and *right of way* are examples of idioms which must be interpreted as a unit since the separate parts do not mean the same thing as the entire expression.

19. **(D)** A comparison is drawn between the method used by mathematicians of the past and those of the present.

20. **(C)** Insulating one's home to help cut down on the amount of fuel needed is one effect of the increase in heating costs.

TEST VII. LOGIC AND ORGANIZATION

1.E	4.B	7.C	10.D	13.D	16.B	19.E	22.C
2.C	5.B	8.E	11.E	14.B	17.B	20.E	23.C
3.A	6.B	9.A	12.C	15.A	18.C	21.C	24.A

TEST VII. EXPLANATORY ANSWERS

1. **(E)** *Diction.* "Inferior," which is an adjective meaning poor in quality or below average, should be changed to "better," a comparative adjective meaning more excellent.

2. **(C)** *Irrelevancy.* The subject of sentence 5 is "radio stations" and since the subject of the passage is "television," the sentence should be omitted.

3. **(A)** *Diction.* "Wasteland," a noun defined as barren land or unproductive activity, accurately completes the meaning of sentence 6.

4. **(B)** *Clarification.* "You will see" is consistent with the imperative tone of the passage.

5. **(B)** *Sentence relationship.* Sentence 8 is not a complete sentence and, since it completes the train of thought of sentence 7, should be joined to sentence 7.

6. **(B)** *Economy.* "Without end," which carries the same meaning as "endlessly," should be omitted to make sentence 9 less wordy.

7. **(C)** *Ordering.* Sentence 11 completes the train of thought running throughout sentences 7, 8 and 9, and thus should follow sentence 9.

8. **(E)** *Economy*. The phrase, "exaggerate and overstate the matter," is verbose and should be simply "exaggerate."

9. **(A)** *Diction*. The phrase, "having a fling," is defined as having a brief time of wild pleasures. It most accurately completes the meaning of the sentence.

10. **(D)** *Clarification*. Sentence 2 is not a complete sentence. The addition of the phrase, "The result has been," completes the sentence and integrates it into the passage.

11. **(E)** *Irrelevancy*. The topic of the sentence, the Norwegian word for teenagers, is irrelevant to the topic of the paragraph which is the Western European youth market. The sentence should thus be omitted.

12. **(C)** *Economy*. "Large, successful, wide-ranging and well established" are all adjectives that convey approximately the same meaning. The elimination of "large" and "successful" prevents verbosity.

13. **(D)** *Sentence relationship*. "Moreover" is an adverb that means in addition to what has been said. It is an inappropriate transition word. Therefore the sentence should begin with "In Western Europe."

14. **(B)** *Diction*. "Diapers" is inappropriate to the meaning of the sentence. "The youth market" is being personified and "infancy" is the word most appropriate to this figure of speech.

15. **(A)** *Ordering*. Sentence 7 accurately completes the train of thought of sentence 6.

16. **(B)** *Paragraphing*. The second paragraph should begin with sentence 5. The third paragraph, which introduces the research done on the subject explained in the first two paragraphs, must begin with sentence 8.

17. **(B)** *Sentence relationship*. Sentence 2 is not a complete sentence. The addition of "in water, in butter and in wine" to sentence 1 amplifies the meaning of sentence 1 and eliminates the unnecessary repetition of the phrase, "To taste right it should swim."

18. **(C)** *Clarification*. As sentence 3 stands it is not clear exactly what is being prepared, preserved and distributed. The addition of "of nutritious food" clarifies this.

19. **(E)** *Sentence relationship*. Sentence 4 is not a complete sentence until joined with sentence 5.

20. **(E)** *Irrelevancy*. Sentence 6 discusses the sense of "touch" which is largely irrelevant to the sensory evaluation of food, the subject of the paragraph.

21. **(C)** *Ordering*. Sentence 8 is an extension of the train of thought in sentence 9 and thus should follow it.

22. **(C)** *Diction*. The adjective, "sufficient," is defined as enough or adequate and most accurately completes the meaning of sentence 9.

23. **(C)** *Economy*. The adjective, "sensory," and the phrase, "according to sight, taste and smell," convey the same meaning. Thus, the elimination of the phrase makes this a better sentence.

24. **(A)** *Paragraphing*. Sentence 7 introduces the research currently being done on the theme set forth in the first six sentences.

GRAMMAR FOR TEST TAKERS

Grammar is a classic stumbling block on the road to lofty examination scores. This section attempts to remove that block, or at least to minimize its damaging effects, by concentrating on material relevant to examination questions.

Immediately below is a series of sentences which are grammatically correct or incorrect. Confronted with a similar series on a test, the candidate would be required to indicate whether or not they were correct. That is exactly what should be done here. Do not guess. If you aren't sure whether a sentence is correct or not, mark it as such. And if you mark a sentence as being correct that isn't, be sure you understand <u>why</u> you made the mistake.

GRAMMAR FUNDAMENTALS IMPARTED BY THE QUESTION AND ANSWER METHOD

EXPLANATIONS OF KEY POINTS BEHIND THESE QUESTIONS ARE GIVEN WITH THE ANSWERS WHICH FOLLOW THE QUESTIONS

All these sentences are followed by judgments of their accuracy in accordance with grammatical principles. These explanations will give you an accurate measure of your strengths and weaknesses in this important test subject.

1. They are as old as us.

2. She is older than him.

3. Whom do you suppose paid us a visit.

4. Punish whomever is guilty.

5. It is me.

6. Can it be them?

7. Can it be her?

8. It would be impossible for you and I.

9. This is the death knell for we individualists.

10. He had a great deal of trouble with the store's management.

11. I, who's older, know better than you.

12. The mans hair is gray.

13. Is there any criticism of Arthur going?

14. Everybody tried their hardest.

15. I do not like these sort of cakes.

16. The government are unanimously agreed upon this action.

17. The government is unanimously agreed upon this action.

18. She don't like to engage in such activity.

19. The use of liquors are dangerous.

20. The district attorney, as well as many of his aides, have been involved in the investigation.

21. Either the fifth or the seventh of the courses they have laid open are to be accepted.

22. The fighting and wrestling of the two men is excellent.

23. The worst feature of the play were the abominable actors.

24. There is present a child and two dogs.

25. I shall go. You will go. He will go. We shall go. You will go. They will go.

26. I will; I repeat, I will. You shall; I say you shall. He shall; I say he shall. We will; we say we will. You shall; I say you shall. They shall; I say they shall.

27. When he saw me he says his prayers.

28. If I only knowed what the results of my action would be I would have restrained myself.

29. He spoke slow and careful.

30. The sun shines bright on my old Kentucky home.

31. She looks beautiful.

32. A Washington Street car accident resulted in two deaths.

33. The man gave the wrong reply.

34. The boy answered wrong.

35. He always has and will do it.

36. We hoped that you would have come to the party.

37. I intended to have gone.

38. In the parlor, my cousin kept a collection of animals which he shot.

39. He said that Venus was a planet.

40. If he was here, I should be happy.

41. I wish that I was a man.

42. By giving strict obedience to commands, a soldier learns discipline, and consequently would have steady nerves in time of war.

EXPLANATORY ANSWERS-GRAMMAR FUNDAMENTALS

Most of the 42 statements are grammatically incorrect. The errors are those of CASE, AGREEMENT, NUMBER, or PRINCIPAL PARTS. The proper form for each incorrect statement is given below. Following the proper form is a brief explanation of the grammatical principle underlying the correction.

STATEMENTS INVOLVING CASE

1. They are as old as we (are).

2. She is older than he (is).
   PRINCIPLE: (1, 2) The subject of a verb is in the nominative case, even when the verb is remote, or understood (not expressed).

   NOTE: T H A N and AS are conjunctions, not prepositions. When they are followed by a pronoun merely, this pronoun is not their object, but part of a clause, the rest of which may be understood. The case of this pronoun is determined by its relation to the rest of the unexpressed clause. Sometimes the understood clause calls for the objective: "I like his brother better than (I like) him."

3. Who do you suppose paid us a visit?
   PRINCIPLE: Guard against the improper attraction of who into the objective case by intervening expressions.

4. Punish whoever is guilty.
   PRINCIPLE: Guard against the improper attraction of who or whoever into the objective case by preceding verbs or prepositions.

5. It is I.

6. Can it be they?

7. Can it be she?

PRINCIPLE: (5, 6, 7) Nouns or pronouns connected by the verb to be (in any of its forms: is, was, were, be, etc.) agree in case. To be never takes an object, because it does not express action.

8. It would be impossible for you and me.

9. This is the death knell for us individualists.
   PRINCIPLE: (8, 9) The object of a preposition or a verb is in the objective case.

10. He had a great deal of trouble with the management of the store.
    PRINCIPLE: It is usually awkward and slightly illogical to attribute possession to inanimate objects.

11. I, who am older, know better than you.
    PRINCIPLE: A pronoun agrees with its antecedent in person, number and gender, but not in case.

12. The man's hair is gray.
    PRINCIPLE: A noun or pronuon used to express possession is in the possessive case. Do not omit the apostrophe from nouns, or from pronouns which require it, such as one's.

13. Is there any criticism of Arthur's going?
    PRINCIPLE: A noun or pronoun linked with a gerund should be in the possessive case.

STATEMENTS INVOLVING NUMBER

14. Everybody tried his hardest.
    PRINCIPLE: Each, every, every one, everybody, anybody, either, neither, no one, nobody, and similar words are singular.

15. I do not like this sort of cakes.
    PRINCIPLE: Do not let this or that, when modifying kind or sort, be attracted into the plural by a following noun.

16, 17. Both statements are correct.
    PRINCIPLE: (16, 17) Collective nouns may be regarded as singular or plural, according to the meaning intended.

18. She doesn't like to engage in such activity.
    PRINCIPLE: Do not use don't in the third person singular. Use doesn't. Don't is a contraction of do not.

STATEMENTS INVOLVING AGREEMENT

19. The use of liquors is dangerous.
    PRINCIPLE: A verb agrees in number with the subject. A verb should not agree with a noun which intervenes between it and the subject.

20. The district attorney, as well as many of his aides, has been involved in the investigation.
    PRINCIPLE: The number of the verb is not affected by the addition to the subject of words introduced by: with, together with, no less than, as well as, etc.

21. Either the fifth or the seventh of the courses they have laid open is to be accepted.
    PRINCIPLE: Singular subjects joined by nor, or, take a singular verb.

22. The fighting and wrestling of the two men are excellent.

PRINCIPLE: A subject consisting of two or more nouns joined by and takes a plural verb.

23. The worst feature of the play was the abominable actors.
    PRINCIPLE: A verb should agree in number with the subject, not with a predicate noun.

24. There are present a child and two dogs.
    PRINCIPLE: In "there is" and "there are," the verb should agree in number with the noun that follows it.

25. The conjugation is correct.
    PRINCIPLE: To express simple futurity or mere expectation, use shall with the first person (both singular and plural) and will with the second and third.

26. All the sentences are correct.
    PRINCIPLE: To express resolution or emphatic assurance, reverse the usage: that is, use will with the first person (both singular and plural) and shall with the second and third.

STATEMENTS INVOLVING PRINCIPAL PARTS

27. When he saw me he said his prayers.

28. If I only knew what the results of my action would be, I would have restrained myself.
    PRINCIPLE: Use the correct form of the past tense and the past participle. Avoid come, done, bursted, knowed, says, for the past tense; and (had) eat, (had) froze, (have) ran, (has) wrote, (are) suppose, for the past participle.

NOTE: Memorize the principal parts of the most common "irregular" verbs. The principal parts are the infinitive (*play*), the first person of the past tense (*played*), and the past participle (*played*). This sample (*play*) is a "regular" verb; that is, the past tense and past participle are formed by adding *ed* to the infinitive. This is not the case with "irregular" verbs. One way to recall the principal parts of "irregular" verbs is to repeat as follows: today I choose; yesterday I chose; often in the past I have chosen. Thus, the principal parts of choose are: choose (infinitive); chose (past tense); and chosen (past participle).

29. He spoke slowly and carefully.
PRINCIPLE: Do not use an adjective to modify a verb.

30. The statement is correct because BRIGHT modifies SUN.
PRINCIPLE: In such sentences as "He stood firm," and "The cry rang clear," the modifier should be an adjective if it refers to the subject, an adverb if it refers to the verb.

31. Statement is correct grammatically.
PRINCIPLE: After a verb pertaining to the senses, an adjective is used to denote a quality pertaining to the subject. (An adverb is used only when the reference is clearly to the verb.)

32. A street car accident in Washington resulted in two deaths.
PRINCIPLE: Use "made" adjectives with caution. When an adjective phrase which normally follows the noun is condensed and placed before the noun as an attributive modifier, the result may be awkward, or even confusing.

33, 34. Both are correct.
PRINCIPLE: Certain adverbs do not differ in form from adjectives. When form does not indicate which of the two parts of speech is intended, the word must be classified according to its use in the sentence.

35. He always has done it, and always will do it.
PRINCIPLE: Do not use a verb, conjunction, preposition, or noun in a double capacity when one of the uses is ungrammatical.

36. We hoped that you would come to the party. (The principal verb HOPED indicates a past time. In that past time our hope was that you WOULD come, not that you WOULD HAVE come.)
PRINCIPLE: In dependent clauses and infinitives, the tense is to be considered in relation to the time expressed in the principal verb.

37. I intended to go. (The principal verb INTENDED indicates a past time. In that past time I intended to do something. What? Did I intend to GO, or to have gone.)

38. In the parlor, my cousin kept a collection of animals which he had shot.
PRINCIPLE: When narration in the past tense is interrupted for reference to a preceding occurrence, the past perfect tense is used.

39. He said that Venus is a planet.
PRINCIPLE: General statements equally true in the past and in the present are usually expressed in the present tense.

40. If he were here, I should be happy.

41. I wish that I were a man.
PRINCIPLE: The subjunctive mode of the verb to be is used to express a condition contrary to fact, or a wish.

42. By giving strict obedience to commands, a soldier learns discipline, and consequently WILL HAVE steady nerves in time of war. war.
PRINCIPLE: Use the correct auxiliary. Make sure that the tense, mode, or aspect of successive verbs is not altered without reason.

CORRECT USAGE TEST

DIRECTIONS: Each of the following questions is of the type you may expect to find on your test. Select the letter next to the sentence that best completes the statement. Following each question is the rule of grammar that applies. Each correct answer is explained.

1. The most acceptable of the following sentences is:

   (A) It is us you meant.
   (B) It is us whom you meant.
   (C) It is us who you meant.
   (D) It is we you meant.

   RULE: The nominative or subject case follows the verb "to be." Nominative pronouns are: I, we, she, they, it and who.

   EXPLANATION: Since US is in the objective case, the only correct choice is "D."

2. The most acceptable of the following sentences is:

   (A) This is entirely between you and he.
   (B) This is completely between you and he.
   (C) This is between you and him.
   (D) This is between he and you.

   RULE: The objective case follows a preposition. Pronouns used in the objective case are: me, us, you, him, her, it, them and whom.

   EXPLANATION: Since BETWEEN is a preposition, it must be followed by objective pronouns. Therefore, "C" is the only correct choice.

3. The most acceptable of the following sentences is:

   (A) As I said, neither of them are guilty.
   (B) As I said neither of them are guilty.
   (C) As I said neither of them is guilty.
   (D) As I said, neither of them is guilty.

   RULE: A singular, indefinite pronoun must be used with a singular verb. Singular pronouns include: anyone, someone, each, neither, everyone, another, somebody, no one.

   EXPLANATION: Eliminate "A," since NEITHER is singular and cannot be used with "are," which is plural. Eliminate "B" for the same reason. Eliminate "C," since a comma should properly be inserted after SAID. "D" is the correct answer since IS is a singular verb.

4. The most acceptable of the following sentences is:

   (A) What kind of a substance is insulin?
   (B) What kind of substance is insulin?
   (C) What kind a substance is insulin?
   (D) Of what kind oi substance is insulin?

   RULE: Before a noun, use "kind of."

   EXPLANATION: KIND A and KIND OF A are corruptions and may not properly be used preceding a noun. "B" is the correct answer.

5. The most acceptable of the following sentences is:

   (A) Your pen is different from mine.
   (B) Your pen is different to mine.
   (C) You pen is different than mine.
   (D) Your pen is different with mine.

   RULE: "Different from" is preferred to "different than." Therefore, "A" is the correct answer.

6. The most acceptable of the following sentences is:

   (A) The lawyer's client sat besides him.
   (B) The client sat beside the lawyer.
   (C) The client sat besides the lawyer.
   (D) His client sat besides him.

   RULE: Do not confuse "beside" with "besides." The former means "by the side of;" the latter means "in addition to."

   EXPLANATION: Since the sentences refer to position, BESIDE, meaning "by the side of," is the desired word. Therefore, "B" is the correct answer.

7. The most acceptable of the following sentences is:

   (A) The prisoners went back to their cells, like they were ordered.
   (B) The prisoners have went back to their cells as they were ordered.
   (C) The prisoners went back to their cells, as they were ordered.
   (D) The prisoners have gone back to their cells, like they were ordered.

   RULE: "Like" means "similar to," and takes an object. It is often incorrectly substituted for "as" and "as if." "Like" may not introduce a clause, while "as" may introduce a subject and a verb.

   EXPLANATION: Eliminate "A" because LIKE may not introduce a subject and a verb. Eliminate "B" because the past participle of TO GO is GONE and not WENT. "C" is the correct answer because WENT is the correct form of the past tense of TO GO, and AS is properly used here, introducing a subject and a verb.

8. The most acceptable of the following sentences is:

   (A) These problems had been laying dormant for centuries.
   (B) These problems has been laying dormant for centuries.
   (C) These problems had been lain dormant for centuries.
   (D) These problems had been lying dormant for centuries.

   RULE: The verb "lie" does not take an object. It means "to rest or stay." Its principal parts are: lie, lay, lying, lain. The verb "lay" takes an object. It means the actual putting down of something. Its principal parts are: lay, laid, laying, laid.

   EXPLANATION: Eliminate "A" since the correct form of the required present participle is LYING. Eliminate "B" for the same reason. Eliminate "C", since LAIN is incorrectly used. "D" is the correct answer, since LYING is correctly used.

9. The most acceptable of the following sentences is:

   (A) The draperies were not hanged well.
   (B) The draperies were not hanged good.
   (C) The draperies were not hung well.
   (D) The draperies were not hung good.

   RULE: "Hanged" is only used when referring to death by hanging. In other cases, "hung" is used. Its principal parts are: hang, hung, hung.

   EXPLANATION: Eliminate "A" since HANGED is improperly used. Eliminate "B" for the same reason. "C" is the correct answer. Eliminate "D," since good is an adjective and cannot modify a verb. WELL is an adverb and is properly used to modify a verb.

THE WATCHLIST

Grammar is a classic stumbling block on the road to lofty examination scores. This section attempts to remove that block, or at least to minimize its damaging effects, by concentrating on material relevant to examination questions.

Watch for the words and phrases on this list. Some of them are overworked. Others are used incorrectly. Many are longer than necessary.

ABOUT. *He will arrive at about 1600 hours* is not a correct sentence. Use *at* or *about*, but not both.

ABOVE should not be used in the sense of *more than*. *His pay is more than* (not *above*) *$5,000 a year*.

ACCOMPANIED BY. The preposition *with* is usually better, as *his letter with* (instead of *accompanied by*) *the application*.

ADVISE. *Tell, inform,* and *say* are fresher words. *You are advised* is a useless phrase.

AFFECT, EFFECT. *Affect* is always a verb meaning to modify or influence. *Effect* may be a noun or a verb. As a verb it means to accomplish or bring about; as a noun, outcome or result. Both *affect* and *effect* are overworked, both correctly and incorrectly.

AFFORD AN OPPORTUNITY. *Allow* is suggested as a replacement for this overworked phrase.

ALL-AROUND is not correct. Use *all-round*.

ALL OF. Say *all the soldiers*, not *all of the soldiers*.

ALL READY, ALREADY. The first is an adjective phrase, correctly used in this sentence: *When the hour came, they were all ready*. The second is an adverb that oftener than not should be omitted: *We have (already) written a letter*.

ALTERNATIVE, CHOICE. *Alternative* refers to two only; *choice*, to two or more. Since there is only one alternative to another, don't say *the only other alternative;* simply say *the alternative*.

AMOUNT, NUMBER are often used loosely. An *amount* is a sum total; *number* as a noun, refers to collective units. You have an *amount of money*, and *a number of errors*.

ANTICIPATE means to foresee or prevent by prior action. Don't use it when you actually mean *expect*.

APT. Don't use this word when you mean *likely*. *Apt* suggests predisposition. *A tactless person is apt to write a blunt letter,* but *delayed replies are likely* (not *apt*) *to damage public relations.*

ASCERTAIN is a big word often used when the little word *learn* is better. Don't use *ascertain* unless you want to put over the idea of effort in getting facts.

ATTACHED—

PLEASE FIND
HERETO } *Attached* is adequate
HEREWITH

ATTENTION IS INVITED OR ATTENTION IS CALLED should be needless. If a sentence doesn't make its point without these emphatics, it needs rewriting.

BETWEEN, AMONG. *Between* properly refers to two only. *Among* is used in referring to more than two.

BIANNUAL, BIENNIAL. *Biannual,* like semiannual, means twice a year. *Biennial* means every 2 years.

BIMONTHLY means every two months. *Semimonthly* is used to express twice monthly.

CANNOT BE OVEREMPHASIZED. A much overworked phrase in military writing. Be careful when writing *the importance of this action cannot be overemphasized.* The chances are its importance can very easily be overemphasized.

COGNIZANCE. Avoid this big word both in its legal meaning of *jurisdiction* and in its common meaning of *heed* or *notice.* Instead of saying *under the cognizance of this office,* be specific, as *this office does not audit travel vouchers.*

CONTINUOUSLY, CONTINUALLY. The first word means *without interruption;* the second, *intermittently, at frequent intervals.*

DURING suggests continuously, throughout. *In* (not *during*) *the meeting he brought up the question of pay raises.*

EVENT should not be used for *incident, affair,* and *happening* unless the occurrence is particularly noteworthy.

EVERY EFFORT WILL BE MADE. In military writing this phrase often means *no effort will be made.* If you intend to make an effort, you will be able to say what effort, when, and by whom.

FACILITATE is a popular military word. It means *make easy,* but it *makes hard* reading for some people.

FARTHER, FURTHER. *Farther* indicates distance; *further* denotes quantity or degree. You go *farther* away; you hear nothing *further.*

FEW, LESS. *Few* is for numbers; *less* is for quantities or amounts. Write *fewer* pages and say *less.*

FULLEST POSSIBLE EXTENT. A meaningless padding.

INDICATE is overworked and *show* is a good substitute.

INFORMED. *You are informed* is a useless phrase in most correspondence.

INITIAL is overworked, but *first* is not used enough.

INITIATE is a favorite for which *begin* is synonymous Sometimes the word can be omitted, as in the phrase *initiate a citation (cite)*.

INTERPOSE NO OBJECTION. Another fancy favorite. Be direct. Say *I approve* or *I do not object*.

KINDLY should not be used for *please. Please reply*, not *kindly reply*.

LAST and LATEST are not interchangeable. *Last* means final; *latest*, most recent. The *last* page of a book, but the *latest* book on the market.

LENGTHY means unduly or tediously long. *Lengthy* may describe some of our letters, but *long* is usually the word.

MEETS WITH OUR APPROVAL is a roundabout way to say *we approve*.

NECESSARY is often used when *need* would do. For example, you may shorten *it is not necessary* to *you need not*.

NOMINAL means *in name*, and by implication, *small*. Why not say *small?*

NONE as a subject is usually plural unless a singular subject is clearly indicated. *None of the jobs are open. None of the work is done.*

NUMEROUS INSTANCES HAVE BEEN REPORTED. A well worn favorite. Instead tell what instances apply to whom, when, where, and in violation of what.

ON is superfluous in stating days and dates. *He arrived Tuesday*, not *on Tuesday*.

OUT is superfluous in phrases like *start out* and *lose out. He started* (not *started out*) *as a private*.

OVER should be avoided when you mean *more than* in referring to a number. *There were more than* (not *over*) *five hundred people at the meeting*.

PART. *Our error* is better than *an error on our part*.

PAST. Say *last year*, not *past year*, if you mean the preceding year.

PORTION. *Part of the time*, not *portion of the time*.

PREDICATED ON THE ASSUMPTION. Forget this one.

PREVENTIVE is better than the irregular doublet *preventative*.

PREVIOUS TO, PRIOR TO. Why not *before?*

PRINCIPAL, PRINCIPLE. The noun *principal* means *head* or *chief*, as well as *capital sum*. The adjective *principal* means *highest* or *best in rank or importance*. Principle means *truth, belief, policy, conviction*, or *general theory*.

PROVEN should not be used as the past participle of *prove*. Use *proved*. Proven may be used as an adjective.

PROMULGATE. A long word for *issue*.

PROVIDING should not be used for *if* or *provided*. *Providing low-cost houses is a problem but we will meet the problem provided the builders get supplies.*

PURSUANT TO. *Under* will usually take the place of this one.

QUITE means *really, truly, wholly, positively*. Avoid its use in phrases like *quite a few*.

RECENT DATE is meaningless. Either give the date of the letter or omit any reference to it.

RENDER. Use *give* in the sense of *giving help*.

RESIDE. The chances are you seldom use this word in talking. The talk word *live* is the natural one for a letter.

STATE is more formal than *say*.

SOME should not be used in the sense of *somewhat, a little*, or *rather*. *His letters are somewhat* (not *some*) *better*.

SORT. Never say *these sort* or *those sort*. Say *this sort* or *those sorts*.

STILL REMAINS. *Still* adds nothing to the meaning of *remains*.

SUBSEQUENT TO. *After*.

TERMINATED. *Ended* may be just as final.

THIS—

IS TO INFORM YOU. Omit.

IS TO ACKNOWLEDGE AND THANK YOU. *Thank you* is enough.

UNKNOWN should be avoided in the sense of *unidentified*.

UNTIL SUCH TIME AS. *Until* is enough.

UTILIZATION is an inflated word for *use*.

WISH TO APOLOGIZE, WISH TO ADVISE. Instead of the first phrase, simply say *we apologize*. Instead of the second phrase, start with what you have to say.

HOW TO ANSWER ESSAY QUESTIONS

There are as many answers to an essay question as there are students taking the exam. This chapter presents some of the points that are considered in the grading of the essay question. The Model Answers provided indicate the kind of treatment of a topic that will gain you college credit.

It is assumed that any student taking the CLEP exams in Composition needs no instruction in writing an essay. He or she has written many essays before and knows the technical requirements of a good composition. But the kind of writing that will award you college credit goes beyond such technical matters as topic sentences, paragraph unity and orderly development. Your essays will also be judged on validity of content, effectiveness of organization, and clarity of expression.

It is generally agreed that a superior essay should possess the following characteristics:
1. approximate perfection in technical matters
2. evident power in thought, vocabulary, and style
3. exceptional smoothness or vividness in expression
4. unusually good development of topic.

Before starting to write your essay, you are advised to take several preliminary steps.

1. Read the question at least twice so that you are certain of what is being asked.

2. Decide what mode of expression is most appropriate to the subject matter. The five major modes of expression are: Exposition, which explains how to do something; Persuasion, which stimulates the reader to some kind of change in attitude or opinion; Description, which creates pictures with words; Narration, which recounts events; and Argument, which encourages the reader to agree with what you write.

3. Write a brief outline of the ideas you wish to express or the points you want to make in your essay. No matter how abbreviated, an outline serves to give organization and direction to your writing. To further understand how to construct a helpful outline, study the two following examples of essay questions and the different types of outlines provided.

S3268

SAMPLE QUESTION I

"He who loves an old house never loves in vain."

Appreciation of one's home has been expressed in many ways, such as in the foregoing quotation. What is there in the make-up of the house or apartment that you return to at the end of the day that makes you like (or dislike) it. In answering this question, give a clear description of your home and its contribution to your life.

OUTLINE OF POINTS TO BE MADE

1. Location, size and style of house.

2. Description of interior space.

3. Inhabitants of the house.

4. Personality of the house.

5. A place you run to or one you run from?

SAMPLE QUESTION II

"The battle of Waterloo was won on the playing fields of Eton."

Rugby, a form of football, is the sport referred to by implication in this famous statement which explains the military success of the English over Napoleon. You probably like to play or watch some sport. Tell about it and emphasize its contributions to the life of your nation.

OUTLINE OF QUESTIONS TO BE ANSWERED

1. What is the game or sport called?

2. Where did it originate?

3. Does it involve individual or team effort?

4. What equipment is required?

5. What are the physical demands of the sport?

6. How did you personally become involved with this particular sport?

7. Does it have personalities on the national scene?

8. Does it have spectators in all levels of society?

The following student written model answers to essay questions meet the requirements for excellent writing. They are technically correct; their treatment shows originality. They display power in expression and in vocabulary and, above all, they are mature in conception and development. The assessments provided after each model essay should make you aware of what is expected of you on an essay exam.

QUESTION 1

The faculty adviser of the Senior Year Book has asked you to prepare an editorial, giving your views of success and offering advice on how to attain success in school and in life.

MODEL ANSWER 1

Most young people who are at all ambitious are in constant search of something that will help them on the road to success. Such aid may be found in many ways and through many channels. It may come through friends; chance acquaintances, books or formal education. It may take the form of wise advice, or searching criticism and disinterested appraisal of character. It may come free or it may be bought and paid for. It may be amateur or professional. It may be found in the lives of great men, in a casual anecdote, in a textbook theory or formula, in one's every-day experiences, or in the mundane observations of your associates or colleagues.

But no outsider, or no outside force can wave a magic wand that will bring success. Fundamentally, it is not to be found in other people, in books or in lectures or even in sage observation or advice. Deeds and not words put men on top. The successful person may get help and inspiration from others, but he always blazes a path of his own. The most valuable advice or analysis that he ever gets is that to which he subjects himself.

The ambitious salesman may take courses in business administration. These may help him, possibly, but there is no fairy wand, and though a belief in fairies adds to the joys of childhood, it only carries adults away from the straight and forward path. A course in salesmanship may do more harm than good, if it is conceived of as anything more than an aid to growth. All outside aids are, in a sense, artificial. One fallacy of so-called "expert" advice from books, articles in newspapers or magazines, and even from business or training courses is that no matter how honestly they are conceived and offered, too many people consider these alone as the basis of their success, forgetting the importance of personal achievement. No search is so frequent and yet so futile and pitiful as the search for a substitute to take the place of the slow and painful process of inner growth that signifies real and genuine success.

ASSESSMENT: This composition shows keen comprehension of subject matter and excellent development of the topic. Its sentence structure is almost professional and the vocabulary shows a wide range of reading and a high degree of competence in use. The theme reads like an editorial in its treatment of the subject and development of the topic.

QUESTION 2

"The most effective way to envision history is to read fiction. Novels —if you choose them with care—will often give you a clear picture of life in the past or life in the present in your own country or some other country."

Show the validity of this statement by referring to two novels that you have read. Give the titles and the authors. Bring out specifically how each novel has given you a vivid understanding of some phase of history.

MODEL ANSWER 2

Two novels that make history come alive are *The Red Badge of Courage* by Stephen Crane and *The Robe* by Lloyd C. Douglas.

The Red Badge of Courage gives us a clear insight into the lives of the men who won the Civil War and preserved the nation. The author takes a youth of the Civil War period, Henry Fleming, and bares his soul to us. We meet Henry's comrades, live with them, fight with them, and sometimes die with them. Through Henry's eyes we see men in the heat of battle influenced by courage or cowardice that turns them into running sheep. We wait with Henry for his first engagement in battle and share his doubts of his courage and his dreams of heroic achievements. His fright is ours when he turns and flees during the battle and then experiences shame after the heat of battle has left him. When he conquers his fear and returns to the battle, we can feel the surge of relief and almost happiness he experiences. Reading Mr. Crane's book gives us the feeling of sharing the hardships and rigors of the Union Army, from the viewpoint of the infantryman. Mr. Crane has painted a vivid picture for all of us. We often think of war in general terms, and use the word casually, but through the author's penetrating analysis we are led to see its wastefulness and its tremendous psychological effect upon the individual soldier.

To most of us, the early days of Christianity are far off in idea as well as in time, and we are inclined to regard them as part of the too-distant past which will always be vague to us. It is only through an author's imagination and vivid writing that these days come alive to us. In *The Robe*, we read a tale of the spiritual regeneration of a soldier who eventually embraces Christianity. We meet a young Roman soldier, Marcellus, who commands the soldiers who crucified Jesus, and who wins the Robe in a dice game on Golgotha. Soon afterward Marcellus begins to realize the spiritual power in the Robe, and is sick at heart as he realizes his own personal guilt and unhappiness. Soon he investigates the Man who wore it. We travel with him to Greece and Asia Minor as he talks to many of the men who knew Jesus. He becomes a Christian himself, and we endure with him the many sufferings which the Romans imposed upon those who followed the new religion. Before he dies for his faith, he predicts Christianity will one day replace the Roman Empire. Throughout the entire story we are intrigued by Mr. Douglas' excellent descriptions of life at this time, and leave the book with a clearer understanding of the sublime nature of the early Christian martyrs and a sense of our comparative weakness in today's world.

ASSESSMENT: *The Red Badge of Courage*. Excellent choice of selection to meet requirements of question. Thorough knowledge of selection, supported by excellent references. Outstanding generalizations. Excellent application to personal experience; mature response. Excellent technique of composition.

The Robe. Excellent choice of selection. Excellent knowledge of selection. Forceful generalizations supported by specific references. Good application to personal experience. Excellent technique of composition. Slight punctuation weakness.

QUESTION 3

"The moral standards of this country are sinking—and sinking lower day by day. It is high time that something was done about this deplorable situation."

If this statement is correct, we must agree that the situation is not only deplorable but quite serious. Give your own view in regard to the quotation.

MODEL ANSWER 3

I believe that the conclusion drawn by the writer of this quotation is just, and I shall try to illustrate its validity by discussing one aspect of the topic.

The morals of our public officials should be beyond reproach, since the faith of the public is vested in them. How much faith can the public have in its officials when important political and social decisions can be swayed by the price of a mink coat or a convertible car? The answer is quite clear.

The moral standards of our elected and appointed officials have been highly questionable in recent years. Many selfishly made decisions on the part of politicians have resulted in disadvantages to the people they are supposed to represent. Decisions for self-profit involving housing, for example, have directly or indirectly caused injury and death to many families. These cleverly neglected areas which we call slums or "underprivileged areas" are virtual death traps. The fact that these places exist, and huge profits are being made by their owners, suggests political corruption at its worst.

Recently city contracts were awarded by a now deposed elected official in return for "special favors" that included the redecorating of his home. Although this act had seemingly involved very little money, it turned out that the city had overpaid thousands of tax dollars by awarding contracts to that corrupt politician's associate.

This case is but one example of public plundering. Take this example and multiply it by other officials in other cities, in other states, and you have a very serious American trend toward immorality.

ASSESSMENT: Expertly organized. Facts expressed convincingly. Expression is correct and effective. Variety of style. Slight weakness in technical English.

PART THREE

Humanities

A Verisimilar General Examination

Literature Glossary

3

THE GENERAL EXAMINATION IN THE HUMANITIES

The more you know about the exam you will have to face, the better your chances of success. That's just what this chapter is for. To set the stage for the exam to come and spotlight the steps toward scoring high. Here you will find valuable information about the General Examination in the Humanities and sample questions that forecast the test.

A MINI-EXAM THAT FORECASTS THE GENERAL EXAMINATION

This chapter presents a miniature General Examination. The "mini-exam" contains good samples of the various types of questions you may expect to encounter. Our purpose is to offer you a bird's eye view of the General Examination in the Humanities. The sample questions show you the subjects that will be included, the different types of questions, and the levels of difficulty you may expect.

The subject areas tested by the Humanities Examination are Literature, Art, Music, and Philosophy. Since the Exam covers a broad range of subjects, you may expect questions on all periods from classical to contemporary, and in fields like Literature, Archaeology, Painting, Sculpture, Architecture, Films, the Mass Media, Dance, Opera, and Jazz. The test attempts to measure your cultural interests and your knowledge of the basic subject matter of the Humanities. You will not be examined on the contents of any particular book or course of study. If you have a lively interest in the arts, and show this by going to museums and concerts, seeing films, attending theater, and reading widely, you are prepared to take this examination.

The time limit for the Humanities Examination is 1½ hours. You will have to answer about 150 questions, approximately half of which are concerned with

Literature and one-third of which are concerned with Art. Many questions call for factual information. (See questions 1-4 following, for samples of questions on Music, Philosophy and Greek Drama.) Other questions require you to show your skill as an observer and your ability to deal with and understand unfamiliar excerpts from literature as well as reproductions of works of art.

ANALYSIS OF TYPICAL QUESTIONS

For example, you might be given a passage like this:

> Myself when young did eagerly frequent
> Doctor and Saint, and heard great argument
> About it and about; but evermore
> Came out by the same door wherein I went.

These lines are from *The Rubáiyát of Omar Khayyám*, as translated by Edward Fitzgerald. These verses once enjoyed wide popularity, but in recent years interest in them has dwindled, and it is unlikely that you would have studied this particular quatrain out of the 101 extant. The questions about this excerpt (Questions 9 and 10) were devised to measure your skill as a careful reader.

In the context of the quatrain quoted above, "about it" (line 3) means

(A) the pursuit of pleasure
(B) religious doctrine
(C) the mystery of life
(D) contemporary politics
(E) the generation gap.

This question concerns itself with the kernel of the poet's philosophy. It points up the words "about it," which express the core of the meaning of this quatrain. Ordinarily, the word "it" is limited and defined somewhere within a passage. In this instance, however, it is not defined. The word "it" represents Omar's continuing preoccupation with the meaning of life and death, hence (C) "the mystery of life," is the correct answer.

As a surface consideration, the reader might construe the phrase "eagerly frequent" to imply the pursuit of social pleasures, choosing (A) "the pursuit of pleasure" as the answer. The inclusion of the phrase "Doctor and Saint" might indicate to a less perceptive reader that the doctor referred to was a doctor of philosophy, debating religious doctrine with a saint, in the sense of a saintly or pious person. Therefore, option (B) "religious doctrine" might be the choice. To a less analytical reader, reference to the word "argument" might lead the reader to the conclusion that (C) "contemporary politics" is the correct answer. Finally, the reader who takes his clue from the phrase "myself when young" and the concluding line "Came out by the same door wherein I went" might choose to interpret "about it" as referring to (E) "the generation gap" as representing the inability of the Establishment to communicate their views to the young.

This question measures your ability to interpret philosophies and points of view expressed by a poet of the 12th century and to begin to understand, from one fragment, the thrust of the entire work.

Other questions on excerpted passages may deal with such matters as poetic devices, style, and rhyme schemes. If the excerpt represents a particular style associated with an author, you may be asked to identify that author. (For example, in question 6, where the lines of poetry bear a distinctive style, you must choose the poet.) You may also need to call upon your knowledge of poetic form to answer questions (for example, question 7). Likewise you may be asked to deal with the subject matter of a building or painting and identify its style.

In another type of question, you will be tested on your ability to relate to works of art. For example, the question below asks about the subject matter of a Diego Rivera fresco:

Which of these significant religious events is depicted in this painting?

(A) The Raising of Lazarus
(B) The Immaculate Conception
(C) The Pietà
(D) The Resurrection
(E) The Descent from the Cross

To answer this question correctly, you must look at the reproduction with care, noting the nature of the event taking place, and then try to relate this information to the listed titles. The central figure in the painting is reclining and is surrounded by three men. One appears to be covering the naked body with a shroud, while another appears to cut the tied hands from a post. The third man holds the head so that it will not fall to the ground once the ropes are severed.

All the themes listed are religious events in the life of Christ. Choice (A), "The Raising of Lazarus," a most famous painting by Peter Paul Rubens, shows Jesus calling Lazarus from his grave. "The Immaculate Conception," choice (B), depicts Mary being borne heavenward by angels in the Murillo painting. "The Pietà," choice (C), is a sculptured work depicting the grieving Mary with her dead Son in her lap. In choice (D), "The Resurrection," by El Greco, Christ is shown being raised from the dead. In choice (E), "The Descent from the Cross," Christ's dead body is being removed from the Cross by several of His disciples, in a manner similar to that in the Diego Rivera fresco. Thus, choice (E) is correct.

SUMMARY OF HUMANITIES EXAMINATION

You will have 1½ hours and 150 questions in which to show what you know and understand in the broad area of humanities. Many questions can be answered from information gained in reading and observation. Highly technical material is avoided. If questions are asked about a specific literary or art work, they will be of a type you have probably encountered before. However, because the test covers such a wide area, you are not expected to be knowledgeable on all questions. Therefore, don't anticipate a perfect score.

A MINI-EXAM IN THE HUMANITIES

Allow about 7 minutes for this Examination.

ANSWER SHEET FOR THIS MINI-EXAMINATION

```
    A B C D E      A B C D E      A B C D E      A B C D E      A B C D E      A B C D E      A B C D E      A B C D E
 1 [] [] [] [] []  2 [] [] [] [] []  3 [] [] [] [] []  4 [] [] [] [] []  5 [] [] [] [] []  6 [] [] [] [] []  7 [] [] [] [] []  8 [] [] [] [] []

    A B C D E      A B C D E      A B C D E      A B C D E      A B C D E      A B C D E      A B C D E      A B C D E
 9 [] [] [] [] [] 10 [] [] [] [] [] 11 [] [] [] [] [] 12 [] [] [] [] [] 13 [] [] [] [] [] 14 [] [] [] [] [] 15 [] [] [] [] [] 16 [] [] [] [] []
```

DIRECTIONS: Each of the questions or incomplete statements below is followed by five suggested answers or completions. Select the one which is best in each case. Blacken your answer sheet A, B, C, D, or E accordingly.

1. Eric Siday and Walter Carlos are both

    (A) violinists
    (B) composers of electronic music
    (C) German lieder singers
    (D) cellists
    (E) innovators in twelve-tone music

2. Technical terms, such as "soffit," "pediment," "nave," "pilaster," and "clerestory" might be used by

    (A) a painter
    (B) a physician
    (C) a clergyman
    (D) a physicist
    (E) an architect

3. The religious philosophy that holds that each man should be free to form his own religious beliefs, and that takes an optimistic view of the nature of man and believes him capable of creating a world society based on justice and cooperation is known as

    (A) Unitarianism
    (B) egoism
    (C) pantheism
    (D) Existentialism
    (E) Subjective Idealism

4. All of the following accurately describe Elizabethan drama EXCEPT:

    (A) Female roles were portrayed by men.
    (B) The producers competed for royal patronage.
    (C) The plays were performed in churches by monks.
    (D) The acting companies operated by royal charter.
    (E) Significant events often happened offstage.

5. The figure shown is

    (A) a Macedonian warrior
    (B) an Aztec deity
    (C) a Roman household guard
    (D) a gargoyle
    (E) a Polynesian tiki

Questions 6–7

'Tis education forms the common mind;
Just as the twig is bent the tree's inclined.

6. The lines above were written by

    (A) John Donne
    (B) Alexander Pope
    (C) William Shakespeare
    (D) Samuel Johnson
    (E) James Whitcomb Riley

9. In the context of the quatrain quoted above "about it" (line 3) means

    (A) the pursuit of pleasure
    (B) religious doctrine
    (C) the mystery of life
    (D) contemporary politics
    (E) the generation gap

7. Which term tells the form of the lines above?

    (A) free verse
    (B) blank verse
    (C) a quatrain
    (D) a couplet
    (E) a triolet

8. Which of the following Greek deities is *not* correctly described?

    (A) Zeus . . . king of the gods
    (B) Eros . . . god of love
    (C) Athena . . . goddess of wisdom
    (D) Aphrodite . . . goddess of the moon
    (E) Apollo . . . god of the sun

Questions 9–10

Myself when young did eagerly frequent
Doctor and Saint, and heard great argument
About it and about; but evermore
Came out by the same door wherein I went.

10. "Came out by the same door wherein I went" (line 4) means

    (A) being as unfulfilled after a quest for knowledge as before
    (B) the monotony of repeating the same chore endlessly
    (C) stubborn pride in being unchangeable
    (D) pleasure at being permitted to use the main entrance
    (E) an indication of the writer's meticulous precision in his daily life

CORRECT ANSWERS FOR THIS MINI-EXAMINATION

1.A	3.A	5.B	7.D	9.C
2.E	4.C	6.B	8.D	10.A

THE HUMANITIES
SECOND VERISIMILAR EXAMINATION

This Verisimilar Examination is patterned after the actual exam. In all fairness we must emphasize that it is not a copy of the actual exam, which is guarded closely and may not be duplicated. The exam you'll take may have more difficult questions in some areas than you will encounter on this Verisimilar Exam. On the other hand, some questions may be easier, but don't bank on it. This book is supposed to give you confidence . . . not over-confidence.

Allow about 1½ hours for this Examination.

In order to create the climate of the actual exam, that's exactly what you should allow yourself . . . no more, no less. Use a watch to keep a record of your time, since it might suit your convenience to try this practice exam in several short takes.

ANALYSIS AND TIMETABLE: VERISIMILAR EXAMINATION II.			
The timetable below is both an index to your practice test and a preview of the actual exam. In constructing this examination, we have analyzed every available announcement and official statement about the exam and thus predict that this is what you may face.			
SUBJECT TESTED	*Time Allowed*	*SUBJECT TESTED*	*Time Allowed*
Literature	45 Minutes	Fine Arts	25 Minutes
Philosophy	10 Minutes	Art	10 Minutes

B 3443

ANSWER SHEET FOR VERISIMILAR EXAMINATION II.

TEST I. LITERATURE

1 A B C D E   2 A B C D E   3 A B C D E   4 A B C D E   5 A B C D E   6 A B C D E   7 A B C D E   8 A B C D E
9 A B C D E   10 A B C D E   11 A B C D E   12 A B C D E   13 A B C D E   14 A B C D E   15 A B C D E   16 A B C D E
17 A B C D E   18 A B C D E   19 A B C D E   20 A B C D E   21 A B C D E   22 A B C D E   23 A B C D E   24 A B C D E
25 A B C D E   26 A B C D E   27 A B C D E   28 A B C D E   29 A B C D E   30 A B C D E   31 A B C D E   32 A B C D E
33 A B C D E   34 A B C D E   35 A B C D E   36 A B C D E   37 A B C D E   38 A B C D E   39 A B C D E   40 A B C D E
41 A B C D E   42 A B C D E   43 A B C D E   44 A B C D E   45 A B C D E   46 A B C D E   47 A B C D E   48 A B C D E
49 A B C D E   50 A B C D E

TEST II. FINE ARTS

1 A B C D E   2 A B C D E   3 A B C D E   4 A B C D E   5 A B C D E   6 A B C D E   7 A B C D E   8 A B C D E
9 A B C D E   10 A B C D E   11 A B C D E   12 A B C D E   13 A B C D E   14 A B C D E   15 A B C D E   16 A B C D E
17 A B C D E   18 A B C D E   19 A B C D E   20 A B C D E   21 A B C D E   22 A B C D E   23 A B C D E   24 A B C D E
25 A B C D E   26 A B C D E   27 A B C D E   28 A B C D E   29 A B C D E   30 A B C D E   31 A B C D E   32 A B C D E
33 A B C D E   34 A B C D E   35 A B C D E   36 A B C D E   37 A B C D E   38 A B C D E   39 A B C D E   40 A B C D E
41 A B C D E   42 A B C D E   43 A B C D E   44 A B C D E   45 A B C D E   46 A B C D E   47 A B C D E

TEST III. PHILOSOPHY

1 A B C D E   2 A B C D E   3 A B C D E   4 A B C D E   5 A B C D E   6 A B C D E   7 A B C D E   8 A B C D E
9 A B C D E   10 A B C D E   11 A B C D E   12 A B C D E   13 A B C D E   14 A B C D E   15 A B C D E

TEST IV. LITERATURE

1 A B C D E   2 A B C D E   3 A B C D E   4 A B C D E   5 A B C D E   6 A B C D E   7 A B C D E   8 A B C D E
9 A B C D E   10 A B C D E   11 A B C D E   12 A B C D E   13 A B C D E   14 A B C D E   15 A B C D E   16 A B C D E
17 A B C D E   18 A B C D E   19 A B C D E   20 A B C D E   21 A B C D E   22 A B C D E   23 A B C D E   24 A B C D E
25 A B C D E   26 A B C D E   27 A B C D E

TEST V. ART

1 A B C D E   2 A B C D E   3 A B C D E   4 A B C D E   5 A B C D E   6 A B C D E   7 A B C D E   8 A B C D E
9 A B C D E   10 A B C D E   11 A B C D E   12 A B C D E   13 A B C D E   14 A B C D E   15 A B C D E   16 A B C D E
17 A B C D E   18 A B C D E   19 A B C D E

TEAR OUT ALONG THIS LINE AND MARK YOUR ANSWERS AS INSTRUCTED IN THE TEXT

TEST I. LITERATURE

TIME: 30 Minutes. 50 Questions.

DIRECTIONS: For each question in this test, read carefully the stem and the five lettered choices that follow. Choose the answer which you consider correct or most nearly correct. Mark the answer sheet for the letter you have chosen: A, B, C, D, or E.

Correct and explanatory answers are provided at the end of the exam. After you have completed the entire exam, read the explanations carefully. They'll reinforce your strengths and pinpoint your weaknesses so that you know just what to study to raise your score.

1. Which of the following novels is concerned with the right of the superior man to commit a crime?

   (A) *Anna Karenina*   (D) *Crime and Punishment*
   (B) *Bleak House*   (E) *Père Goriot*
   (C) *Middlemarch*

2. Taking for his theme the arrest of time through memory, which of the following French novelists wrote *Remembrance of Things Past*?

   (A) Emile Zola   (D) Andre Gide
   (B) Victor Hugo   (E) Honoré de Balzac
   (C) Marcel Proust

3. Which of the following characters does *not* appear in *The Odyssey*?

   (A) Circe   (D) Andromache
   (B) Calypso   (E) Telemachus
   (C) Nestor

4. In which of the following works does the hero sell his soul to the devil for unlimited knowledge?

   (A) *Don Quixote*   (D) *Tom Jones*
   (B) *Faust*   (E) *Eugene Onegin*
   (C) *Don Juan*

5. In which of the following works does the poet John Milton attempt to "justify the ways of God to men"?

   (A) *Areopagitica*   (D) *Paradise Lost*
   (B) *King Lear*   (E) *The Faerie Queene*
   (C) *Comus*

6. Which of the following writers is concerned with what he calls our intellectual overdevelopment and sexual underdevelopment?

   (A) George Eliot
   (B) James Joyce
   (C) Samuel Richardson
   (D) Rainer Maria Rilke
   (E) D.H. Lawrence

7. Lytton Strachey, known for his work *Eminent Victorians* was

   (A) a poet
   (B) an essayist
   (C) a novelist
   (D) a playwright
   (E) a writer of children's stories

Questions 8 to 9

"Because I am mad about women,
I am mad about the hills,"
Said that wild old wicked man
Who travels where God wills.
"Not to die on the straw at home,
Those hands to close these eyes,
That is all I ask, my dear,
From the old man in the skies."

Daybreak and a Candle-end

8. This is the first stanza of a poem in which of the following forms?

   (A) Villanelle
   (B) Sonnet
   (C) Ballad
   (D) Sestina
   (E) Limerick

9. It was written by the Irish poet

   (A) O'Casey
   (B) Yeats
   (C) Shaw
   (D) Wilde
   (E) Tennyson

10. Which of the following Shakespeare heroines is *incorrectly* matched with the hero of the play in which she appears?

    (A) Ophelia ... Hamlet
    (B) Cordelia ... Macbeth
    (C) Cressida ... Troilus
    (D) Cleopatra ... Antony
    (E) Beatrice ... Benedick

11. Who is the author of the famous short story, *The Necklace*, about a woman who has ruined her health working to replace a necklace she borrowed from a friend and lost, only to discover, at the end of the story, that the original was a piece of costume jewelry, and far less costly than the necklace she has substituted for it?

    (A) Gustave Flaubert
    (B) Katherine Mansfield
    (C) O. Henry
    (D) Anton Chekhov
    (E) Guy de Maupassant

12. In which of the following novels does the hero try, unsuccessfully, to organize a strike in the mines?

    (A) *Sons and Lovers*
    (B) *Cousine Bette*
    (C) *Germinal*
    (D) *The Magic Mountain*
    (E) *David Copperfield*

13. Which of the following is *not* a national epic?

    (A) *The Song of Roland*
    (B) *The Iliad*
    (C) *El Cid*
    (D) *The Niebelungenlied*
    (E) *The Brothers Karamazov*

Questions 14 to 15:

> O wild West Wind, thou greath of Autumn's being,
> Thou, from whose unseen presence the leaves dead
> Are driven, like ghosts from an enchanter fleeing, . . .

14. The lines above begin

    (A) an ode by Shelley
    (B) an epithalamion by Donne
    (C) an epic by Spenser
    (D) a tragedy by Shakespeare
    (E) a sestina by Dante

15. Which of the following describes the lines above?

    (A) A couplet
    (B) A tercet
    (C) An octave
    (D) Blank verse
    (E) A quatrain

16. Which of the following characters is correctly paired with the novel in which he or she appears?

    (A) Sue Bridehead . . . *Tess of the d'Urbervilles*
    (B) Elizabeth Bennett . . . *Little Dorrit*
    (C) Benjy Compson . . . *The Sound and the Fury*
    (D) Mrs. Dalloway . . . *To the Lighthouse*
    (E) Isabel Archer . . . *Tristram Shandy*

17. Which of the following poems is composed largely of lines written by other writers?

    (A) Wordsworth's "Ode: Intimations of Immortality from Recollections of Early Childhood"
    (B) Pope's "The Dunciad"
    (C) Tennyson's "In Memoriam"
    (D) Eliot's "The Wasteland"
    (E) Whitman's "O Captain! My Captain!"

18. In which short story does a human being wake up to find that he has become an insect?

(A) "The Penal Colony"   (D) "The Metamorphosis"
(B) "The Bear"   (E) "Bliss"
(C) "The Rocking Horse Winner"

19. Which of the following is a symbol of sexual love?

(A) White rose   (D) Diadem
(B) Cross   (E) Red rose
(C) Unicorn

20. Which of the following is a play?

(A) *War and Peace*   (D) *Beowulf*
(B) *Pygmalion*   (E) *The Canterbury Tales*
(C) *Ulysses*

21. Which of the following is *not* a Shakespearean hero?

(A) King Arthur   (D) Shylock
(B) Prince Hal   (E) Lear
(C) Romeo

22. Which of the following novels is *not* by Henry James?

(A) *The Wings of the Dove*   (D) *The Pickwick Papers*
(B) *The Princess Casamassima*   (E) *The Portrait of a Lady*
(C) *The Ambassadors*

23. Dryden, known for his work *Marriage à la Mode,* was

(A) an English playwright   (D) an Irish poet
(B) an American novelist   (E) an English diarist
(C) a German biographer

24. *The Oresteia* was written by

(A) Seneca   (D) Plautus
(B) Sophocles   (E) Aeschylus
(C) Euripides

25. Which of the following novels is about a woman whose life is ruined by reading novels?

(A) *Anna Karenina*   (D) *Moll Flanders*
(B) *Emma*   (E) *Heidi*
(C) *Madame Bovary*

26. Which of the following is a work by Thomas Mann that has recently been made into a film?

    (A) *Death in Venice*
    (B) *The Waves*
    (C) *The Flowers of Evil*
    (D) *Dubliners*
    (E) *Walden*

27. Which of the following Shakespeare heroes is correctly matched with the heroine of the play in which he appears?

    (A) Malvolio . . . Juliet
    (B) Lear . . . Desdemona
    (C) Romeo . . . Olivia
    (D) Othello . . . Hermia
    (E) Prospero . . . Miranda

28. Which of the following Shakespeare plays is *not* based on Roman history?

    (A) *Antony and Cleopatra*
    (B) *Macbeth*
    (C) *Titus Andronicus*
    (D) *Coriolanus*
    (E) *Julius Caesar*

29. Which of the following is a novel about writing a novel?

    (A) *Vanity Fair*
    (B) *Nostromo*
    (C) *The Counterfeiters*
    (D) *Huckleberry Finn*
    (E) *The Hunchback of Notre Dame*

30. Which of the following novels takes place at sea?

    (A) *The Mayor of Casterbridge*
    (B) *Pamela*
    (C) *The Grapes of Wrath*
    (D) *Moby Dick*
    (E) *Arrowsmith*

31. Which of the following writers was a Pole who, nevertheless, wrote all of his novels in English?

    (A) Nabokov
    (B) Conrad
    (C) Dostoevski
    (D) Turgenev
    (E) Swift

32. Which of the following novels is a polemic against slavery?

    (A) *The Nigger of the "Narcissus"*
    (B) *The Way of All Flesh*
    (C) *Of Human Bondage*
    (D) *Uncle Tom's Cabin*
    (E) *The Lord of the Rings*

33. Which playwright shocked his audiences by championing the cause of women's rights in the mid-nineteenth century?

    (A) Ibsen
    (B) Strindberg
    (C) Chekov
    (D) Congreve
    (E) Synge

34. Which of the following is *not* a *bildungsroman*, or novel of development?

    (A) *David Copperfield*
    (B) *Wilhelm Meister*
    (C) *Frankenstein*
    (D) *The Red and the Black*
    (E) *Portrait of the Artist as a Young Man*

35. Which of the following writers is out of chronological order?

    (A) Chaucer
    (B) Shakespeare
    (C) Joyce
    (D) Milton
    (E) Dickens

36. Which of the following plays of Shakespeare is in the genre of romance?

    (A) *Twelfth Night*
    (B) *Romeo and Juliet*
    (C) *Antony and Cleopatra*
    (D) *The Winter's Tale*
    (E) *The Merchant of Venice*

37. Jupiter was the

    (A) father of the gods
    (B) god of the sea
    (C) god of light
    (D) god of the lower world
    (E) god of war

38. The Sirens were creatures that

    (A) warned people of their impending deaths
    (B) signalled the outbreak of war to alarm the population
    (C) sang for people in love and put them under a spell
    (D) sang for sailors, beguiling them towards the rocks where they shipwrecked
    (E) sang for the drowning as they went under

39. "It was the best of times, it was the worst of times." This is the first sentence of

    (A) "The Collar" by Herbert
    (B) *A Tale of Two Cities* by Dickens
    (C) *The Rape of the Lock* by Pope
    (D) *Orlando Furioso* by Ariosto
    (E) "The Open Window" by Saki

40. Which of the following books is an *anti*-Utopia?

    (A) *Rasselas* by Dr. Johnson
    (B) "Dejection: An Ode" by Coleridge
    (C) *Nightwood* by Djuna Barnes
    (D) *Brave New World* by Huxley
    (E) *Humphrey Clinker* by Smollett

41. Which of the following is an allegory?

    (A) *Joseph Andrews* by Fielding
    (B) *Don Quixote* by Cervantes
    (C) *Saint Joan* by Shaw
    (D) *Pilgrim's Progress* by Bunyan
    (E) *The Forsyte Saga* by Galsworthy

42. Which of the following is a famous poet *and* critic, the author of *Culture and Anarchy*?

    (A) Keats
    (B) Goldsmith
    (C) Arnold
    (D) Beckett
    (E) Austen

43. The archetype of desire on the part of the male child to replace the father in the affections of the mother is called

    (A) the Oedipus complex
    (B) libido
    (C) the myth of Narcissus
    (D) the Christ complex
    (E) the myth of Sisyphus

44. The author of the epic whose hero, Gargantua, has become an archetype of gigantism and excess is

    (A) Swift
    (B) Rabelais
    (C) Cervantes
    (D) Chaucer
    (E) Tasso

45. The words, "Do not go gentle into that good night," begin a

    (A) villanelle by Dylan Thomas
    (B) narrative poem by Alfred Lord Tennyson
    (C) ballad by William Wordsworth
    (D) satire by John Donne
    (E) novel by H.G. Wells

46. The writer's thesis in the work that begins, "Do not go gentle into that good night," is that old men should

    (A) accept what life brings stoically
    (B) try to stay as young as possible
    (C) seek ways to enjoy life
    (D) protest against death
    (E) seek ways to gain political power

47. Which of the following, hailed as a great novel of the women's movement, deals with a writer trying to liberate herself from a conventional role?

(A) *Emma* by Jane Austen
(B) *Slouching Towards Bethlehem* by Joan Didion
(C) *One Hundred Years of Solitude* by Gabriel Garcia Marquez
(D) *Mrs. Dalloway* by Virginia Woolf
(E) *The Golden Notebook* by Doris Lessing

48. Herman Hesse's celebrated novel about the experience of becoming a religious adept in India is called

(A) *Steppenwolf*   (D) *The Tin Drum*
(B) *Siddhartha*   (E) *Passage to India*
(C) *I'm Not Stiller*

49. A children's classic, this book has had perhaps even more impact as a satire of a world of arbitrary and illogical pronouncements, where language is used to confuse rather than clarify. The statement above describes

(A) *Tom Swift*   (D) *Alice in Wonderland*
(B) *The Adventures of Robin Hood*   (E) *The Wind in the Willows*
(C) *Winnie the Pooh*

50. *Ivanhoe*, by Sir Walter Scott, falls in the category of

(A) an historical novel   (D) a tragedy
(B) an epic poem   (E) a satire
(C) a sonnet

END OF TEST

Go on to do the following Test in this Examination, just as you would be expected to do on the actual exam.

TEST II. FINE ARTS

TIME: 25 Minutes. 47 Questions.

DIRECTIONS: Each of the questions or incomplete statements below is followed by five suggested answers or completions. Select the one that is best in each case. Blacken your answer sheet A, B, C, D, or E accordingly.

Correct and explanatory answers are provided at the end of the exam.

1. Which of the following painters was NOT one of the "Blue Four"?

   (A) Picasso
   (B) Klee
   (C) Kandinsky
   (D) Feininger
   (E) Jawlensky

2. Which of the following sculptors was a Baroque master?

   (A) Donatello
   (B) Peter Flötner
   (C) Nikolaus Gerhaert
   (D) Gianlorenzo Bernini
   (E) Antonio Pollaiuolo

3. A term developed in the present century to describe the artistic manifestations, principally Italian, of the period *c.* 1520-1600 is

   (A) Rococo
   (B) Neoclassicism
   (C) Mannerism
   (D) Gothic
   (E) Baroque

4. Which of the following painters is INCORRECTLY paired with the group or movement with which he was associated?

   (A) Bellows...Ashcan School
   (B) Mirò...Impressionism
   (C) Millet...Barbizon School
   (D) Dali...Surrealism
   (E) Feininger...Cubism

5. In his hands the dashes of pure color turned and twisted, tracing invisible and unstable lines of force. They were woven into rhythmical and convulsive patterns reflecting the mounting intensity of his own feelings.

   The painter referred to in the sentences above is

   (A) Vuillard
   (B) Whistler
   (C) Modigliani
   (D) Gauguin
   (E) van Gogh

S3265

6. His bronze "Bird in Space" became a *cause célèbre* when United States customs refused to admit it duty free as a work of art.
   The sculptor referred to in the sentence above is
   (A) Alexander Calder
   (B) Constantin Brancusi
   (C) Marcel Duchamp
   (D) Vladimir Tatlin
   (E) Pablo Picasso

7. Which of the following is a method of painting in which the powdered pigment is mixed with hot glue-size?
   (A) gouache
   (B) acrylic
   (C) fresco
   (D) pastel
   (E) size color

8. In Germany *Art Nouveau* was called
   (A) *Neue Sachlichkeit*
   (B) *Die Brücke*
   (C) *Jugendstil*
   (D) *Der Blaue Reiter*
   (E) The School of Paris

9. Matisse was the principal artist of which of the following?
   (A) the Fauve group
   (B) *Die Brücke*
   (C) the Barbizon School
   (D) *Les Nabis*
   (E) *Art Nouveau*

10. They combined several views of any given object all more or less superimposed, expressing the idea of the object rather than any one view of it.
    Which of the following are referred to in the sentence above?
    (A) Fauvists
    (B) Impressionists
    (C) Cubists
    (D) Surrealists
    (E) Symbolists

11. The sculpture above is
    (A) an Etruscan funerary figure
    (B) a symbol of a Polynesian fertility god
    (C) an artifact of Peking man
    (D) an artifact of Java man
    (E) a Venus figurine (from Willendorf, Austria)

12. Which is by Marcel Duchamp?

13. Which is a Constructivist sculpture?

14. Which is by Alberto Giacometti?

(A)

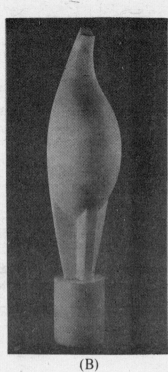

(B)

(C)

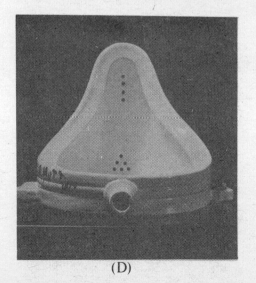

(D)

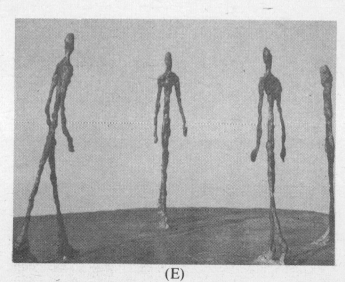

(E)

15. Which is by Canaletto?

16. Which is a Pre-Raphaelite painting?

17. Which is by Rubens?

(A)

(B)

(C)

(D)

(E)

18. Which is by Diego Rivera?

19. Which is a Futurist painting?

20. Which is by Max Ernst?

(B)

(A)

(C)

(D)

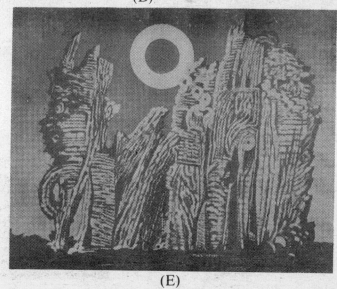

(E)

21. In *Vers une architecture*, published in 1923, he said that the forms of ships, turbines, grain elevators, airplanes, and machine products were indexes to 20th-century imagination.

The architect referred to in the sentence above is

(A) Louis H. Sullivan
(B) Le Corbusier
(C) Frank Lloyd Wright
(D) Mies van der Rohe
(E) Walter Gropius

22. The pointed arch was a motif of which of the following architectural styles?

(A) Roman
(B) Renaissance
(C) Neoclassical
(D) Greek
(E) Gothic

Questions 23 to 25:

23. Which was designed by Walter Gropius?
24. Which is in the Neoclassical style?
25. Which was designed by Louis H. Sullivan?

(A)

(B)

(C)

(D)

(E)

26. Which of Beethoven's symphonies bears the title *Eroica*, the "Heroic Symphony"?

    (A) the Ninth Symphony
    (B) the Second Symphony
    (C) the Fifth Symphony
    (D) the Sixth Symphony
    (E) the Third Symphony

27. The music of which of the following composers was constantly motivated from three main sources: English folk song, English hymnody, and English seventeenth-century literature?

    (A) (Franz) Joseph Haydn
    (B) Ralph Vaughan Williams
    (C) George Frederick Handel
    (D) Virgil Thomson
    (E) John Cage

28. In music, impressionism was associated particularly with the name of

    (A) Claude-Achille Debussy
    (B) Erik Satie
    (C) Béla Bartók
    (D) Virgil Thomson
    (E) Aaron Copland

29. Her vaguely formed idea was that dance is the expression of an inner urge or impulse and that the source of this impulse comes, physically, from the solar plexus.

    The dancer referred to in the sentence above is

    (A) Martha Graham
    (B) Doris Humphrey
    (C) Isadora Duncan
    (D) Ruth St. Denis
    (E) Loie Fuller

Questions 30 to 31 refer to the following operas:

    (A) *Lucia di Lammermoor*
    (B) *Pagliacci*
    (C) *Don Giovanni*
    (D) *Fidelio*
    (E) *Tosca*

30. In which opera does the drama on a mimic stage become the players' real-life tragedy?

31. Which opera was composed by Puccini?

32. In ballet, a beating step of elevation in which the dancer makes a weaving motion in the air is called

    (A) a *pirouette*
    (B) an *entrechat*
    (C) an *arabesque*
    (D) a *variation*
    (E) a *divertissement*

33. An outstanding jazz pianist is

    (A) William "Count" Basie
    (B) Charlie Parker
    (C) Sonny Rollins
    (D) Scott Joplin
    (E) James Scott

34. He was an untiring collector of folk songs not only in his native Hungary but also in other eastern European countries, and both the rhythms and the melodic intervals of folk songs powerfully affected his style.

    Which of the following composers is referred to in the sentence above?

    (A) Béla Bartók
    (B) Erik Satie
    (C) Franz Liszt
    (D) George Gershwin
    (E) Wolfgang Amadeus Mozart

35. Which of the following is an extended choral work with or without solo voices, and usually with orchestral accompaniment?

    (A) cantata
    (B) sonata
    (C) symphony
    (D) opera
    (E) Gregorian Chant

Questions 36 to 37 refer to the following ballets:

    (A) *The Judgment of Paris*
    (B) *Orpheus*
    (C) *The Age of Anxiety*
    (D) *Dark Elegies*
    (E) *Illuminations*

36. Which ballet was inspired by Leonard Bernstein's Second Symphony and the poem by W. H. Auden on which this symphony is based?

37. Which ballet is a contemporary treatment of the ancient myth of the Greek musician who descended into Hades in search of his dead wife?

38. *Messiah* is an oratorio composed by

    (A) Richard Strauss
    (B) Gustav Mahler
    (C) George Handel
    (D) (Franz) Joseph Haydn
    (E) Johann Sebastian Bach

39. Ruth St. Denis cofounded a dance company with

    (A) Merce Cunningham
    (B) Michel Fokine
    (C) Paul Taylor
    (D) Ted Shawn
    (E) Alwin Nikolais

40. In a normal 20th-century orchestra, a tuba would be located in which of the following sections?

    (A) woodwind
    (B) strings
    (C) percussion
    (D) unclassified
    (E) brass

41. The star of Josef von Sternberg's *The Blue Angel* and *Morocco* was

    (A) Gloria Swanson
    (B) Mae West
    (C) Marlene Dietrich
    (D) Lillian Gish
    (E) Jeanette MacDonald

42. The director of *Battleship Potemkin* was

    (A) Sergei Yutkevitch
    (B) Alexander Dovzhenko
    (C) Vsevolod Pudovkin
    (D) Vsevolod Meyerhold
    (E) Sergei Eisenstein

43. Which of the following films openly praised the Ku Klux Klan and implicitly condemned miscegenation?

    (A) Arthur Penn's *Bonnie and Clyde*
    (B) D. W. Griffith's *Intolerance*
    (C) Jean Renoir's *The Rules of the Game*
    (D) D. W. Griffith's *The Birth of a Nation*
    (E) Man Ray's *Return to Reason*

44. Which of the following is a renowned portrait photographer?

    (A) Yousuf Karsh
    (B) Minor White
    (C) W. Eugene Smith
    (D) Margaret Bourke-White
    (E) Brett Weston

45. The film *Blow-Up* used which of the following as a source?

    (A) *The Daybooks of Edward Weston*
    (B) a short story by Julio Cortázar
    (C) a series of photographs by Man Ray
    (D) a short story by Jean Genet
    (E) a short story by Franz Kafka

46. *Let Us Now Praise Famous Men* contained a series of photographs by

    (A) Paul Strand
    (B) Walker Evans
    (C) Ansel Adams
    (D) Imogen Cunningham
    (E) Edward Weston

47. Between 1864 and 1874, she produced a remarkable series of portraits of her literary and artistic friends that were based on Pre-Raphaelite paintings.

    The photographer referred to in the sentence above is

    (A) Margaret Bourke-White
    (B) Laura Gilpin
    (C) Imogen Cunningham
    (D) Julia Margaret Cameron
    (E) Dorothea Lange

END OF TEST

TEST III. PHILOSOPHY

TIME: 10 Minutes. 15 Questions.

DIRECTIONS: *For each of the following questions, select the choice which best answers the question or completes the statement.*

Correct and explanatory answers are provided at the end of the exam. After you have completed the entire exam, read the explanations carefully. They'll reinforce your strengths and pinpoint your weaknesses so that you know just what to study to raise your score.

1. Aesthetics is that branch of philosophy whose subject matter is

   (A) morality
   (B) existence
   (C) art
   (D) history
   (E) meaning

2. According to the French philosopher Descartes, the only thing a person cannot doubt is

   (A) the existence of God
   (B) his own existence
   (C) the existence of physical objects
   (D) the immortality of the soul
   (E) the truths of mathematics

3. "There will be no end to political troubles until kings become philosophers, or philosophers become kings" is a view held by

   (A) Plato
   (B) Aristotle
   (C) Hobbes
   (D) Locke
   (E) Rousseau

4. The earliest known Greek philosopher, Thales, believed that everything in the universe was made out of

   (A) earth
   (B) air
   (C) fire
   (D) water
   (E) atoms

5. According to the Utilitarian philosopher Jeremy Bentham, a person should always

   (A) do unto others as he would have others do unto him
   (B) act in his own best interest
   (C) put others' interests before his own
   (D) promote the interests of the working classes
   (E) act so as to promote the greatest happiness for the greatest number

6. Epistemology is defined as which of the following?

   (A) Government of the church by bishops
   (B) The theory of the method of knowledge
   (C) Pertaining to letters or letter-writing
   (D) A syllogism the major premise of which is proved by a preceding syllogism
   (E) An incidental narrative or digression

7. What is the original definition of the term "metaphysics"?

   (A) Ontology
   (B) After physics
   (C) The concept of final causes
   (D) First principles of things
   (E) The science of transcendent things

8. Bertrand Russell's *Metaphysics* uses which of the following as its basis for discussion?

   (A) Linguistics
   (B) Anthropology
   (C) Sociology
   (D) Religion
   (E) Psychology

9. Socrates' philosophy comes to us as reported chiefly by which of the following?

   (A) Aristotle
   (B) Plato
   (C) Herodotus
   (D) Ptolemy
   (E) Zeno

10. The philosophy of indifference to pleasure or pain is termed *Stoicism* after which of the following sources?

    (A) The name of its founder
    (B) The Latin word for "numbness"
    (C) The Greek word for "portico"
    (D) The name of a city in Asia Minor
    (E) The name of an ancient god

11. Lucretius's "On the Nature of Things" is best described as

    (A) a heroic epic
    (B) a long philosophical poem
    (C) an elegy on the death of a friend
    (D) a hymn to the gods
    (E) a fable

12. What ancient Greek philosopher stated that "You cannot step into the same river twice," i.e., no action or condition of being can ever be repeated?

    (A) Anaxagoras
    (B) Aristotle
    (C) Heraclitus
    (D) Plato
    (E) Epicurus

13. The evil that men do lives after them;
    The good is oft interred with their bones.

    These lines from a speech in Shakespeare's *Julius Caesar* are best described as a

    (A) syllogism   (D) corollary
    (B) maxim   (E) euphemism
    (C) theorem

14. What is the philosophical term for a moral obligation or command that is unconditionally and universally binding?

    (A) Categorical imperative   (D) Self-fulfilling prophecy
    (B) Tautology   (E) The golden mean
    (C) First principle

15. We owe all of the following dramatic concepts to a single seminal work of literary criticism, Aristotle's *Poetics*, EXCEPT for

    (A) the unities of time, place, and action
    (B) denouement
    (C) the central importance of spectacle
    (D) hubris, or overweening pride, as the tragic hero's tragic flaw
    (E) catharsis

END OF TEST

*Go on to do the following Test in this Examination, just as you would be
expected to do on the actual exam.*

TEST IV. LITERATURE

TIME: 15 Minutes. 27 Questions.

DIRECTIONS: For each question in this test, read carefully the stem and the five lettered choices that follow. Choose the answer which you consider correct or most nearly correct. Mark the answer sheet for the letter you have chosen: A, B, C, D, or E.

Correct and explanatory answers are provided at the end of the exam. After you have completed the entire exam, read the explanations carefully. They'll reinforce your strengths and pinpoint your weaknesses so that you know just what to study to raise your score.

1. It is the story of a tragic, adulterous love. The heroine meets and falls in love with Aleksei Vronski, a handsome young officer. She abandons her child and husband in order to be with Vronski. When he tires of her and leaves her to go to war, she kills herself by leaping under a train.

   The passage above discusses

   (A) Tolstoi's *Anna Karenina*
   (B) Dostoevski's *The Possessed*
   (C) Sholokhov's *And Quiet Flows the Don*
   (D) Pasternak's *Doctor Zhivago*
   (E) Turgenèv's *Fathers and Children*

2. Which of the following is a satirical novel, set in the society of the future, in which placards everywhere say: "Big Brother is watching you"?

   (A) Robbe-Grillet's *In the Labyrinth*
   (B) Huxley's *Brave New World*
   (C) Malraux's *Man's Fate*
   (D) Orwell's *1984*
   (E) Rand's *The Fountainhead*

3. Set in a London back street, amid a group of anarchists, it is the story of Verloc, an agent provocateur.

   The sentence above discusses
   (A) Conrad's *The Secret Agent*
   (B) Orwell's *Coming Up for Air*
   (C) Hughes' *A Fox in the Attic*
   (D) Greene's *A Burnt-Out Case*
   (E) Mann's *Confessions of Felix Krull: Confidence Man*

4. In Greek mythology, which of the following stole fire from heaven?

   (A) Sisyphus   (D) Hades
   (B) Prometheus   (E) Icarus
   (C) Zeus

5. The play centers on Alceste, who has vowed to speak and act with complete honesty and no longer to adhere to the conventions of a hypocritical society.

   The sentence above discusses

   (A) Shaw's *Man and Superman*
   (B) Wilde's *The Importance of Being Earnest*
   (C) Eliot's *The Cocktail Party*
   (D) Molière's *The Misanthrope*
   (E) Ibsen's *The Wild Duck*

6. Which of the following has as its central themes creative evolution and the eternal pursuit of the male by the female?

   (A) O'Neill's *Desire Under the Elms*
   (B) Albee's *Who's Afraid of Virginia Woolf?*
   (C) Shaw's *Man and Superman*
   (D) Williams' *A Streetcar Named Desire*
   (E) Genet's *The Maids*

7. Which of the following was a metaphysical poet?

   (A) Ezra Pound   (D) Alexander Pope
   (B) H. D. (Hilda Doolittle) (E) John Dryden
   (C) John Donne

8. The poem entitled "The People, Yes" was written by

   (A) Gerard Manley Hopkins   (D) Robinson Jeffers
   (B) Dylan Thomas   (E) Carl Sandburg
   (C) Theodore Roethke

9. Her famous soliloquy, in one uninterrupted long sentence, ends with the word yes—her affirmation of life and love.

   The sentence above discusses

   (A) Catherine Sloper   (D) Hester Prynne
   (B) Molly Bloom   (E) Justine
   (C) Daisy Miller

10. Which of the following novels was NOT written by Aldous Huxley?

   (A) *Eyeless in Gaza*   (D) *Crome Yellow*
   (B) *Point Counter Point*   (E) *Animal Farm*
   (C) *Brave New World*

11. "Beowulf" is

    (A) an unfinished poetic work by Geoffrey Chaucer
    (B) a narrative poem in blank verse
    (C) an unfinished epic satire by Lord Byron
    (D) a Middle English poem in alliterative verse
    (E) an Old English (Anglo-Saxon) epic in alliterative verse

12. Which of the following is a famous series of essays by Joseph Addison and Richard Steele?

    (A) *New Masses*
    (B) *Broom*
    (C) *The Spectator*
    (D) *transition*
    (E) *The Rambler*

13. Its subject is the quest of its *décadent* hero, Des Esseintes, for the rare and perverse in sensation. Restless and discontent, Des Esseintes seeks release from the ennui of existence in perfumes, music, painting, the love of circus acrobats, or the study of medieval Latin literature.

    The passage above discusses

    (A) Dostoevski's *The Possessed*
    (B) Huysmans' *Against the Grain* (or *Against Nature*)
    (C) Hesse's *Steppenwolf*
    (D) Hardy's *Jude the Obscure*
    (E) Durrell's *The Black Book*

14. *A Shropshire Lad*, a collection of poems, was written by

    (A) Robert Graves
    (B) William Blake
    (C) Elizabeth Barrett Browning
    (D) Alfred Tennyson
    (E) A. E. Housman

15. Which of the following Shakespearean characters is INCORRECTLY paired with the play in which he appears?

    (A) Prospero . . . *The Tempest*
    (B) Shylock . . . *The Merchant of Venice*
    (C) Christopher Sly . . . *The Taming of the Shrew*
    (D) Dogberry . . . *The Comedy of Errors*
    (E) Francis Flute . . . *A Midsummer Night's Dream*

16. Jack Burden, a young intellectual, narrates the story of the rise and fall of Willie Stark, a Southern demagogue apparently modeled on Huey Long.

    The passage above discusses

    (A) Osborne's *Look Back in Anger*
    (B) Miller's *Death of a Salesman*
    (C) Warren's *All the King's Men*
    (D) O'Neill's *The Great God Brown*
    (E) Williams' *The Glass Menagerie*

17. Born of peasant parents, he used the theme of the passing of rural Russia in his poetry. One of the finest lyric poets of the early Soviet period, he was for a time connected with a literary group called the Imaginists.

The passage above discusses

(A) Sergei Yesenin   (D) Vladimir Mayakovski
(B) Boris Pasternak   (E) Osip Mandelshtam
(C) Aleksandr Blok

18. Which of the following characters is INCORRECTLY paired with the novel in which he/she appears?

(A) Mellors . . . *Lady Chatterley's Lover*
(B) Eugene Gant . . . *Look Homeward, Angel*
(C) Catherine Sloper . . . *Washington Square*
(D) Raskolnikov . . . *War and Peace*
(E) Antoine Roquentin . . . *Nausea*

19. *Dubliners*, a collection of short stories, was written by

(A) Samuel Beckett   (D) Brendan Behan
(B) F. Scott Fitzgerald   (E) D. H. Lawrence
(C) James Joyce

20. It is concerned with young Hans Castorp and his personal development at a tuberculosis sanatorium in the Swiss Alps.

The sentence above discusses

(A) Rand's *The Fountainhead* (D) Vidal's *The City and the Pillar*
(B) Faulkner's *Sanctuary*   (E) Mann's *The Magic Mountain*
(C) Styron's *Lie Down in Darkness*

21. Which of the following plays was NOT written by Samuel Beckett?

(A) *Happy Days*   (D) *Krapp's Last Tape*
(B) *Waiting for Godot*   (E) *No Exit*
(C) *Endgame*

22. The author of *Frankenstein* was married to which of the following poets?

(A) John Keats   (D) Percy Shelley
(B) Dante Gabriel Rossetti (E) Alfred Tennyson
(C) William Wordsworth

23. The novel, which is rich in fantasy throughout, ends in what is called the magic theater, a kind of allegorical sideshow. Here, the hero, Harry Haller, learns that in order to relate successfully to humanity and reality without sacrificing his ideals, he must overcome his own social and sexual taboos, including his prejudice against technology.

The passage above discusses

(A) Grass' *Local Anaesthetic* (D) Orwell's *1984*
(B) Ellison's *Invisible Man*   (E) Hesse's *Steppenwolf*
(C) Huxley's *Brave New World*

24. Which of the following stories was written by H. G. Wells?

    (A) "The Pit and the Pendulum"   (D) "The Metamorphosis"
    (B) "Babylon Revisited"   (E) "The Time Machine"
    (C) "The Killers"

25. The character Hercule Poirot was created by

    (A) Leslie Charteris   (D) Arthur Conan Doyle
    (B) Agatha Christie   (E) C. Day-Lewis
    (C) André Gide

26. The novel describes conditions in a Soviet prison camp during the Stalin era. It traces in excruciating detail the struggle of one prisoner to stay alive and to snatch what meager comforts he can find during a typical day in the camp.

    The passage above discusses

    (A) Ellison's *Invisible Man*
    (B) Pasternak's *Doctor Zhivago*
    (C) Maugham's *Of Human Bondage*
    (D) London's *The Iron Heel*
    (E) Solzhenitzyn's *One Day in the Life of Ivan Denisovich*

27. Which of the following characters is INCORRECTLY paired with the play in which he/she appears?

    (A) Willy Loman . . . *The Caretaker*
    (B) Abbie . . . *Desire Under the Elms*
    (C) King Creon . . . *Antigone*
    (D) Maggie Pollitt . . . *Cat on a Hot Tin Roof*
    (E) Claire . . . *The Maids*

END OF TEST

Go on to do the following Test in this Examination, just as you would be expected to do on the actual exam.

TEST V. ART

TIME: 10 Minutes. 19 Questions.

DIRECTIONS: For each question in this test, read carefully the stem and the five lettered choices that follow. Choose the answer which you consider correct or most nearly correct. Mark the answer sheet for the letter you have chosen: A, B, C, D, or E.

Correct and explanatory answers are provided at the end of the exam.

1. Which of the following is a group of Impressionist painters?

    (A) Picasso, Gris, Braque   (D) Millais, Burne-Jones, Rossetti
    (B) Ernst, Schwitters, Tanguy   (E) Nolde, Kollowitz, Kandinsky
    (C) Monet, Renoir, Degas

2. Which of the following created massive, heroic sculptures, marked by a quality of repose in action, and figures which look as though they are trying to free themselves from the stone block?

    (A) Michelangelo   (D) Donatello
    (B) Rodin   (E) Callimachus
    (C) Giacometti

3. Often using the poor for his models and the Old Testament for his subject, which painter is known for his moving portraits, with startling, brilliant light emerging from a dark canvas?

    (A) Franz Hals   (D) Rembrandt
    (B) Caravaggio   (E) Vermeer
    (C) Ingres

4. *Chiaroscuro* is a technique involving the use of

    (A) light and shade   (D) geometric forms
    (B) color   (E) biomorphic forms
    (C) pictorial illusionism

5. A Greek statue of a youth is called a

    (A) krater   (D) pediment
    (B) kylix   (E) amphora
    (C) kouros

6. Picasso's *Les Demoiselles d'Avignon*, the first Cubist painting, was influenced by

    (A) Japanese *netsuke*   (D) African masks
    (B) Byzantine enamels   (E) Inca statuary
    (C) Indian temple statuary

7. Which of the following is thought of as an "anti-art" art movement?

    (A) Surrealism   (D) Pointillism
    (B) Dada   (E) Symbolism
    (C) Mannerism

8. Which of the following artists is associated with "drip-painting"?

    (A) de Kooning   (D) Rothko
    (B) Motherwell   (E) Johns
    (C) Pollock

9. Which of the following is a Constructivist sculptor?

    (A) Matisse   (D) Brancusi
    (B) Rodin   (E) Bernini
    (C) Gabo

10. Who organized the artistic focal point or "salon" in Paris that in the 1920s had attracted nearly all the young talent of the time, many of whom became recognized masters of their various crafts?

    (A) Eric Satie   (D) Jean Cocteau
    (B) Manuel de Falla   (E) Princesse Edmond de Polignac
    (C) Pablo Picasso

11. With which of the following did Pablo Picasso NOT collaborate in some way?

    (A) Eric Satie   (D) Dmitri Shostakovitch
    (B) Igor Stravinsky   (E) Arthur Honegger
    (C) Jean Cocteau

12. Although generally considered one of the leaders of the Cubist School of painting, which of the following Schools was Picasso also heavily involved in simultaneously with his cubist work?

    (A) Romantic   (D) Impressionist
    (B) Classical   (E) Pointillist
    (C) Neo-Classical

13. Which of the following kinds of scenes are most often associated with Paul Cézanne?

    (A) Still life   (D) Action study
    (B) Formal portrait   (E) Architectural rendering
    (C) Informal portrait

14. Albrecht Dürer is best known for his use of which of the following mediums?

    (A) Oils   (D) Charcoal and pastels
    (B) Water colors   (E) Pen and ink
    (C) Woodcuts and engravings

15. Which of the following explains why it is often misleading to refer to a painting of Peter Paul Rubens as "genuine"?

   (A) Most are modern forgeries.
   (B) Most were begun by Rubens but detailed or completed by others.
   (C) He never actually painted anything but only managed a painting workshop.
   (D) Only copies of his work by his pupils now exist.
   (E) "Rubens" was one of Rembrandt's pseudonyms.

16. A "casting" in sculpture refers to the use of which of the following materials?

   (A) Stone
   (B) Wood
   (C) Metal
   (D) Ivory
   (E) Papier-mâché

17. A "frieze" is best associated with which of the following terms?

   (A) Bas-relief
   (B) Pediment
   (C) Caryatid
   (D) Free-standing
   (E) Entablature

18. Which of these is not a 20th-century sculptor?

   (A) Giacometti
   (B) Moore
   (C) Brancusi
   (D) Donatello
   (E) Arp

19. Famous for his sculptures, Auguste Rodin was also known in which of the following fields?

   (A) Oil painting
   (B) Inventing
   (C) Philosophy
   (D) Drawing
   (E) Poetry

END OF EXAMINATION

If you finish before the allotted time is up, check your work on this part only. When time runs out, compare your answers for this test and all the other tests in the examination with the correct key answers that follow.

CORRECT ANSWERS FOR VERISIMILAR EXAMINATION II.

TEST I. LITERATURE

1.D	8.C	15.B	22.D	29.C	36.D	43.A	50.A
2.C	9.B	16.C	23.A	30.D	37.A	44.B	
3.D	10.B	17.D	24.E	31.B	38.D	45.A	
4.B	11.E	18.D	25.C	32.D	39.B	46.D	
5.D	12.C	19.E	26.A	33.A	40.D	47.E	
6.E	13.E	20.B	27.E	34.C	41.D	48.B	
7.B	14.A	21.A	28.B	35.C	42.C	49.D	

TEST I. EXPLANATORY ANSWERS

1. **(D)** *Crime and Punishment*, whose hero, Raskolnikov, decides he has a moral right to murder a pawnbroker he has long considered a social parasite, and who suffers remorse afterwards.

2. **(C)** Marcel Proust, who in this work discovered what he called "involuntary memory," the ability of a sensory stimulus to evoke an entire past experience—in this case, the famous episode of the "tea and madeleines."

3. **(D)** Andromache, who figures in the *Iliad*.

4. **(B)** *Faust*, whose hero of the same name, an alchemist, makes a contract with the devil, gains infinite knowledge—and lives to regret it.

5. **(D)** *Paradise Lost*, the great Protestant epic, which places the responsibility for the fall of man on his own shoulders. The (A) *Areopagitica* is Milton's pamphlet on divorce, and (C) *Comus* his masque on the subject of chastity. (B) *King Lear* is a tragedy by Shakespeare. (E) *The Faerie Queene* is an epic by Spenser.

6. **(E)** D.H. Lawrence, who expressed such views in the celebrated *Lady Chatterley's Lover*, as well as his masterpieces *The Rainbow* and *Women in Love*.

7. **(B)** An essayist, whose best known book is *Eminent Victorians*, a book which is largely responsible for the way we view the Victorian world.

8. **(C)** A ballad; neither (A) villanelle, (B) sonnet, (D) sestina, nor (E) limerick have a stanza form that ends in a refrain, as this does, characteristic of the ballad form.

9. **(B)** Yeats; (A) O'Casey and (C) Shaw are Irish playwrights; (D) Wilde is an Irish essayist and novelist; (E) Tennyson was Poet Laureate of England.

10. **(B)** Cordelia... Macbeth; Cordelia is the youngest and only true daughter of Lear in *King Lear*, and Macbeth is the hero in the play of the same title.

11. **(E)** Guy de Maupassant; it is perhaps his most famous story, and is virtually universally read.

12. **(C)** *Germinal*, though Zola reiterates, at the end of the novel, his conviction that the working classes will eventually be organized. The life of the poor workers was Zola's constant theme.

13. **(E)** *The Brothers Karamazov*, which is a novel by the Russian writer Dostoevski. (A) *The Song of Roland* is the epic of France. (B) *The Iliad* is the epic of Greece, along with *The Odyssey*, (C) *El Cid* is the epic of Spain. (D) *The Niebelungenlied* is the epic of Germany.

14. **(A)** An ode by Shelley, his greatest, and characteristically emotional. The apostrophe to the wind would be unlikely at the beginning of (B) an epithalamion, (C) an epic, (D) a tragedy, or (E) a sestina.

15. **(B)** A tercet, three lines whose rhyme scheme is a-b-a.

16. **(C)** Benjy Compson... *The Sound and the Fury*. Benjy is the idiot brother who narrates the first of the four sections of the book. (A) Sue Bridehead is the heroine of *Jude the Obscure*. (B) Elizabeth Bennett is the heroine of *Pride and Prejudice*. (D) Mrs. Dalloway is the heroine of the novel of the same name. (E) Isabel Archer is the heroine of *The Portrait of A Lady*.

17. **(D)** Eliot's "The Wasteland," whose collage technique is intended, among other things, to make the point that all works of literature are in some sense a revision of the tradition from which they derive.

18. **(D)** "The Metamorphosis," whose hero—or anti-hero—a miserable clerk wakes up one day to find that his abject lot has been objectified in his metamorphosis into a dung beetle.

19. **(E)** A red rose. (A) a white rose and (C) a unicorn are symbols of chastity. (B) a cross is the symbol of Christianity. (D) a diadem is a symbol of rule.

20. **(B)** *Pygmalion*, by George Bernard Shaw; the long-running Broadway play, *My Fair Lady*, is based on this. (A) *War and Peace* and (C) *Ulysses* are novels. (D) *Beowulf* is an epic. (E) *The Canterbury Tales* is a collection of verse narratives.

21. **(A)** King Arthur, the hero of legend, and among other treatments, of the verse narrative by Tennyson.

22. **(D)** *The Pickwick Papers* by Charles Dickens.

23. **(A)** An English playwright of the Restoration, best known for *Marriage à la Mode*.

24. **(E)** Aeschylus. It narrates the story of the fall of the house of Atreus, and is the only complete trilogy in the body of Greek tragedy that remains to us.

25. **(C)** *Madame Bovary*, whose heroine, Emma Bovary, is dissatisfied with her life in provincial France, and longs to live like the heroines of the novels she reads.

26. **(A)** *Death in Venice*, a novella about decadence and homosexuality, by Thomas Mann.

27. **(E)** Prospero . . . Miranda. Prospero is Miranda's father in *The Tempest*.

28. **(B)** *Macbeth*, which is based on an incident in Scottish history narrated in Holinshed's *Chronicles*, undoubtedly Shakespeare's source for this play.

29. **(C)** *The Counterfeiters* purports to be the journal of the hero, the novelist, Edouard, and outlines his plans for the novel he is "about to write."

30. **(D)** *Moby Dick*, the tale of a whaler's obsessive desire to kill the whale, Moby Dick, that caused him to lose his leg.

31. **(B)** Conrad, who made a conscious decision to write in a foreign language. (A) Nabokov, who is of Russian origin but now lives in Switzerland, and who began to write in English during his long stay in America, made a similar decision, but he has also written novels in his native Russian and in French (his great works, though, were written in English). (C) Dostoevski and (D) Turgenev wrote in their native Russian, (E) Swift, in his native English.

32. **(D)** *Uncle Tom's Cabin* is an impassioned outcry against the system of slavery. The author, Harriet Beecher Stowe, a fervent Abolitionist, claimed that the book was dictated to her by God; she was only "God's secretary," she said, claiming for the book the authority of a third testament.

33. **(A)** Ibsen, in such works as a *Doll's House* which depicts the limiting nature of a stuffy, conventional bourgeois marriage.

34. **(C)** *Frankenstein*, by Mary Shelley, is the story of the monster whose name has become a household word.

35. **(C)**   Joyce, who lived from 1882 to 1941. The dates for the others are as follows: A) Chaucer, 1340?—1400; B) Shakespeare, 1564—1616; D) Milton, 1608—74; E) Dickens, 1812—70.

36. **(D)**   *The Winter's Tale*, which along with *Pericles, Prince of Tyre; Cymbeline*, and *The Tempest* forms a group known as the romances. (A) *Twelfth Night* and (E) *The Merchant of Venice* are comedies. (B) *Romeo and Juliet* and (C) *Antony and Cleopatra* are tragedies.

37. **(A)**   **The father** of the gods (Greek mythology: Zeus). (B) The god of the sea was Neptune (Greek: Poseidon). (C) The god of light was Phoebus Apollo (a name used by both Romans and Greeks). (D) The god of the lower world was Pluto (Greek: Hades). (E) The god of war was Mars (Greek: Ares).

38. **(D)**   Sang for sailors, beguiling them towards the rocks where they shipwrecked. In the twelfth book of *The Odyssey*, Ulysses steers past them by stuffing his mariners' ears with wax so they will not hear the singing and be tempted. He alone may hear the sirens, but as a precaution, he has himself lashed to the mast so he cannot forget himself and, taking charge of the ship, drive it onto the rocks.

39. **(B)**   *A Tale of Two Cities* by Charles Dickens. The subject of the book is the French Revolution, and the opening sentence summarizes Dickens' attitude through the whole book, his mixture of elation and pessimism about the Revolution.

40. **(D)**   *Brave New World*, a fantasia of a technological world of horrors, not unlike the more celebrated *1984* by George Orwell.

41. **(D)**   *Pilgrim's Progress* by Bunyan is the most famous allegory in the English language. Its characters, such as Christian and Ignorance, are named for the virtues and vices they represent.

42. **(C)**   Arnold was a poet (''Dover Beach'' is his best known poem) and, perhaps even more important, the greatest culture critic of the Victorian era. His greatest concern is the rift between so-called ''popular culture'' and ''high culture.''

43. **(A)**   The Oedipus complex, based on the myth of Oedipus, who accidentally slays his father and proceeds to marry a woman who, though he does not know it, is his own mother, Jocasta. The complex was analyzed by Freud, who insists that these events take place on an unconscious level, and this interpretation is a major theme in Western literature.

44. **(B)**   Rabelais, in his bawdy epic, *Gargantua*.

45. **(A)** Villanelle by Dylan Thomas, whose title is the first line of the poem. The first and third lines are repeated alternately at the close of stanzas, and form the final couplet, with which a villanelle always ends.

46. **(D)** Protest against death. We are aware that some form of protest is involved from Thomas' use of the words "burn" and "rave," which rules out the passive or possibly stoic alternatives.

47. **(E)** *The Golden Notebook* by Doris Lessing appeared in 1962, just at the beginning of the Women's Liberation Movement, of which it was to become, in a sense, the epic. The central character, Molly, has become an archetype of the intelligent and talented woman struggling to shuck off a form of behavior which she feels confines her, but which, she finds, has become a kind of second nature.

48. **(B)** *Siddhartha* is Hesse's great work about the mystical experience. (A) *Steppenwolf* is another of Hesse's novels, whose hero is a tortured personality apparently based on Nietzsche. (C) *I'm Not Stiller* is by the German novelist Max Frisch. (D) *The Tin Drum* is by another German novelist, Gunter Grass. (E) *Passage to India* is the masterpiece of the English novelist E.M. Forster.

49. **(D)** *Alice in Wonderland*. Lewis Carroll, who wrote the book for a little girl he knew, Alice Liddell, was a logician, and the book is filled with all sorts of logical absurdities, spoofs, games, and other delightful kinds of nonsense.

50. **(A)** An historical novel, whose subject is twelfth-century England. Scott's works, which were enormously popular throughout Europe, started a vogue of historical novel writing. Victor Hugo, for example, was influenced by him.

TEST II. FINE ARTS

1.A	7.E	13.C	19.C	25.D	31.E	37.B	43.D
2.D	8.C	14.E	20.E	26.E	32.B	38.C	44.A
3.C	9.A	15.B	21.B	27.B	33.A	39.D	45.B
4.B	10.C	16.C	22.E	28.A	34.A	40.E	46.B
5.E	11.E	17.D	23.A	29.C	35.A	41.C	47.D
6.B	12.D	18.A	24.B	30.B	36.C	42.E	

TEST II. EXPLANATORY ANSWERS

4. **(B)** Mirò was associated with surrealism.

Explanatory Notes: Questions 12 to 14

    (A) Barbara Hepworth: Single Form, 1962-63
    (B) Constantin Brancusi: Bird, 1912
    (C) Vladimir Tatlin: Relief, 1914
    (D) Marcel Duchamp: Fountain, 1917
    (E) Alberto Giacometti: City Square, 1948-49

Explanatory Notes: Questions 15 to 17

    (A) Leonardo Da Vinci: Mona Lisa
    (B) Giovanni Antonio Canaletto: Feast of the Ascension in Venice
    (C) Holman Hunt: The Light of the World, 1853
    (D) Rubens: An Allegory of Peace and War, 1629
    (E) Michelangelo: Creation of Man, Sistine Chapel, Rome, 1508-12

Explanatory Notes: Questions 18 to 20

    (A) Diego Rivera: Uprising (detail), a fresco
    (B) Paul Cézanne: Bathers, *c.* 1900-05
    (C) Marcel Duchamp: Nude Descending a Staircase, No. 2, 1912
    (D) Pablo Picasso: Guernica, 1937
    (E) Ernst: Grey Forest, 1927

Explanatory Notes: Questions 23 to 25

    (A) Gropius: Bauhaus, Dessau, 1925-26
    (B) Nash: Cumberland Terrace, London, begun 1826-27
    (C) Burnham and Root: Monadnock Block, Chicago, 1891
    (D) Louis H. Sullivan: Guaranty Building, Buffalo, New York, 1895
    (E) Chartres, Cathedral, southwest buttresses

TEST III. PHILOSOPHY

1.C	3.A	5.E	7.B	9.B	11.B	13.B	15.C
2.B	4.D	6.B	8.A	10.C	12.C	14.A	

TEST III. EXPLANATORY ANSWERS

1. **(C)** Art. Aesthetics is defined as ''the study of the qualities perceived in works of art, with a view to the abstraction of principles.'' (Random House Dictionary of the English Language)

2. **(B)** His own existence. Descartes tried to doubt everything that was susceptible to doubt, to see if anything could withstand such doubt and thus serve as a foundation for knowledge. He concluded that everything could be doubted except the existence of the doubter, since he at least must exist in order to doubt.

3. **(A)** Plato, in *The Republic*, where he outlines his ideal state, which is to be governed by the philosopher king.

4. **(D)** Water. Medieval philosophers believed that everything was made out of the "four elements," (A) earth, (B) air, (C) fire, *and* (D) water. Democritus held the theory that everything was made out of (E) atoms, and in this he has been proven correct.

5. **(E)** Act so as to promote the greatest happiness for the greatest number. Utilitarianism is defined as "the ethical doctrine that virtue is based on utility, and that conduct should be directed toward promoting the greatest happiness of the greatest number of people." (Random House Dictionary of the English Language) Bentham was the single greatest exponent of Utilitarianism.

6. **(B)** Epistemology is one of the branches of traditional metaphysics.

7. **(B)** Aristotle's *Metaphysics* was literally the following work in a series after his treatise on physics.

8. **(A)** Russell attempts to demonstrate the interrelationship of concepts and their verbal expression as determined by grammar.

9. **(B)** Socrates' ideas are set forth in Plato's dialogues.

10. **(C)** The word is derived from the Greek, *stŏĭkos*, referring to the Painted Portico in Athens where Zeno of Citium taught his ideas about 300 B.C.

11. **(B)** Born 96 B.C., died 55 B.C. The Roman Stoic poet's full name was Titus Lucretius Carus.

12. **(C)** 6th-5th centuries B.C. The foundation of his philosophy is a belief in the impermanence and mutability of existing things.

13. **(B)** According to Webster's Seventh New Collegiate Dictionary, "a saying of proverbial nature."

14. **(A)** As opposed to a hypothetical imperative, the categorical imperative is an imperative of conduct arising from expediency or necessity rather than from moral law.

15. **(C)** A concept associated in the 20th century with the polemical writings on the theater of Antonin Artaud, French poet and playwright (1896 to 1948). His most notable work on the subject is the collection entitled *The Theater and its Double*, published in 1938.

TEST IV. LITERATURE

1.A	5.D	9.B	13.B	16.C	19.C	22.D	25.B
2.D	6.C	10.E	14.E	17.A	20.E	23.E	26.E
3.A	7.C	11.E	15.D	18.D	21.E	24.E	27.A
4.B	8.E	12.C					

TEST IV. EXPLANATORY ANSWERS

10. **(E)** *Animal Farm* was written by George Orwell.

15. **(D)** Dogberry appears in *Much Ado about Nothing*.

18. **(D)** Raskolnikov appears in *Crime and Punishment*.

21. **(E)** *No Exit* was written by Jean-Paul Sartre.

27. **(A)** Willy Loman appears in *Death of a Salesman*.

TEST V. ART

1.C	4.A	7.B	10.E	13.A	16.C	19.D
2.A	5.C	8.C	11.D	14.C	17.E	
3.D	6.D	9.C	12.C	15.B	18.D	

TEST V. EXPLANATORY ANSWERS

1. **(C)** Monet, Renoir, Degas are Impressionists, a group concerned with the fleeting moment and the use of light. The others are, respectively, (A) Cubists, (B) Surrealists, (D) Pre-Raphaelites, and (E) Expressionists.

2. **(A)** Michelangelo; some examples are the colossal David and the Louvre sculptures of the slaves. (B) Rodin and (C) Giacometti worked principally in metal; (D) Donatello's sculpture is architectural, and no work of (E) Callimachus remains.

3. **(D)** Rembrandt, who combines all of these qualities. (B) Caravaggio's paintings are characterized by a light much like Rembrandt's and (A) Franz Hals and (E) Vermeer used the poor for models. (C) Ingres painted beautiful, voluptuous studies, usually of the rich.

4. **(A)** Light and shade. *Chiaroscuro* refers to a dramatic disposition of light and shade in a picture.

5. **(C)** Kouros is the ancient Greek name for a sculpture of a boy (fem. koure). (B) kylix is a ceremonial dish. (A) krater and an (E) amphora are vases. (D) pediment is a low gable, usually triangular in shape.

6. **(D)** African masks, which the faces of the *Demoiselles*, with their cubist forms, resemble.

7. **(B)** Dada, which questioned why a signed object, such as Duchamp's urinal (now in the Museum of Modern Art) should not be a museum piece. The other movements are far more strictly traditional.

8. **(C)** Jackson Pollock, who was interested in the idea of painting as process, employed random and chance effects, such as dripping his paint on the canvas.

9. **(C)** Gabo, who was committed to the use of modern techniques and materials, and interested primarily in the use of space. (A) Matisse, (B) Rodin, and (E) Bernini are classical in their sculpture, and (D) Brancusi was concerned with form rather than space in his work.

10. **(E)** A wealthy woman, she commissioned many now famous works, and many were dedicated to her.

11. **(D)** Picasso made a vast contribution in designing settings and costumes for staged productions. He also provided sketches for published works. No Soviet artist of the period could have been involved in such a thing outside the Soviet Union.

12. **(C)** It is quite difficult to name schools or styles Picasso did not indulge in at some time or another. However, at the time he produced his masterpiece, *Three Musicians* (1921), he was also monumentalizing the classics graphically as Stravinsky was doing musically.

13. **(A)** An impressionist who refined the use of color as subject in and of itself, Cézanne has been referred to as "the father of modern painting." His famous still-lifes are not pictures of fruit as such but studies of tone as a concrete object.

14. **(C)** Dürer (1471-1528) is considered the greatest of German artists and the only European artist of his caliber to devote himself primarily to these two mediums.

15. **(B)** Only a small number of Rubens' paintings were conceived and executed by himself alone. In most cases, specialists in certain figures, such as Frans Snyders, an animal painter, did the backgrounds and detail, or Rubens' pupils would do the bulk of the work, Rubens himself merely sketching it out and adding final touches.

16. **(C)** Casting involves the use of a mold into which is poured molten metal.

17. **(E)** A frieze is the center part of an entablature, that section of a building supported on columns and which supports the roof. Especially with classical Greek buildings such as the Parthenon, it is often sculpted; but a bas-relief per se consists of only a slight projection from its surrounding surface—it is never undercut, whereas a sculpted frieze often consists of undercut though attached figures, not true bas-relief.

18. **(D)** He worked during the Italian Renaissance (1386-1466).

19. **(D)** Rodin's drawing was influential in the development of Amedeo Modigliani's painting style.

SCORE YOURSELF

Compare your answers to the Correct Key Answers at the end of the Examination. To determine your score, count the number of correct answers in each test. Then count the number of incorrect answers. Subtract ¼ of the number of incorrect answers from the number of correct answers. Plot the resulting figure on the graph below by blackening the bar under each test to the point of your score. Plan your study to strengthen the weaknesses indicated on your scoring graph.

EXAM II HUMANITIES	Very Poor	Poor	Average	Good	Excellent
LITERATURE 77 Questions	1-10	11-29	30-53	54-69	70-77
FINE ARTS 47 Questions	1-6	7-17	18-32	31-41	42-47
PHILOSOPHY 15 Questions	1-2	3-6	7-10	11-13	14-15
ART 19 Questions	1-3	4-7	8-12	13-16	17-19

GLOSSARY OF LITERARY TERMS

This is some of the language you're likely to see on your examination. You may not need to know all the words in this carefully prepared glossary, but if even a few appear, you'll be that much ahead of your competitors. Perhaps the greater benefit from this list is the frame of mind it can create for you. Without reading a lot of technical text you'll steep yourself in just the right atmosphere for high test marks.

allegory: A poem or story in which the characters, objects, places, etc. may stand for certain ideas or ideals. For example, in *The Pilgrim's Progress*, a book by John Bunyan, the leading character, Christian, is really any man who struggles through life searching for goodness.

alliteration: Sometimes poets create a certain effect when they use the same consonant in quick repetition. This is called *alliteration*. Usually, the consonant used appears as the first letter of the words, as you will see in the following examples:

"The mother of months in meadow or plain."
"And watching his luck was the girl he loved,
The lady that's known as Lou."

In the first example, the poet created an alliterative effect by the repetition of the letter "m" in "mother," "months," and "meadow."
The second poet used the letter "l" to get an alliterative effect. Can you pick out the alliterative words?

apostrophe: a direct address to a dead or absent person or thing. Examples:

"O Spirit, that dost prefer the upright heart and pure."
"O Captain! my Captain! rise up and hear the bells."

assonance: Assonance is a cousin to alliteration. It is the appearance of the same vowel sounds in quick repetition. Here are examples:

"Mid hushed, cool-rooted flowers fragrant-eyed"
"A weed by the stream
Put forth a seed
And made a new breed"

In the first example, the sound of "oo" occurs twice. In the second example, the poet used the sound of "ee" and "ea" four times.

ballad: A story in poetic form. Somtimes this form is called a *narrative*.

cliche: A word or phrase which has been used so often in common speech that it has lost its freshness, its "spark."

colloquialism: A word or phrase that is identified with a certain locality. For example the phrase, "How you'all" is identified with the southern part of the United States.

dirge: A sad poem in which the poet speaks of a dead friend, hero, or relative. Another term for dirge is *elegy*.

euphemism: a substitution of a mild expression for a harsh one. Examples:

The departed (for the dead).
A slow student (for a stupid one).

foot: a group of two or three syllables upon one of which the accent, or stress of the voice, falls in reading.

Free verse: Poetry that is not necessarily rhymed nor has any special meter.

hyperbole: An exaggeration which the reader knows is not true. Examples:

"He was the best card player that ever was or ever will be."
"We are immensely obliged."
"I'd walk a million miles for one of your smiles."

imagery: The poet often tries to arouse in the reader certain pictures or feelings, which is summed up as imagery. For example, when you read the lines,

The Owl and the Pussy-cat went to sea
    In a beautiful pea-green boat,

the poet hopes that you will see this ridiculous scene in your mind.

Sometimes a poet may wish you to feel rather than to see. The poet wishes you to feel cold when you read the following lines:

Talk of your cold! Through the jacket's fold
It stabbed like a driven nail.
If our eyes we'd close, then the lashes froze
Till sometimes we couldn't see.

inversion: The changing of the usual order of words. Usually this is done in order to maintain the meter of the poem. Examples of inversion are:

"Holy, fair, and wise is she"
(the usual order would be "She is holy, fair, and wise.")

"Let me not to the marriage of true minds
Admit impediments. . ."
(The usual order would be "Let me not admit there are impediments to the marriage of true minds.")

irony: says something but means the opposite. Examples:

"Here's a pretty how-d'ye-do (if one gets a cold shoulder.)"
"You must love me (if one hates you.)"

limerick: A short humorous poem with a characteristic meter and rhyme structure:

There was a young lady of Niger
Who smiled as she rode on a tiger:
 They came back from the ride
 With the lady inside
And the smile on the face of the tiger.

litotes: an understatement in which the negative of the opposite meaning is used: Examples:

Not bad at all.
A matter of no slight importance.
Not entirely unsatisfactory.

metaphor: a comparison between persons or things without the use of like or as. Examples:

The road was a ribbon of moonlight.
He was a lion in strength.

metonymy: a figure by which a thing is designated, not by its own name, but by the name of something that resembles or suggests it. Examples:

glasses (for spectacles)
the knife (for surgery)

monologue: A story told by one person.

mood: The feeling that the poet wishes the reader to achieve when reading his work. For example, the poet wishes you to have a feeling of well-being and happiness after you read

The year's at the spring,
And day's at the morn;
Morning's at seven;
The hill-side's dew-pearl'd;
The lark's on the wing;
The snail's on the thorn;
God's in His Heaven—
All's right with the world!

onomatopoeia: Certain words are supposed to imitate the events they represent. Here are a few examples:

"Crack! was the sound of the rifle in the night!"
"The fire bells clanged their alarm."
"The ball plopped into the water."
"Crack!", "clanged", and "plopped" are examples of *onomatopoeia*.

oxymoron: Words that seemingly are opposed, such as "a wickedly moral man" and "thunderous silence."

paradox: A statement which seems to contradict itself. However, upon close investigation, it turns out to have an element of truth.

personification: a figure in which an inanimate object is given human qualities. Examples:

Old Sol is really shining today.
Death, be not proud!

scan a line: to mark the feet and tell what kind they are.

simile: a comparison between persons or things with the use of like or as. Examples:

He is as restless as a windshield wiper.
The sky looks like a burning ship.

stanza: a regularly recurring group of lines. For examples of stanzas, see Longfellow's "Psalm of Life" and "Village Blacksmith."

synechdoche: a figure of speech in which a part is used for the whole. Examples:

The cutthroat (for murderer) was finally caught.
This ranch has sixty head (of cattle).

PART FOUR

Mathematics

A Verisimilar General Examination

4

GLOSSARY OF MATHEMATICAL SYMBOLS

Here is a list of conventional mathematical symbols and notations used in arithmetic, algebra, geometry, and in the areas of sets and logic. Familiarity with these symbols is an important prerequisite for success on your exam. Should you run across a mathematical notation with which you are unfamiliar you may refer to this list. Now is the time to study this glossary carefully, because you will not be permitted to use it when you sit for the exam.

+   Plus; Positive
−   Minus; Negative
or ×   Times; Multiplied by; Multiplication
÷   Divided by; Division
≠   Is Not Equal
>   Greater Than
<   Less Than
∪   Union of Two Sets
∩   Intersection of Two Sets
⊂   Is Included in, Is a Subset of
⊃   Contains as a Subset
∈   Is an Element of
∉   Is Not an Element of
∧ or ○ or φ or {}
     Empty Set, Null Set
√   Root
:   Ratio of; Is to
∴   Therefore
∠   Angle
∟   Right Angle
⊥   Perpendicular; Is Perpendicular to
‖   Parallel; Is Parallel to
○   Circle
△   Triangle
□   Square
▭   Rectangle
()   Parentheses,

[]   Brackets,
{}   Braces: the Quantities
     Enclosed by Them
     Are To Be Taken Together.
f or *F*   Function
d   Differential
δ   Variation
∫   Integral; Integral of
s   Standard Deviation of a Sample
σ   Standard Deviation of a Population
Σ   Sum; Summation
$\bar{\chi}$ Arithmetic Mean of a
     Sample of a Variable x
μ   Arithmetic Mean of a Population
π   Pi; The Number 3.14159265+; The Ratio
     of the Circumference of a Circle
     To Its Diameter
!   Indicates the Product of All
     the Whole Numbers Up To and
     Including a Given Preceding Number
′   Minute
″   Second
i   Imaginary Unit
∞   Infinity
0   Zero
*   Indicates That An Unknown Mathematical Operation Is To Take Place

THE GENERAL EXAMINATION IN MATHEMATICS

A great deal depends on your examination score, as you know. And this book will help you achieve your highest possible score. You'll get plenty of practice with relevant test subjects and questions. But first we want you to pick up a few facts about the test which may make things easier for you. Then, if you decide to take the General Examination in Mathematics, you'll benefit from the intensive practice provided in CLEP: THE GENERAL EXAMINATION IN MATHEMATICS which is available from Arco Publishing Company, 219 Park Avenue South, New York, New York 10003.

A MINI-EXAM THAT FORECASTS THE GENERAL EXAMINATION

This chapter presents a miniature General Examination. This "mini-exam" contains good samples of the various types of questions you may expect to encounter. Our purpose is to offer you a bird's eye view of the **Mathematics** Examination. The sample questions show you the subjects that will be included, the different types of questions, and the levels of difficulty you may expect.

The Mathematics Examination covers basic principles and concepts likely to be included in a general college course in mathematics. The examination covers the kind of math that is used in courses such as business, economics, social science or psychology. The examination covers a wide range of mathematical ideas and skills. It does not examine your knowledge of the math you would study if you majored in mathematics in college. The questions are mainly below the college calculus level.

The examination takes about 90 minutes and includes 90 questions. There are two parts to the exam: Basic Skills and Math Content. Although you have 90 minutes to complete the entire exam, it is best to spend about 30 minutes on the Basic Skills section and 60 minutes on the Math Content section.

The Basic Skills section of the examination utilizes a kind of question in which you compare two quantities and decide if they are equal; if one is greater than the other; or if the relationship cannot be determined. Topics are taken from arithmetic, algebra, geometry, and data interpretation.

The Math Content section of the examination utilizes the common multiple choice question in which you are given a problem and must choose the correct answer from among four choices. Topics include sets, logic, the real number system, functions and their graphs, mathematical systems, elementary probability and statistics.

The content of the test is not derived from any particular textbook or course, but the topics are frequently included in courses for elementary education majors in the structure of math, or in courses to meet general education requirements.

SUMMARY OF MATHEMATICS EXAMINATION

The questions on this test are designed to measure your familiarity with the kind of mathematics that can be applied to fields of study such as business, economics, social science and psychology. The questions are not posed to mislead or trick you. Some questions will test your independent mathematical reasoning, while other questions will ask only for routine application of knowledge.

A MINI-EXAM IN MATHEMATICS

Allow about 30 minutes for this Examination.

ANALYSIS OF THIS MINI-EXAM

This table is both an analysis of the exam that follows and a price-less preview of the actual test. Look it over carefully and use it well. Since it lists both subjects and times, it points up not only what to study, but also how much time to spend on each topic. Making the most of your study time adds valuable points to your examination score.

SUBJECT TESTED	Time Allowed	SUBJECT TESTED	Time Allowed
BASIC SKILLS IN MATHEMATICS	5 Minutes	MATH CONTENT. (Functions, Sets, Number Systems, and Statistics.)	25 Minutes
Total time to allow for all questions and all Test Categories in this Miniature Examination in Mathematics:			30 Minutes
Total number of questions on this particular Verisimilar Examination in Mathematics:			30 Questions
Time allowed for all Test Categories and all questions on the actual General Examination in Mathematics:			90 Minutes
Total number of questions on the actual General Examination in Mathematics:			90 Questions

After you have finished the entire Examination, not now, you can check your answers with our Key Answers which are consolidated at the end of this Examination. In addition to the Key Answers for this Test we have provided Explanatory Answers there. They should help you considerably with clarification of points you may have missed in arriving at incorrect answers.

ANSWER SHEET FOR THIS MINI-EXAM

Make only ONE mark for each answer. Additional and stray marks may be counted as mistakes. In making corrections, erase errors COMPLETELY. Make glossy black marks.

TEST I. BASIC SKILLS

1 A B C D E 2 A B C D E 3 A B C D E 4 A B C D E 5 A B C D E 6 A B C D E 7 A B C D E 8 A B C D E

9 A B C D E 10 A B C D E

TEST II. MATH CONTENT

1 A B C D E 2 A B C D E 3 A B C D E 4 A B C D E 5 A B C D E 6 A B C D E 7 A B C D E 8 A B C D E

9 A B C D E 10 A B C D E 11 A B C D E 12 A B C D E 13 A B C D E 14 A B C D E 15 A B C D E 16 A B C D E

17 A B C D E 18 A B C D E 19 A B C D E 20 A B C D E

A NOTE ABOUT TEST TIMES.

The time allotted for each Test in each Examination in this book is based on a careful analysis of all the information now available. The time we allot for each test, therefore, merely suggests in a general way approximately how much time you should expend on each subject when you take the actual Exam. We have not, in every case, provided precisely the number of questions you will actually get on the examination. It's just not possible to know what the examiners will finally decide to do for every Test in the Examination. It might be a good idea to jot down your "running" time for each Test, and make comparisons later on. If you find that you're working faster, you may assume you're making progress. Remember, we have timed each Test uniformly. If you follow all our directions, your scores will all be comparable.

TEST I. BASIC SKILLS

TIME: 5 Minutes. 10 Questions.

DIRECTIONS: For each of the following questions two quantities are given . . . one in Column A; and one in Column B. Compare the two quantities and mark your answer sheet with the correct, lettered conclusion. These are your options:
  A: if the quantity in Column A is the greater;
  B: if the quantity in Column B is the greater;
  C: if the two quantities are equal;
  D: if the relationship cannot be determined from the information given.

Questions 1 to 5

These questions refer to the bar graph below which shows the percent of each type of extra-curricular activity (A, B, C, D, E,) in which seniors of a certain high school are involved.

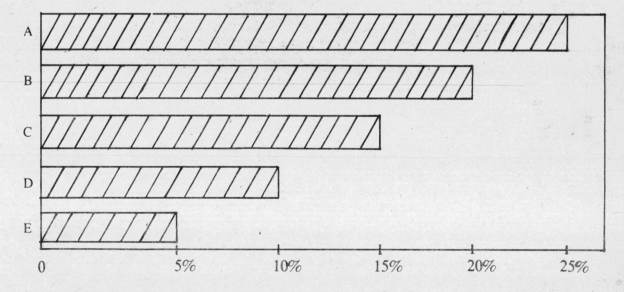

COMMON INFORMATION	COLUMN A	COLUMN B
1.	The combined ratios of seniors participating in activities C and D	The ratio of seniors participating in activity A
2.	If there were 400 seniors the number of seniors participating in activity B	If there were 600 seniors the number of seniors participating in activity E
3. 45 seniors participate in activity C	The number of seniors in the school	325 seniors
4. The ratio between boys and girls in among these seniors is 3:2	The number of senior girls participating in activity B	The number of senior girls participating in activity A
5. 50 seniors participate in activity B	The number of seniors in activity D	30 seniors

Questions 6 to 10

These questions refer to the circle graph below which illustrates how a certain school district spends the school budget during a particular school year. The school budget was $1,112,000.

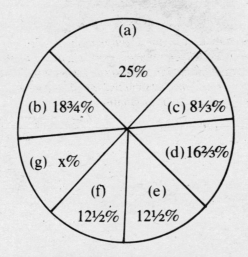

Key: (a) teacher salaries
   (b) school bonds
   (c) textbooks
   (d) administrative salaries

   (e) school maintenance
   (f) office help
   (g) school supplies

COMMON INFORMATION	COLUMN A	COLUMN B
6.	The percent of money spent for school supplies	8%
7.	$280,000	The amount of money spent for teacher salaries
8.	The ratio between category b and category g	3:1
9.	The amount of money spent on administrative salaries	$185,000
10.	The amount of money spent on teacher salaries	The combined total amount spent on administrative salaries and textbooks

END OF TEST

Go on to the next Test in the Examination, just as you would do on the actual exam. Check your answers when you have completed the entire Examination. The correct answers for this Test, and all the other Tests, are assembled at the conclusion of this Examination.

TEST II. MATH CONTENT

TIME: 25 Minutes. 20 Questions.

DIRECTIONS: For each question in this test, read carefully the stem and the four lettered choices that follow. Choose the answer which you consider correct or most nearly correct. Mark the answer sheet for the letter you have chosen: A, B, C, or D.

Correct and explanatory answers are provided at the end of the exam. After you have completed the entire exam, read the explanations carefully. They'll reinforce your strengths and pinpoint your weaknesses so that you know just what to study to raise your score.

1. If m is an even integer, which of the following is an even integer?

(A) $m^2 + 1$ (C) $m^2 + m$

(B) $2m + 3$ (D) $4m - 1$

2. If $\log_{49} 1/7 = x$, then x =

(A) 7   (B) 1/7   (C) 1/2   (D) −1/2

3. $(\sqrt{-4})^2$ equals

(A) 4i   (B) ±4   (C) −4   (D) 4

4. If $f(x) = x^3 - 2x^2 + x$, then $f(-3)$ equals

(A) −54   (B) −48   (C) 0   (D) 18

5. One card is picked at random from a deck of 52 cards. What is the probability of picking the ten of spades?

(A) 1/4   (B) 1/16   (C) 1/48   (D) 1/52

6. The value of $(1/2)y^° + (3x/2)^° - 27^{-1/3}$ equals

(A) 1   (B) 1 1/6   (C) 2   (D) 4 1/2

7. If $M = \{2, 3\}$ and $N = \{4\}$, then $M \times N$ equals

(A) {(2,4),(3,4)}   (C) {8, 12}

(B) {24}   (D) {2, 3, 4}

8. If $2x^3 = y$, then dy/dx equals

(A) x^2 (B) $2x^2$ (C) $6x$ (D) $6x^2$

9.

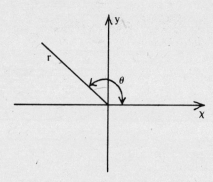

In the above figure tan θ equals

(A) x/y   (B) y/x   (C) $-$y/x   (D) $-$x/y

10. In the geometric progression 2x/3, 4...the next term would be

(A) 40   (B) 24   (C) 24x   (D) $24(x)^{-1}$

11. Solve for a in the equation 3 sin (a + 5) = m$-$4

(A) a = 5$-$(m$-$4) sin   (C) a = 3 sin (m$-$4) + 5

(B) a = $-5+\dfrac{(m-4)}{3}$ sin^{-1} (D) a = $\dfrac{m-4}{3}$ sin $-$ 5

12. If $a^{-1} -2$ is divided by 2a$-$1 the quotient is

(A) a   (B) 2a   (C) $-\frac{1}{2}$a   (D) $-$1/a

13. 8! × 5! ÷ 10! equals

(A) 4!   (B) 4   (C) 2   (D) 4/3

14. The complex conjugate of 9 + 2i is

(A) $-$9$-$2i   (C) 9$-$2i
(B) $-$9+2i   (D) 2+9i

15. An inscribed angle and a central angle intercept the same arc on a given circle. If the arc is 1/6 the length of the circumference, then the number of degrees in the intercepted arc equals

(A) 30°   (B) 45°   (C) 60°   (D) 90°

16.

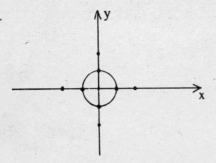

The equation for the above graph is

(A) $x + y = 1$

(B) $x^2 - 1 = -y^2$

(C) $x^2 - y^2 = 1$

(D) $x^2 = y^2 + 1$

17. If the tan of an angle equals 5/12 then the sin of the same angle equals

(A) 5/12   (B) 1/25   (C) 1/35   (D) 5/13

Questions 38 to 40 refer to the following truth table:

p	q	~p	~q	p∨q
T	T			
T	F			
F	T			
F	F			

18. In the truth table (~p) column would be

(A)	(B)	(C)	(D)
T	T	T	F
F	F	T	F
F	T	T	T
T	F	T	T

19. In the truth table (~q) column would be

(A)	(B)	(C)	(D)
F	T	F	T
F	F	T	T
T	T	F	F
T	F	T	F

20. In the truth table (p∨q) column would be

(A)	(B)	(C)	(D)
F	T	T	F
F	T	F	T
F	T	T	F
T	F	F	T

END OF EXAMINATION

CORRECT ANSWERS FOR THIS MINI-EXAM

TEST I. BASIC SKILLS

1.C	3.B	5.B	7.A	9.A
2.A	4.B	6.B	8.C	10.C

TEST I. EXPLANATORY ANSWERS

1. **(C)**
Activity C = 15%   Activity A = 25%
Activity D = 10%
Combined = 25%
$$25\% = \tfrac14 = 1:4$$
∴ Column A = Column B

2. **(A)**
Activity B = 20%   Activity E = 5%
20% = .20   5% = .05
.20(400) = 80   .05(600) = 30
80 > 30
∴ Column A > Column B

3. **(B)**
Let x = the number of seniors
.15x = 45
x = 300
325 > 300
∴ Column B > Column A

4. **(B)**
If the ratio between boys and girls is 3:2, then the ratio between girls and the entire class is 2:5.
Activity B = 20% seniors = 8% senior girls
Activity A = 25% seniors = 10% senior girls
10% > 8%
∴ Column B > Column A

5. **(B)**
Let x = the total number of seniors
.20x = 50
x = 250 (total no. of seniors)
Activity D = 10%
.10(250) = 25
30 > 25
∴ Column B > Column A

6. **(B)**
The percents in the circle must total 100%
∴ school supplies = 6¼%
8% > 6¼%
∴ Column B > Column A

7. **(A)**
Teacher salaries = 25% of the budget
25% = ¼
¼(1,112,000) = 278,000
280,000 > 278,000
∴ Column A > Column B

8. **(C)**
Category b = 18¾% of the budget
Category g = 6¼% of the budget
18¾%: 6¼% = .1875: .625 = 3:1
∴ Column A = Column B

9. **(A)**
Administrative salaries = 16⅔% of the budget
16⅔% = 1/6
1/6(1,112,000) = $185,333.67
185,333.67 > 185,000
∴ Column A > Column B

10. **(C)**
Teacher salaries = 25% of the budget
Administrative salaries = 16⅔%
Textbooks = 8⅓%
16⅔ + 8⅓ = 25%
∴ Column A = Column B

TEST II. MATH CONTENT

1.C	4.B	7.A	10.D	13.D	16.B	19.C
2.D	5.D	8.D	11.B	14.C	17.D	20.B
3.C	6.B	9.C	12.D	15.A	18.D	

TEST II. EXPLANATORY ANSWERS

1. **(C)** Let $m = 2$
    then $m^2 + m = (2)^2 + 2 = 6$ (an even integer)

2. **(D)** $\log_{49} 1/7 = x$
    $$49^x = 1/7$$
    $$(7^2)^x = 1/7$$
    $$7^{2x} = 7^{-1}$$
    $$2x = -1$$
    $$x = -1/2$$

3. **(C)** $(\sqrt{-4})^2 = -4$

4. **(B)** $f(-3) = (-3)^3 - 2(-3)^2 + (-3)$
    $$= -27 - 18 - 3$$
    $$= -48$$

5. **(D)** $P(10) = 4/52 = 1/13$
    $P(\text{spade}) = 1/4$
    $P(10 \text{ of spades}) = 1/13 \cdot 1/4 = 1/52$

6. **(B)** $(1/2)y° = 1/2$
    $(3 \times 12) = 1$
    $27^{-1/3} = 1/3$
    $\therefore 1/2 + 1 - 1/3 = 1\ 1/6$

7. **(A)** $M \times N = \{(2,4), (3,4)\}$

8. **(D)** $y = 2x^3$
    $dy/dx = 6x^2$

9. **(C)** $\tan \theta = \dfrac{\text{opposite}}{\text{adjacent}} = \dfrac{y}{-x} = -y/x$

10. **(D)** To find the third term divide the second by the first to find the
ratio $4 \div 2x/3 = 4 \cdot 3/2x = 6/x$
Then multiply the second term by the ratio $4(6/x) = 24/x = 24(x)^{-1}$

11. **(B)** $3 \sin (a+5) = m-4$
$$\sin (a+5) = \frac{m-4}{3}$$

$$(a+5) = \left(\frac{m-4}{3}\right) \sin^{-1}$$

$$a = -5 + \left(\frac{m-4}{3}\right) \sin^{-1}$$

12. **(D)** $(a^{-1}-2) \div 2a-1$
$(1/a - 2) \div 2a - 1$
$$\frac{1-2a}{a} \times \frac{1}{2a-1} = \frac{1}{-a} = -\frac{1}{a}$$

13. **(D)** $\dfrac{8! \times 5!}{10!} = \dfrac{5!}{10 \cdot 9} = \dfrac{5 \cdot 4 \cdot 3 \cdot 2 \cdot 1}{10 \cdot 9} = 4/3$

14. **(C)** The conjugate of $9 + 2i$ is $9 - 2i$

15. **(A)** $1/6 \cdot 360 = 60°$
$\therefore$ inscribed angle equals $30°$

16. **(B)** The equation of a circle whose radius is one unit from the origin is
$x^2 + y^2 = 1$
$x^2 = 1 - y^2$
$x^2 - 1 = - y^2$

17. **(D)**

If $\tan A = 5/12$
then $\sin A = 5/13$

18. **(D)** $\sim p$ is the opposite of p

19. **(C)** $\sim q$ is the opposite of q

20. **(B)** If both p and q are T or if either p or q is T then $p \lor q$ is T. $p \lor q$ is
only F when both p and q are F.

MATHEMATICS
THIRD VERISIMILAR EXAMINATION

"A thousand mile journey begins with a single step." To begin your studies test yourself with this professionally constructed Examination. It's quite similar to the one you'll actually get. It's a practical yardstick for finding out how your beginning knowledge and ability measure up to the requirements. If you get right to work on it and score yourself objectively, you'll be able to chart your progress and plan further study to concentrate on improving your weaknesses.

Allow about 1½ hours for this Examination.

In order to create the climate of the actual exam, that's exactly what you should allow yourself . . . no more, no less. Use a watch to keep a record of your time, since it might suit your convenience to try this practice exam in several short takes.

ANALYSIS AND TIMETABLE: A VERISIMILAR EXAMINATION III.				
This table is both an analysis of the exam that follows and a priceless preview of the actual test. Look it over carefully and use it well. Since it lists both subjects and times, it points up not only what to study, but also how much time to spend on each topic. Making the most of your study time adds valuable points to your examination score.				
SUBJECT TESTED	*Time Allowed*	*SUBJECT TESTED*		*Time Allowed*
BASIC SKILLS IN MATHEMATICS	30 Minutes	MATH CONTENT. (Functions, Sets, Number Systems, and Statistics.)		60 Minutes
Total time to allow for all questions and all Test Categories in this Verisimilar Examination in Mathematics:				90 Minutes
Total number of questions on this particular Verisimilar Examination in Mathematics:				90 Questions

ANSWER SHEET FOR VERISIMILAR EXAMINATION III.

Practice using Answer Sheets. Make ONE mark for each answer. Additional and stray marks may be counted as mistakes. In making corrections erase errors COMPLETELY. Make glossy black marks. To arrive at an accurate estimate of your ability and progress cover the Correct Answers with a sheet of white paper while you are taking this test.

TEST I. BASIC SKILLS

TEST II. MATH CONTENT

TEST III. MATH CONTENT

SCORE YOURSELF

Compare your answers to the Correct Key Answers at the end of the Examination. To determine your score, count the number of correct answers in each test. Then count the number of incorrect answers. Subtract ¼ of the number of incorrect answers from the number of correct answers. Plot the resulting figure on the graph below by blackening the bar under each test to the point of your score. Plan your study to strengthen the weaknesses indicated on your scoring graph.

EXAM III MATHEMATICS	Very Poor	Poor	Average	Good	Excellent
BASIC SKILLS 40 Questions	1-7	8-16	17-27	28-35	36-40
MATH CONTENT 50 Questions	1-7	8-18	19-33	34-44	45-50

TEST I. BASIC SKILLS

TIME: 30 Minutes. 40 Questions.

COMMON INFORMATION: In each question, information concerning one or both of the quantities to be compared is given in the Common Information column. A symbol that appears in any column represents the same thing in Column A as in Column B.
NUMBERS: All numbers used are real numbers.
FIGURES: Assume that the position of points, angles, regions, and so forth, are in the order shown.

Assume that the lines shown as straight are indeed straight. Figures are assumed to lie in a plane unless otherwise indicated.

Figures accompanying questions are intended to provide information you can use in answering the questions. However, unless a note states that a figure is drawn to scale, you should solve the problems by using your knowledge of mathematics, and NOT by estimating sizes by sight or by measurement.

DIRECTIONS: For each of the following questions two quantities are given . . . one in Column A; and one in Column B. Compare the two quantities and mark your answer sheet with the correct, lettered conclusion. These are your options:
  A: if the quantity in Column A is the greater;
  B: if the quantity in Column B is the greater;
  C: if the two quantities are equal;
  D: if the relationship cannot be determined from the information given.

Correct and explanatory answers are provided at the end of the exam. After you have completed the entire exam, read the explanations carefully. They'll reinforce your strengths and pinpoint your weaknesses so that you know just what to study to raise your score.

	COMMON INFORMATION	COLUMN A	COLUMN B
1.		The average of 18, 20, 22, 24, 26	The average of 19, 21, 23, 25
2.		$8 + 14 (8 - 6)$	$14 + 8 (8 - 6)$
3.		6% of 30	The number 30 is 6% of
4.		$(1/5)^3$	$(1/5)^2$

S3041

	COMMON INFORMATION	COLUMN A	COLUMN B
5.		2^2	$\sqrt[3]{64}$
6.		$8 - 6 \times 2 + 7$	$9 + 12 \times 4 - 6$
7.	The ratio of boys to girls in a math class is 3:1	Ratio of girls to the entire class	1:3
8.	A sport jacket priced $48 after a 20% discount	Original price of the sport coat	$60
9.		(Base 2 Number) 10101	(Base 3 Number) 121
10.		A package of meat weighing 1.8 lbs. (unit price 92.6¢ per lb.)	A package of meat weighing 2.3 lbs. (unit price 67.5¢ per lb.)
11.	$\begin{cases} x - y = -6 \\ x + y = -2 \end{cases}$	x	y
12.	$(x - 6)(x + 4) = 0$	The smallest root of the equation	The negative of the greatest root of the equation
13.	$x/4 = y^2$	x	y
14.	$x = -1$	$3x^2 - 2x + 4$	$2x^3 + x^2 + 4$
15.	$6 > y > -2$	$y/4$	$4/y$
16.	$\begin{cases} x < 0 \\ y < 0 \end{cases}$	$x + y$	$x - y$
17.	$A * B = A^2 + B$	$1/3 * 1/2$	$1/2 * 1/3$
18.	$t < 0$	t^3	t^2
19.		The sum of the factors of: $x^2 + 5x + 6 = 0$	The product of the factors of: $x^2 - x - 6 = 0$
20.	$a/b = c/d$	$a+b$	$c+d$

COMMON INFORMATION	COLUMN A	COLUMN B

21.

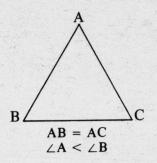

AB = AC
∠A < ∠B

COLUMN A: BC

COLUMN B: AB

22.

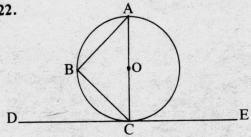

AC is a diameter of circle 0

DE is tangent to circle 0

COLUMN A: ∠ ACE

COLUMN B: ∠ ABC

23.

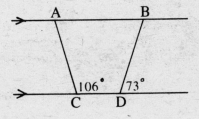

COLUMN A: AC

COLUMN B: BD

24.

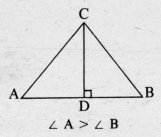

∠ A > ∠ B

COLUMN A: ∠BCD

COLUMN B: ∠ ACD

25.

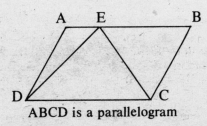

ABCD is a parallelogram

COLUMN A: Areas of △ AED + △ EBC

COLUMN B: Area of △ DEC

COMMON INFORMATION	COLUMN A	COLUMN B

26.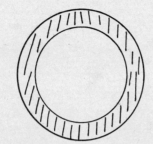

Diameter of large circle = 16
Diameter of small circle = 12

Area of shaded portion | Area of small circle

27.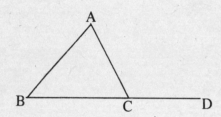

∠ ACD | ∠ A + ∠ B

28.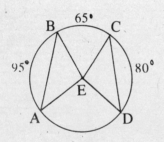

∠ AED | ∠ B

29. | The edge of a cube whose volume is 64 cubic feet | The edge of a cube whose total surface area is 96 square feet

30.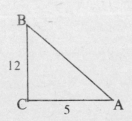

$(AB)^2 - 5\,AC$ | $(BC)^2$

COMMON INFORMATION	COLUMN A	COLUMN B

The *Common Information* for questions 31 to 35 consists of the following circle graph. This circle graph shows how Mr. X spends his monthly paycheck of $1,000.

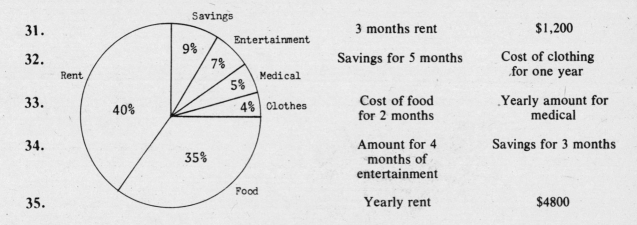

	COLUMN A	COLUMN B
31.	3 months rent	$1,200
32.	Savings for 5 months	Cost of clothing for one year
33.	Cost of food for 2 months	Yearly amount for medical
34.	Amount for 4 months of entertainment	Savings for 3 months
35.	Yearly rent	$4800

Questions 36 to 40 refer to the following table:

Based on available information, the tax rate on a gallon of gasoline in certain states is shown in the table below. If your car had 4 cylinders or less, use half the table amount.

Alabama	7¢	Iowa	7¢
Alaska	8¢	Kansas	7¢
Arkansas	7.5¢	Kentucky	9¢
Connecticut	10¢	Minnesota	7¢
Delaware	9¢	Nebraska	8.5¢
Florida	7.5¢	New Jersey	8¢
Hawaii	5¢	North Dakota	7¢
Idaho	8.5¢	Texas	5¢
Indiana	8¢	Wyoming	5¢

Compare the taxes paid for gasoline for the situation described in Column A with the situation described in Column B.

COMMON INFORMATION	COLUMN A	COLUMN B
36.	A 4-cylinder car drives 1200 miles in Wyoming	An 8-cylinder car drives 600 miles in Texas
37.	A 6-cylinder car using 800 gallons in Delaware	4-cylinder car using 1200 gallons in Connecticut

COMMON INFORMATION	COLUMN A	COLUMN B
38.	An 8-cylinder car using 2400 gallons in Kentucky	A 6-cylinder car using 3200 gallons in Arkansas
39.	An 8-cylinder car that averages 14 miles to a gallon—driving 2800 Miles in Iowa	An 8-cylinder car that averages 10 miles to a gallon—driving 1900 miles in Delaware
40.	Two 4-cylinder cars using 40,000 gallons combined—driving in Texas	An 8-cylinder car using 14,000 gallons in Kansas and 14,000 gallons in Connecticut

END OF TEST

Go on to do the following Test in this Examination, just as you would be expected to do on the actual exam.

TEST II. MATH CONTENT

TIME: 48 Minutes . 40 Questions.

DIRECTIONS: For each question in this test, read carefully the stem and the four lettered choices that follow. Choose the answer which you consider correct or most nearly correct. Mark the answer sheet for the letter you have chosen: A, B, C, or D.

Correct and explanatory answers are provided at the end of the exam. After you have completed the entire exam, read the explanations carefully. They'll reinforce your strengths and pinpoint your weaknesses so that you know just what to study to raise your score.

1. If 120 is divided into three parts proportioned to 3, 5 and 7, the largest part is

   (A) 17 1/7   (C) 40
   (B) 24   (D) 56

2. If the digit 1 is placed after a two digit number whose tens' digit is t, and units' digit is u, the new number is

   (A) $10t + u + 1$ (C) $1000t + 10u + 1$
   (B) $100t + 10u + 1$ (D) $t + u + 1$

3. If the radius of a circle is increased 50%, the area is increased

   (A) 25%   (B) 50%   (C) 100%   (D) 125%

4. If in the formula $C = en/R + nr$, n is decreased, while e, R, and r remain constant, then C

   (A) decreases   (C) remains constant
   (B) increases   (D) increases and then decreases

5. Which of the following is a valid equation if only real numbers are used?

   I. $a (b - c) = ab - ac$
   II. $x^{a-b} = x^a - x^b$
   III. $\log (a - b) = \log a - \log b$
   IV. $\dfrac{\log a}{\log b} = \log a - \log b$

   (A) I only   (C) III only
   (B) II only   (D) IV only

6. The equation $y + \sqrt{y - 2} = 4$ has

   (A) no roots (C) 2 real roots
   (B) 1 real root (D) 2 imaginary roots

7. If the expressions $\begin{vmatrix} x & y \\ p & q \end{vmatrix}$ has the value $xq - yp$

   for all values of x, y, p and q, then the equation

   $\begin{vmatrix} 2a & 1 \\ a & a \end{vmatrix} = 3$

   (A) is satisfied for no values of a (C) is satisfied for 2 values of a
   (B) is satisfied for 1 value of a (D) is satisfied for 3 values of a

8. If the length of a diagonal of a square is $x + y$, then the area of the square is

   (A) $(x + y)^2$ (C) $\frac{1}{2}(x + y)^2$
   (B) $x^2 + y^2$ (D) $\frac{1}{2}(x^2 + y^2)$

9.

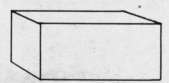

   The dimensions of the front, side and top of the pictured rectangular box are known. The product of their areas is equal to

   (A) the volume of the box (C) twice the volume
   (B) the square root of the volume (D) the square of the volume

10. Given: $a > 0, b > 0, a > b$ and $c \neq 0$. The inequality which is not always correct is

    (A) $a + c > b + c$ (C) $\dfrac{a}{c^2} > \dfrac{b}{c^2}$
    (B) $a - c > b - c$ (D) $ac > bc$

11. From a deck of 52 cards one card is drawn at random. What is the probability that the random card is either a king or a queen?

    (A) 1:52 (B) 1:26 (C) 1:13 (D) 2:13

12. If A = {2, 4, 6} and B = {1, 3, 5} then A ∪ B equals

(A) {1, 2, 3, 4, 5, 6}   (C) {2, 1}
(B) ∅   (D) {2, 4, 3, 5}

13. If f (x) = x² + x + 1, then f (−1) equals

(A) 0   (B) 1   (C) 2   (D) 3

14. The y−intercept of the equation

3y + 4x = 6 is

(A) 6   (B) 4   (C) 2   (D) 0

15. Sin 70° equals

(A) −cos 70°   (C) −cos 20°
(B) cos 20°   (D) cos 70°

16.

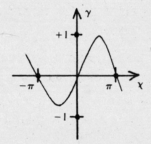

The above graph is for the following equation
(A) y = 2 cos x   (C) y = tan x
(B) y = 2 sin x   (D) y = sin x

17. If A = {1, 3, 5} and B = {5, 7, 9} then A ∩ B =

(A) {5}
(B) {1, 3, 7, 9}
(C) {1, 3, 5, 5, 7, 9}
(D) {1, 3, 5, 7, 9}

18. The magnitude of the vector (4, 7) is

(A) 4/7   (C) √65
(B) 7/4   (D) 11

19. If y = 3 (x² + 5)³ then $\frac{dy}{dx}$ equals

(A) 9 (x² + 5)²   (C) 18 (x² + 5)³
(B) 18 (x² + 5)²   (D) 18x (x² + 5)²

20. Three German books and three French books are placed at random on a shelf that holds exactly six books. What is the probability that all books of the same language will be placed together?

(A) 1/20   (B) 1/10   (C) 1/6   (D) 1/4

21.

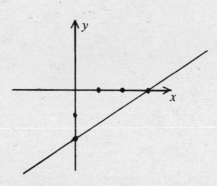

The linear equation for the above graph is

(A) y = − 3/2x −2   (C) y = 3x − 2
(B) y = 3/2x + 2   (D) y = 2/3x − 2

22. Which of the following statements is true?

(A) If $A \subseteq B$, then $A \cap B = A$ (C) If $A \subseteq B$, then $A \times A = A \times B$
(B) $A \times A \subset A$ (D) If $A \subset B$, then $A \cap B = B$

23. If $x = \log_{16} 32$, then x =

(A) 1/2   (B) 2/3   (C) 3/4   (D) 5/4

24. If $(x + 3)(x − 2) < 0$, then

(A) 2 < x < 3   (C) − 2 < x < 3
(B) − 3 < x < 2   (D) − 3 < x < 3

25. If x = {1, 2} and y = {3}, then the number of pairs in the Cartesian product (x) x (y) is

(A) 0   (B) 1   (C) 2   (D) 3

26.

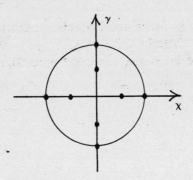

The equation for the circle shown is

(A) $x^2 + y^2 = 4$ (C) $x^2 - y^2 = 4$
(B) $x^2 + y^2 = 2$ (D) $x^2 - y^2 = 2$

27. The slope of the line $3y = 9x - 6$ is

(A) 9   (B) 6   (C) 3   (D) 2

28. $-\sqrt{-49x^2}$ equals

(A) $-7x$ (C) $7x\,i$
(B) $7x$ (D) $-7x\,i$

29. If $f(x) = \dfrac{x + 2}{x - 2}$, then $f(3)$ equals

(A) 4   (B) 5   (C) 6   (D) 7

30. Find the arithmetic mean of 96, 24, 18, 6, 1.

(A) 96   (B) 29   (C) 18   (D) 6

31. The inverse of the statement $p \to q$ is

(A) $\sim p \to q$ (C) $p \to \sim q$
(B) $\sim p \to \sim q$ (D) $q \to p$

32. In base 3, the number following 212 is

(A) 213   (B) 215   (C) 218   (D) 220

33. Find the coordinates of the point of inflection of the curve

    $y = 2/3\ x^3 + 3\ x^2 - 4x + 1$

    (A) $(-6/4, 16)$
    (B) $(6/4, -16)$
    (C) $(4/6, 16)$
    (D) $(16, 4/6)$

34. $2^{1/3} \cdot 5^{1/2}$ equals:

    (A) $15^{1/6}$
    (B) $8^{1/6}$
    (C) $500^{1/6}$
    (D) $15^{5/6}$

35. A drawer contains 5 brown and 4 blue socks. A man pulls out two socks at random. What is the probability that they match?

    (A) 4/5   (B) 5/9   (C) 3/8   (D) 4/9

36. There are 5 chocolates and 1 mint in a box. If 2 candies are chosen at random, what is the probability that the mint is one of them?

    (A) 1/5   (B) 2/5   (C) 1/3   (D) 2/7

37. Change .0530 to scientific notation.

    (A) 530×10^{-4}
    (B) 5.30×10^2
    (C) 5.30×10^{-2}
    (D) 53.0×10^3

38. It takes 5 seconds for a clock to strike 6 o'clock beginning at 6 o'clock precisely. If the strikings are uniformly spaced, how long, in seconds, does it take to strike 12 o'clock?

    (A) 9 1/5
    (B) 10
    (C) 11
    (D) 14 2/5

39. The number of distinct points common to the graphs, $x^2 + y^2 = 9$ and $y^2 = 9$ is

    (A) infinite   (B) 4   (C) 2   (D) 1

40. The sum of two numbers is 10; their product is 20. The sum of their reciprocals is

    (A) 1/10   (B) 1/2   (C) 1   (D) 2

END OF TEST

*Go on to do the following Test in this Examination, just as you would
be expected to do on the actual exam.*

TEST III. MATH CONTENT

TIME: 12 Minutes. 10 Questions.

DIRECTIONS: For each of the problems in this test calculate the correct answer, and mark the letter of that choice on your answer sheet. Figures that accompany problems are intended to provide information useful in solving the problem. They are drawn accurately EXCEPT when it is stated in a specific problem that its figure is not drawn to scale. All figures lie in a plane unless otherwise indicated.

Correct and explanatory answers are provided at the end of the exam. After you have completed the entire exam, read the explanations carefully. They'll reinforce your strengths and pinpoint your weaknesses so that you know just what to study to raise your score.

①

A cylindrical tank is 1/2 full. When 6 quarts are added, the tank is 2/3 full. The capacity of the tank, in quarts, is:

(A) 18   (B) 24   (C) 36   (D) 40   (E) 48

②

The diameters of two wheels are 10 inches and 14 inches. The smaller makes 50 more revolutions than the larger in going a certain distance. This distance, in inches, is:

(A) 3500   (D) 3500π

(B) 1750   (E) none of these

(C) 1750π

③

The graphs of the equations $2x - 3y = 5$ and $4x - 6y = 7$

(A) form an acute angle

(B) intersect in two points

(C) are parallel lines

(D) are coincident lines

(E) are perpendicular lines

④

If 2 is a root of $x^3 + hx + 10 = 0$, then the remaining two roots are:

(A) real and equal

(B) imaginary

(C) unequal and rational

(D) irrational

(E) integral

⑤

Circles O and O' are tangent to each other. Circle O' passes through the center of O. If the area of circle O is 16, then the area circle O' is

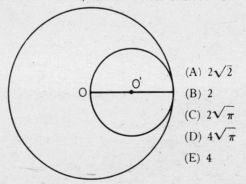

(A) $2\sqrt{2}$

(B) 2

(C) $2\sqrt{\pi}$

(D) $4\sqrt{\pi}$

(E) 4

The graph of $y^2 - 9x^2 = 0$ is:

    (A) a pair of straight lines
    (B) a parabola
    (C) an ellipse
    (D) a circle
    (E) a hyperbola

A circle is inscribed in a square and then a smaller square is inscribed in the circle. The ratio of the area of the smaller square to that of the larger square is:

(A) 1:4   (B) $\sqrt{2}$:2   (C) 1:2   (D) 1:$\sqrt{2}$ (E) 2:3

One root of the equation $x^2 + px + q = 0$ is $1 + i\sqrt{3}$, where p and q are rational numbers and $i = \sqrt{-1}$. It then follows that:

    (A) $p = q$
    (B) $p = 1$ and $q = 2$
    (C) $p = -q$
    (D) $p = -2$ and $q = 4$
    (E) $p = 3, q = 4$

Quadrilateral $PQRS$ is inscribed in a circle of radius 10. If angle PQR is 150°, and L is the length of arc PQR, then

    (A) $L < 10$
    (B) $10 < L < 10.5$
    (C) $10.5 < L < 11$
    (D) $11 < L < 12$
    (E) $L > 12$

(10)

The diagonals of a parallelogram are 20 and 10 and form an angle of 60°. The length of the shorter side is:

(A) 7.5   (B) $10\sqrt{3}$ (C) $5\sqrt{2}$ (D) 8   (E) $5\sqrt{3}$

END OF EXAMINATION

If you finish before the allotted time is up, check your work on this part only. When time runs out, compare your answers for this test and all the other tests in the examination with the correct key answers that follow.

CORRECT ANSWERS FOR VERISIMILAR EXAMINATION III.

TEST I. BASIC SKILLS

1.C	6.B	11.B	16.B	21.B	26.B	31.C	36.D
2.A	7.B	12.A	17.A	22.C	27.C	32.B	37.A
3.B	8.C	13.D	18.B	23.B	28.A	33.A	38.B
4.B	9.A	14.A	19.A	24.A	29.C	34.A	39.B
5.C	10.A	15.D	20.D	25.C	30.C	35.C	40.B

TEST I. EXPLANATORY ANSWERS

1. **(C)**
   The average of Column A is 22
   The average of Column B is 22
   $\therefore$ Column A = Column B

2. **(A)**
$8 + 14(8 - 6)$	$14 + 8(8 - 6)$
$8 + 14(2)$	$14 + 8(2)$
$8 + 28$	$14 + 16$
36	30

   $\therefore$ Column A > Column B

3. **(B)**
$6\% = .06$	$6/100 = 30x$
$.06(30) = 1.80$	
1.8	$6x = 3000$
	$x = 500$

   $\therefore$ Column B > Column A

4. **(B)**
   $(1/5)^3 = 1/125$ $(1/5)^2 = 1/25$
   $\therefore$ Column B > Column A

5. **(C)**
   $2^2 = 4$ $\sqrt[3]{64} = 4$
   $\therefore$ Column A = Column B

6. **(B)**
   $8 - 6 \times 2 + 7$
$8 - 12 + 7$	$9 + 12 \div 4 - 6$
3	$9 + 3 - 6$
	6

   $\therefore$ Column B > Column A

7. **(B)**
   The ratio of girls to entire class is 1:4
   The ratio 1:3 > the ratio 1:4
   $\therefore$ Column B > Column A

8. **(C)**
   Let x = the original price
   $x - 20\%$ of $x = 48$
   $x - 1/5x = 48$
   $4/5x = 48$
   $x = 60$
   $\therefore$ Column A = Column B

9. **(A)**

16	8	4	2	1		9	3	1
1	0	1	0	1		1	2	1

   $16 + 0 + 4 + 0 + 1$ $9 + 6 + 1$
   21   16
   $\therefore$ Column A > Column B

10. **(A)**
.926	.675
$\times\ 1.8$	$\times\ 2.3$
7408	2025
926	1350
$1.6668 = \$1.67$	$1.5525 = \$1.55$

    $\therefore$ Column A > Column B

11. **(B)**
$x - y = -6$	Substituting x = -4
$x + y = -2$	$x - y = -6$
$2x = -8$	$-4 - y = -6$
$x = -4$	$-y = -2$
	$y = 2$

    $\therefore$ Column B > Column A

12. **(A)**
    $(x - 6)(x + 4) = 0$
    $x + 4 = 0$
    $x - 6 = 0$ $x = -4$
    $x = 6$
    $-6 =$ the negative of greatest root
    $-4 =$ smallest root
    $-4 > -6$
    $\therefore$ Column A > Column B

13. **(D)**
There is insufficient information to determine the values of x and y. Hence, it cannot be determined which variable is greater.

14. **(A)**

$3x^2 - 2x + 4$	$2(-1)^3 + (-1)^2 + 4$
$3(-1)^2 - 2(-1) + 4$	$2(-1) + 1 + 4$
$3(1) + 2 + 4$	$-2 + 1 + 4$
9	3

$\therefore$ Column A > Column B

15. **(D)**
Y could equal $\{5, 4, 3, 2, 1, 0, -1\}$

There is insufficient information to determine the value of Column A or Column B.

16. **(B)**
Since x and y are both less than zero, then x and y are both negative. It is also known that two negatives subtracted is greater than the same two negatives added.

$\therefore$ Column B > Column A

17. **(A)**
If $A*B = A^2 + B$
then $\frac{1}{3} * \frac{1}{2} = (\frac{1}{3})^2 + \frac{1}{2}$, and $\frac{1}{2} * \frac{1}{3} = (\frac{1}{2})^2 + \frac{1}{3}$

$1/9 + \frac{1}{2}$	$\frac{1}{4} + \frac{1}{3}$
$2/18 + 9/18$	$3/12 + 4/12$
$11/18$	$7/12$
$22/36$	$21/36$

$\therefore$ Column A > Column B

18. **(B)**
Since t is less than zero, then t is negative. A negative squared is greater than a negative cubed.

$\therefore$ Column B > Column A

19. **(A)**

$x^2 + 5x + 6 = 0$	$x^2 - x - 6 = 0$
$(x + 3)(x + 2) = 0$	$(x - 3)(x + 2) = 0$
$x = -3$	$x = 3$
$x = 2$	$x = -2$

Their sum $= -1$ Their product $= -6$

$\therefore$ Column A > Column B

20. **(D)**
There is insufficient information to determine the values of the four variables.

21. **(B)**
Since AB = AC
then $\angle$ B = $\angle$ C (an isosceles $\triangle$)
since $\angle$ A < $\angle$ B
then $\angle$ A < $\angle$ C (substitution)
$\therefore$ BC < AB (the greater side lies opposite the greater $\angle$)

$\therefore$ Column B > Column A

22. **(C)**
A diameter forms a perpendicular when drawn to a tangent, therefore, $\angle$ ACE = 90°. Also, a triangle inscribed in a semi-circle is a right triangle, therefore $\angle$ ABC = 90°.

$\therefore$ Column A = Column B

23. **(B)**
The shortest line that can be drawn between two parallel lines is a perpendicular line. A transversal increases in size when the angle it makes with one of the parallels gets further away from 90°.
$106° - 90° = 16°$
$90° - 73° = 17°$
$\therefore$ BD > AC

$\therefore$ Column B > Column A

24. **(A)**
Since $\angle$ CDB = $\angle$ CDA = 90° (given)
then $\angle$ A + $\angle$ ACD = $\angle$ B + $\angle$ BCD = 90°
(the acute angles of a right triangle equal 90°)
and since $\angle$ A > $\angle$ B (given)
then $\angle$ ACD > $\angle$ BCD (equals minus unequals are unequal in reverse order)

$\therefore$ Column A > Column B

25. **(C)**
A triangle inscribed in a parallelogram is equal in area to one-half the area of the parallelogram. Since $\triangle$ DEC is equal in area to $\frac{1}{2}$ the area of parallelogram ABCD, then triangles ADE and EBC equal the other half of the parallelogram.

$\therefore$ Column A = Column B

26. **(B)**
Area of circle $= \pi r^2$
Area of large circle $= \pi (8)^2 = 64\pi$
Area of small circle $= \pi (6)^2 = 36\pi$
Shaded portion $= 64\pi - 36\pi = 28\pi$
$36\pi > 28\pi$
$\therefore$ Column B > Column A

27. **(C)**
Since an exterior $\angle$ is equal in degrees to the sum of the two interior remote angles, then $\angle$ ACD $= \angle$ A $+ \angle$ B.
$\therefore$ Column A = Column B

28. **(A)**
$\angle$ AED $= \frac{1}{2} (\overset{\frown}{AD} + \overset{\frown}{BC})$ B $= \frac{1}{2} \overset{\frown}{AD}$
$\quad\quad = \frac{1}{2} (120 + 65)$ $= \frac{1}{2} (120)$
$\quad\quad = \frac{1}{2} (185)$ $= 60°$
$\quad\quad = 92\frac{1}{2}°$
$\therefore$ Column A > Column B

29. **(C)**
Volume cube $= (\text{edge})^3$ Total surface
$\quad\quad 64 = e^3$ area $= 6e^2$
$\quad\quad 4 = e$ $96 = 6e^2$
$\quad\quad\quad\quad\quad\quad 16 = e^2$
$\quad\quad\quad\quad\quad\quad 4 = e$
$\therefore$ Column A = Column B

30. **(C)**
$\triangle$ ABC = 13, 12, 5 right $\triangle$
$(AB)^2 = (BC)^2 + (AC)^2$
(pythagorean theorem)
$(AB)^2 - (AC)^2 = (BC)^2$ (subtraction)
$(AC)^2 = (5)^2 = 25$
$5AC = 5(5) = 25$
$\therefore (AC)^2 = 5AC$
$\therefore (AB)^2 - 5AC = (BC)^2$ (substitution)
$\therefore$ Column A = Column B

31. **(C)**
$40\% = .40$
$1000 (.40) = \$400$ (monthly rent)
$3 (400) = \$1200$ (3 months rent)
$\therefore$ Column A = Column B

32. **(B)**
$9\% = .09$
$1000 (.90) = \$90$ (saving for 1 mo.)
$5 (90) = \$450$ (savings for 5 mos.)
$4\% = .04$
$1000 (.04) = \$40$ (clothing for 1 mo.)
$12 (40) = \$480$ (clothing for 1 yr.)
$\therefore$ Column B > Column A

33. **(A)**
$35\% = .35$
$1000 (.35) = \$350$ (food for 1 mo.)
$2 (350) + \$700$ (food for 5 mos.)
$5\% = .05$
$1000 (.05) = \$50$ (medical for 1 yr.)
$12 (50) = \$600$ (medical for 1 yr.)
$\therefore$ Column A > Column B

34. **(A)**
$7\% = .07$
$1000 (.07) = \$70$ (Entertainment for 1 mo.)
$4 (70) = \$280$ (Entertainment for 4 mos.)
$9\% = .09$
$1000 (.09) = \$90$ (savings for 1 mo.)
$3 (90) = \$270$ (savings for 3 mos.)
$\therefore$ Column A > Column B

35. **(C)**
$40\% = .40$
$1000 (.40) = \$400$ (rent for 1 mo.)
$12 (400) = \$4800$ (rent for 1 yr.)
$\therefore$ Column A = Column B

36. **(D)**
Since the amount of gallons of gasoline consumed by the car cannot be determined, the problem does not contain sufficient information.

37. **(A)**
Delaware   Connecticut
$\quad\quad\quad\quad\quad\quad 1200 (.10) = \$120$
$800 (.09) = \$72.00$ $\frac{1}{2} (120) = \$60$ (4 cyl.)
$\therefore$ Column A > Column B

38. **(B)**
Kentucky   Arkansas
$2400 (.09) = \$216$ $3200 (.075) = \$240$
$\therefore$ Column B > Column A

39. **(B)**
Iowa   Delaware
$2800 \div 14 = 200$ gal. $1800 \div 10 = 180$ gal.
$200 (.07) = \$14$ $180 (.09) = \$16.20$
$\therefore$ Column B > Column A

40. **(B)**
Texas   Kansas
$40,000 (.05) = \$2000$ $14,000 (.07) = \$980$
Since there are two 4 Connecticut
cylinders involved it $14,000 (.10) = \$1400$
is not necessary to $\$1400 + \$980 = \$2380$
take $\frac{1}{2}$ the answer.
$\therefore$ Column B > Column A

TEST II. MATH CONTENT

1.D	6.B	11.D	16.D	21.D	26.A	31.B	36.C
2.B	7.C	12.A	17.A	22.A	27.C	32.D	37.C
3.D	8.C	13.B	18.C	23.D	28.D	33.A	38.C
4.A	9.D	14.C	19.D	24.B	29.B	34.C	39.C
5.A	10.D	15.B	20.B	25.C	30.B	35.D	40.B

TEST II. EXPLANATORY ANSWERS

1. **(D)** Numbers proportioned to 3, 5, 7 are 3x, 5x, 7x.
$$3x + 5x + 7x = 120$$
$$15x = 120$$
$$x = 8$$
$$7x = 7(8) = 56$$

2. **(B)** Placing 1 as indicated shifts the given digit to the left, so that it is now the hundreds' digit and u is now the tens' digit.
$$100t + 10u + 1$$

3. **(D)** Let r = the original radius
then 1½ r = new radius
πr^2 = original area
$9/4 \pi r^2$ = new area
Percent increase in area = $\dfrac{9/4 \pi r^2 - \pi r^2}{\pi r^2} \cdot 100 = 125$

4. **(A)** $C = \dfrac{en}{R + nr} = \dfrac{e}{\dfrac{R + r}{n}}$

Therefore, a decrease in "n" makes the denominator larger and consequently, the fraction C smaller.

5. **(A)** Of the three distributive laws given in statements (1), (2) and (3), only (1) holds in the real number field. Statement (4) is not to be confused with log (a/b) = log a − log b.

6. **(B)**
$$y + \sqrt{y - 2} = 4$$
$$\sqrt{y - 2} = 4 - y$$
$$y - 2 = 16 - 8y + y^2$$
$$0 = y^2 - 9y + 18$$
$$0 = (y - 6)(y - 3)$$
$$y = 6, y = 3$$
A check is obtained only with y = 3.

7. **(C)**

$$\begin{vmatrix} 2a & 1 \\ a & a \end{vmatrix} = 2a^2 - a = 3$$

$2a^2 - a - 3 = 0$
$(2a - 3)(a + 1) = 0$
$\therefore a = 3/2, -1$

8. **(C)**
Area of a square = ½ (diagonal)²
$\therefore$ ½ $(x + y)^2$

9. **(D)**
Let the dimensions be 1, w, and h, then the 3 areas are lw, hw, and lh.
Their product = lw · hw · lh
$\qquad\qquad\quad = 1^2\ w^2\ h^2$
$\qquad\qquad\quad = (lwh)^2$
$\qquad\qquad\quad$ = volume squared

10. **(D)**   If c is negative, then ac < bc.

11. **(D)**
The probability of drawing a king = 4/52 = 1/13.
The probability of drawing a queen = 4/52 = 1/13.
The probability of either a queen or a king = 1/13 + 1/13 = 2/13.

12. **(A)**   "∪" denotes union. A∪B consists of all the elements in A and B.

13. **(B)**   If f (x) = x^2 + x + 1
then f (−1) = $(-1)^2$ + (−1) + 1
$\qquad\qquad = 1 - 1 + 1$
$\qquad\qquad = 1$

14. **(C)**   Write 3y + 4x = 6 in the form y = mx + b where b is the
y− intercept
3y + 4x = 6
$\qquad$ 3y = − 4x + 6
$\qquad\quad$ y = − 4/3x + 2

$\therefore$ y− intercept = 2

15. **(B)**   Since sin and cos are cofunctions,
$\qquad$ sin x° = cos (90 − x)
$\therefore$ sin 70° = cos (90 − 70) = cos 20°

16. **(D)**   The pictured graph is the graph for y = sin x.

17. **(A)** "∩" denotes intersection. A ∩ B consists of the element A and B have in common.

18. **(C)** $|(4, 7)| = \sqrt{(4)^2 + (7)^2} = \sqrt{16 + 49} = \sqrt{65}$
    The vector (x_1, x_2) is the vector from $(0, 0)$ to the point with coordinates (x_1, x_2)

19. **(D)** If $y = 3(x^2 + 5)^3$
    then $\dfrac{dy}{dx} = 9(x^2 + 5)^2 \cdot 2x$
    $= 18x(x^2 + 5)^2$

20. **(B)** The total number of permutations of the 6 books is: $6! = 6 \times 5 \times 4 \times 3 \times 2 \times 1 = 720$. The permutations in which books of the same language are together: $3!\,3!\,2! = 3 \times 2 \times 1 \times 3 \times 2 \times 1 \times 2 \times 1 = 72$ Hence desired probability is $72/720 = 1/10$

21. **(D)** Using the form $y = mx + b$
    slope $= m = \dfrac{0 - (-2)}{3 - 0} = \dfrac{2}{3}$

    $y -$ intercept $(b) = -2$
    $\therefore y = \frac{2}{3}x - 2$

22. **(A)** A × A is not contained in A because A × A is a set of ordered pairs (whose elements are from A). A is a subset of B. Therefore, all the elements of A are common to A and B.

23. **(D)** $x = \log_{16} 3$

    $16^x = 32$
    $(2^4)^x = 2^5$
    $2^{4x} = 2^5$
    $4x = 5$
    $x = 5/4$

24. **(B)** If $(x + 3)(x - 2) < 0$
    then $x + 3 < 0$ and $x - 2 > 0$
    or $x + 3 > 0$ and $x - 2 < 0$
    $x < -3$ and $x > 2$
    (no solution)

    $x > -3$ and $x < 2$
    $-3 < x < 2$

25. **(C)** $x \cdot y = \{ (1,3)(2,3) \}$

26. **(A)** The equation for a circle is $x^2 + y^2 = r^2$
$$x^2 + y^2 = (2)^2$$
$$x^2 + y^2 = 4$$

27. **(C)** Using the form $y = mx + b$, where m = slope
$$3y = 9x - 6$$
$$y = 3x - 2$$
$$\therefore m = 3$$

28. **(D)**
$$-\sqrt{-49x^2} = -(\sqrt{-1})(\sqrt{49x^2}) = -(i)(7x) = -7x\,i$$

29. **(B)**
$$f(3) = \frac{3+2}{3-2} = \frac{5}{1} = 5$$

30. **(B)**
$$\frac{96 + 24 + 18 + 6 + 1}{5} = \frac{145}{5} = 29$$

31. **(B)** The inverse of $p \rightarrow q$ is $\sim p \rightarrow \sim q$

32. **(D)** In base 3, $212 = 2 \times 9 = 18$
$$1 \times 3 = 3$$
$$2 \times 1 = 2$$
$$\overline{23}$$

In base 3, number $24 = 220$

33. **(A)** Points of inflection occur when $y'' = 0$
$$y = \tfrac{2}{3}x^3 + 3x^2 - 4x + 1$$
$$y' = 2x^2 + 6x - 4$$
$$y'' = 4x + 6$$
$$y'' = 0 \text{ when } x = -6/4$$
$$\text{when } x = -6/4, y = 16$$
$$(-6/4, 16)$$

34. **(C)** $2^{1/3} \cdot 5^{1/2} = 2^{2/6} \cdot 5^{3/6} = \sqrt[6]{2^2} \cdot \sqrt[6]{5^3} =$
$$\sqrt[6]{4} \cdot \sqrt[6]{125} = \sqrt[6]{500} = 500^{1/6}$$

35. **(D)** The probability of brown = 5/9 · 4/8
The probability of blue = 4/9 · 3/8
The probability of drawing either brown or blue =
(5/9 · 4/8) + (4/9) · (3/8)
  (20/72) + (12/72)
    32/72 = 4/9

36. **(C)** $\dfrac{5\,!}{1\,!} \div \dfrac{6\,!}{2\,!}$
$120 \div 360 = \frac{1}{3}$

37. **(C)** $.0530 = 5.30 \times 10^{-2}$

38. **(C)** For the six strokes there are 5 equal intervals, so that the time interval between successive strokes is 1 second. For 12 strokes, then, 11 seconds are required.

39. **(C)** Substitute $y^2 = 9$ into $x^2 + y^2 = 9$
$$x^2 + 9 = 9$$
$$x = 0$$

when x = 0, then $x^2 + y^2 = 9$
$$0 + y^2 = 9$$
$$y = \pm 3$$
∴The intersection points are (0, 3) and (0, −3)

40. **(B)** $\dfrac{1}{x} + \dfrac{1}{y} = \dfrac{y + x}{xy} = \dfrac{10}{20} = \dfrac{1}{2}$

TEST III. MATH CONTENT

1.C	3.C	5.E	7.C	9.B
2.C	4.D	6.A	8.D	10.E

TEST III. EXPLANATORY ANSWERS

① **(C)**

Let x quarts = capacity then
$$\frac{1}{2}x + 6 = \frac{2}{3}x$$
$$3x + 36 = 4x$$
$$36 = x$$

② **(C)** Let N = revolutions
$$\frac{10}{14} = \frac{N}{N + 50} = \frac{5}{7}$$
$$7N = 5N + 250$$
$$2N = 250$$
$$N = 125$$

distance = 125 × circumference
= 125 × 14π
= 1750π

③

(C) These graphs have the same slope but different y-intercept.

Hence, the graphs of the equations are parallel lines.

④

(D) If 2 is a root of $x^3 + hx + 10 = 0$,
then $8 + 2h + 10 = 0$ and $h = -9$
By synthetic division,

$$
\begin{array}{rrrr|r}
1 & 0 & -9 & 10 & \underline{2} \\
  & 2 & 4 & -10 & \\
\hline
1 & 2 & -5 & |0 &
\end{array}
$$

$x^2 + 2x - 5 = 0$
The discriminant $b^2 - 4ac$
$\qquad\qquad = 4 - 4 \cdot 1\,(-5) = 4 + 20 = 24$
Hence, the roots are irrational.

⑤

(E) The radius of O' is one-half that of O. Therefore, the area of circle O' is 1/4 that of O. Hence the area of O' is 1/4 of 16 or 4.

⑥

(A) If $y^2 - 9x^2 = 0$
then $y^2 = 9x^2$
and $y = \pm 3x$ which graphs as two straight lines.

⑦

(C)

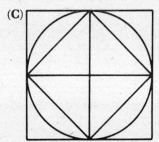

The smaller square is made up of 4 congruent triangles, and the larger square is made up of 8 congruent triangles. Hence, the ratio of their areas is 1:2.

⑧

(D) If one root of $x^2 + px + q = 0$ is $1 + i\sqrt{3}$, then $1 - i\sqrt{3}$ is also a root. Thus the sum of the roots, 2, is equal to $-p$ and the product of the roots 4, is equal to q. Thus $p = -2$ and $q = 4$.

⑨

(B)

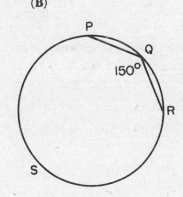

Minor $\overset{\frown}{PQR} = L$

Since $\overset{\frown}{PSR} = 300°$,

$\overset{\frown}{PQR} = 60°$

Thus $L = \dfrac{60}{360} \times 2\pi 10$

$\qquad = \dfrac{1}{6} \times 20\pi = \dfrac{10\pi}{3}$

$\qquad = \dfrac{10 \times 3.14}{3} \approx 10.4$

Thus $10 < L < 10.5$

⑩

(E)

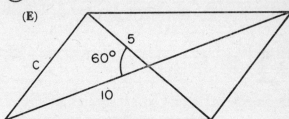

By the Law of Cosines,
$c^2 = 5^2 + 10^2 - 2 \cdot 5 \cdot 10 \cos 60°$
$c^2 = 125 - 100 \cdot \dfrac{1}{2} = 125 - 50 = 75$
$c = \sqrt{75} = 5\sqrt{3}$

ALGEBRA AND GEOMETRY FOR TEST-TAKERS

The mathematics part of your test requires some algebra and geometry background. You do not have to know a great deal about these math areas—certainly not as much as you knew when you took your algebra and geometry courses in high school. But you should, to do well on the test to come, know at least the fundamental algebraic and geometric operations.

NECESSARY BACKGROUND

An **angle** is the figure formed by two lines meeting at a point.

The point B is the **vertex** of the angle and the lines BA and BC are the **sides** of the angle.

ILLUSTRATION

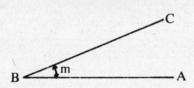

There are three common ways of naming an angle:
1. By a small letter or figure written within the angle, as ∠ m.
2. By the capital letter at its vertex ∠ B.
3. By three capital letters, the middle letter being the vertex letter, as ∠ ABC.

Kinds of angles:

When two straight lines intersect (cut each other), four angles are formed. If these four angles are equal, each angle is a **right angle** and contains 90°.

When one line forms a right angle with another line, the lines are **perpendicular** to each other.

An angle less than a right angle is an **acute angle.**

If the two sides of an angle extend in opposite directions forming a straight line, the angle is a **straight angle.**

ILLUSTRATIONS

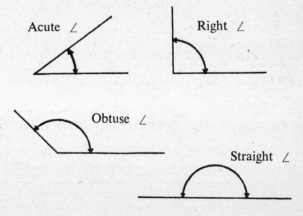

Acute ∠   Right ∠

Obtuse ∠

Straight ∠

An angle greater than a right angle (90°) and less than a straight angle (180°) is an **obtuse angle.**

Kinds of triangles:

If a triangle has two equal sides, it is **isosceles.** If a triangle has its three sides equal, it is **equilateral.**

ILLUSTRATIONS

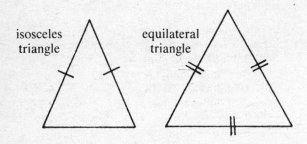

isosceles triangle

equilateral triangle

A **right triangle** is a triangle that has one right angle.

The sum of the angles of any triangle is 180 degrees.

A **circle** is a closed plane curve, all points of which are equidistant from a point within called the center.

A **chord** is a line segment connecting any two points on the circle.

A **radius** of a circle is a line segment connecting the center with any point on the circle.

A **diameter** is a chord passing through the center of the circle.

A **secant** is a chord extended in either one or both directions.

A **tangent** is a line touching a circle at one point and only one.

The **circumference** is the curved line bounding the circle.

An **arc** of a circle is any part of the circumference.

ILLUSTRATIONS

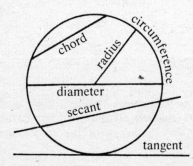

An angle is inscribed in an arc if its vertex is on the arc and its sides are chords joining the vertex to the end points of the arc. ∠ DCE is inscribed in arc DCE.

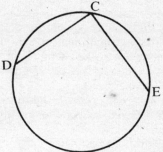

A **central angle,** as ∠ AOB in the figure, is an angle whose vertex is the center of the circle and whose sides are radii. A central angle is equal in degrees to (or has the same number of degrees as) its intercepted arc.

An **inscribed angle,** as ∠ MNP, is an angle whose vertex is on the circle and whose sides are chords.

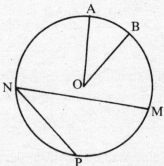

PERFECT SQUARES AND SQUARE ROOTS

To square a number means to multiply the number by itself.

If we know the product of two equal numbers, one of these numbers is called the square root of the given product:

Since $12^2 = 144$, the square root of $144 = 12$.

The symbol for square root is $\sqrt{}$; it is read—"the square root of." $\sqrt{144} = 12$

It may mean any of the following:
a) What number multiplied by itself will give 144?
b) What number squared will give 144?
c) What number has been used twice as a factor to produce 144?
d) What is one of the two equal factors of 144?
e) What is the square root of 144?

METHOD FOR FINDING SQUARE ROOT

1. Locate the decimal point.
2. Mark off the digits in groups of two in both directions beginning at the decimal point.
3. Mark the decimal point for the answer just above the decimal point of the number whose square root is to be taken.
4. Find the largest perfect square contained in the left-hand group.
5. Place its square root in the answer. Subtract the perfect square from the first digit or pair of digits.
6. Bring down the next pair.
7. Double the partial answer.
8. Add a trial digit to the right of the doubled partial answer. Multiply this new number by the trial digit. Place the correct new digit in the answer.
9. Subtract the product.
10. Repeat Steps 6-9 as often as necessary.

You will notice that you get one digit in the answer for every group you marked off in the original number.

To find the square root of a fraction, extract the square of both the numerator and the denominator.

$$\sqrt{\frac{4}{9}} = \frac{2}{3} \qquad \sqrt{\frac{1}{16}} = \frac{1}{4}$$

Examples of Finding Square Root

Example I: Let us extract the square root of 138,384 by the usual method.

1. The number must first be pointed off in groups of two figures each, beginning at the decimal point, which, in the case of a whole number, is at the right. The number of figures in the root will be the same as the number of groups so obtained.

$$
\begin{array}{r}
3 \\
\sqrt{13'83'84} \\
3^2 = 9 \\
\hline
483
\end{array}
$$

2. The largest square less than 13 is 9
   $$\sqrt{9} = 3$$
3. Place its square root in the answer.
4. Subtract the perfect square from the first digit or pair of digits.
5. Bring down the next pair.
6. To form our trial divisor, annex 0 to this root "3" (making 30) and multiply by 2. 483 ÷ 60 = 8. Multiplying the trial divisor 68 by 8, we obtain 544, which is too large.
7. We then try multiplying 67 by 7. This is correct.
8. Add the trial digit to the right of the doubled partial answer. Place the new digit in the answer.
9. Subtract the product. Bring down the final group.
10. Annex 0 to the new root 37 and multiply by 2 for the trial divisor:
    $$2 \times 370 = 740$$
    $$1484 \div 740 = 2$$
    Complete divisor = 740 + 2

$$
\begin{array}{r}
3\ 7\ 2 \\
\sqrt{13'83'84} \\
3 = 9 \\
\hline
483 \\
7 \times 67 = 469 \\
\hline
1484 \\
2 \times 742 = 1484 \\
\hline
\end{array}
$$

Hence, the positive square root of 138,384 is 372.

Example II: Find the positive square root of 3 to the nearest hundredth.

$$
\begin{array}{r}
1.\ 7\ 3\ 2 \\
\sqrt{3.00'00'00} \\
1 \\
\hline
\end{array}
$$

20	200
7 × 27 =	189
340	1100
3 × 343 =	1029
3460	7100
2 × 3462 =	6924

Hence, the positive square root of 3 is 1.73 to the nearest hundredth and 1.7 to the nearest tenth.

RULES FOR ALGEBRA

Rules for signed numbers:

1. **Addition**—To add signed numbers whose signs are alike, find the sum of their absolute values and use the common sign.

To add unlike signed numbers, find the difference between their absolute values and use the sign of the number with the larger absolute value.

2. **Subtraction**—To subtract signed numbers. mentally change the sign of the subtrahend and proceed as in algebraic addition.

3. **Multiplication**—To mu'tiply two monomials:
   1) Multiply the coefficients;
   2) Give each letter in the product an exponent which is the sum of the exponents which that letter has in the original expressions. When two numbers having like signs are multiplied the product is positive. When two numbers having unlike signs are multiplied the product is negative.

4. **Division**—To divide one monomial by another:
   1) Divide the coefficients:
   2) Give each letter in the quotient an exponent which is the difference between the exponents of that letter in the dividend and the divisor.
   The quotient of two numbers with like signs is positive.
   The quotient of two numbers with unlike signs is negative.

DIRECTIONS FOR SOLVING PROBLEMS

1) Read the problem, and determine what number (or numbers) you are asked to find.

2) Represent the unknown number (or numbers) algebraically.
   a. If you are asked to find only one number. let some letter equal or represent it.
   b. If you are asked to find more than one number, then let some letter equal one of them; then represent each of the other numbers in terms of this letter.
   c. When possible, make a drawing to show steps a and b above, and the number relations of the problem.

3) From the condition of the problem—find two expressions that are equal. Then connect these two equal expressions by an equal sign, forming an equation.

4) Solve this equation for the unknown letter. If you are asked to find more than one number, do this from step 2b above.

5) Prove by seeing that your answer satisfies all the conditions of the problem.

FACTORS

When two or more numbers are multiplied together to form a product, the numbers multiplied are called **factors** of that product. For example, 3 and 5 are factors of 15, a and b are factors of ab, and x and x are factors of x^2. Every number is divisible by itself and 1. $15 \times 1 = 15$. $x(1) = x$. It is customary, however. to consider as factors **only whole numbers other than 1.** Numbers which have no factors, other than themselves and one, are said to be prime. The numbers 2. 3. 5. 7. 11. etc., are prime as are x, y, a, or any other literal number.

Find the factors of $3x^3 + 6x^2y + 9x^2z + 3x^2$.

Solution: A study of the terms of this polynomial shows that the monomial expression $3x^2$ is contained in each. $3x^2$, then, is one of the factors of the polynomial. The other factor may be obtained by dividing the given expression by the monomial factor already found.

$$\frac{3x^3 + 6x^2y + 9x^2z + 3x^2}{3x^2} = x + 2y + 3z + 1$$

We thus obtain the factors

$$3x^2 (x + 2y + 3z + 1)$$

RULE:

To find the factors of an expression which is the product of a monomial and a polynomial
1. Study the terms of the given expression to obtain the largest monomial factor common to them all.
2. Divide the expression mentally by this monomial to obtain the polynomial factor.
3. Indicate the product of the factors found.

Let us consider the product of the binomials $x - 2y$ and $3x + 4y$ in which the terms of one are respectively similar to those of the other. If the multiplication is performed in the usual way, it is seen that the first term of the product. $3x^2$. is obtained by multiplying the first terms of the binomials: namely. 3x and x. In like manner the last term of the product, $- 8y^2$. is obtained by multiplying the last terms of the binomials: namely, 4y and $- 2y$. The middle term of the product, $- 2xy$, is obtained by adding to the product of x and 4y the product of 3x and $-2y$. These are called **cross products.**

$$
\begin{array}{r}
3x + 4y \\
x - 2y \\
\hline
3x^2 + 4xy \\
- 6xy - 8y^2 \\
\hline
3x^2 - 2xy - 8y^2
\end{array}
$$

Factors of Quadratic Trinomials

We see that the product of two binomials having similar terms is usually a trinomial. This trinomial always contains the squares of the letters involved and hence is called a quadratic trinomial (from the Latin word **quadratus,** meaning "square"). Find the factors of $x^2 - 6x + 8$.

From what we have just learned we know that the trinomial will factor into two binomials, so we write two parentheses next to each other ( ) ( ). What will be the first term in each binomial? They will have to be factors of x^2, so x and x. Likewise, the second term in each binomial will be factors of 8. Will they be 4 and 2, or 8 and 1? We will have to make our choice on the basis of the middle term of the trinomial. (x-4) (x-2) will be our choice. So $x^2 - 6x + 8 = (x - 4) \ (x - 2)$. Check by multiplying the factors.

Solving Quadratic Equations by Factoring

A **quadratic** equation is an equation which contains the second power of the unknown quantity, but no higher power. For example:
$x^2 - bx = c^2$; $x^2 = 9$; $2x^2 + 6x \quad 10$; $x^2 - 4x + 3 = 0$ are quadratic equations.

Quadratic equations as well as literal equations may often be solved by factoring. In many cases we require more advanced methods, which are explained later. But the method of solving by factoring, where it is possible, is shown by the following example:

Solve: $\quad x^2 - 3x = 28$

Solution: $\quad x^2 - 3x - 28 = 0$

Transposing the 28.

$(x - 7) \ (x + 4) = 0 \quad$ factoring the left member.

$x - 7 = 0 \quad x + 4 = 0$
$\quad x = 7 \quad\quad x = -4$

By setting each factor equal to 0, we obtain two simple equations and solve each.

It is important for you to remember that **a quadratic equation always has two roots.** These roots may be equal. The equation above states that this product equals 0. No product can equal 0 unless one of the factors equals 0, but the product will equal 0 if any factor in it equals 0.

RULE: To solve a quadratic equation by factoring:
1. Transpose every term to the left member of the equation, thus making the right member 0.
2. Factor the left member.
3. Set each factor which contains the unknown quantity equal to 0, and solve the resulting simple equations.

The results obtained are the roots of the quadratic equation.

Solution of Complete Quadratic Equations by a Formula:

$ax^2 + bx + c = 0$ represents **any** complete quadratic equation, since a, b, c may have **any** numerical values. When a complete quadratic equation is arranged in this form, with descending powers of x in the left member, and with the right member 0, it is in standard form.

The roots of this equation in terms of coefficients a, b, and c are expressed by the formula:

$$x = \frac{-b \pm \sqrt{b^2 - 4ac}}{2a}$$

This is called the quadratic formula. This formula is of the greatest importance, since, as you know, not all quadratic equations can be factored. You should memorize this formula thoroughly.

The way in which this formula is used to solve quadratic equations is shown by the following:

Solve $2x^2 + x = 6$.

SOLUTION: Transpose every term to the left member as in the equation $ax^2 + bx + c = 0$

We obtain $\quad\quad 2x^2 + x - 6 = 0$

Then $\quad$ a (the coefficient of x^2) = 2
$\quad\quad$ b (the coefficient of x) = 1
$\quad\quad$ c (the term without x) = -6

Substituting these values in the formula

$$x = \frac{-b \pm \sqrt{b^2 - 4\ ac}}{2a}$$

gives us $x = \dfrac{-1 \pm \sqrt{(1)^2 - 4 \cdot 2(-6)}}{2 \cdot 2}$

$$= \frac{-1 \pm \sqrt{1 + 48}}{4}$$

$$= \frac{-1 \pm 7}{4} = \frac{-1 + 7}{4} \text{ and } \frac{-1 - 7}{4}$$

$$= \frac{3}{2} \text{ and } - 2$$

(1) Write the equation in standard form.
(2) Write down the values of a, b, and c.
(3) Substitute these values in the formula.
(4) Perform all operations.
(5) Check each root.

RULE: Roots are sometimes the same.

ANGLE OF ELEVATION:

PC is a pole, standing on level ground. The sun casts a shadow, AC · 6. A line segment drawn from A (the end of the shadow) through P (the top of the pole) would be directed at the sun. The angle (< CAP) is called the **angle of elevation** of the sun.

ILLUSTRATION

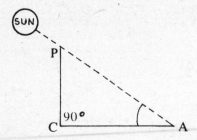

CONGRUENT TRIANGLES:

CONGRUENT TRIANGLES: Triangles whose vertices can be made to correspond so that lengths of corresponding sides and the measures of corresponding angles are equal.

Some problems involve Trigonometry. The following is a brief explanation to give you some knowledge of Trigonometry.

The word "trigonometry" is derived from two Greek words which mean "triangle measurement." It is that branch of mathematics which deals with the relations between the sides and the angles of triangles.

One of the main purposes of trigonometry is to obtain formulas by means of which distances and angles may be measured (indirectly). Trigonometry will enable you to compute the values of the unknown parts.

The value of the ratios of the sides of the right triangles depends upon the size of angle A and not upon the size of the right triangles. The values of these ratios change as angle A changes and for this reason are called **functions** of angle A.

ILLUSTRATION

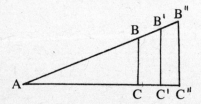

Trigonometric functions of an acute angle:

1. The **sine** of an acute angle of a right triangle is the ratio of the opposite leg to the hypotenuse.
2. The **cosine** of an acute angle of a right triangle is the ratio of the adjacent leg to the hypotenuse.
3. The **tangent** of an acute angle of a right triangle is the ratio of the opposite leg to the adjacent leg.

It is customary, in the study of trigonometry, to let the capital letters A, B, and C denote the angles of a right triangle, C being the right angle, and the small letters a, b, and c denote the corresponding opposite sides.

From the right △ ABC,

the sine of ∠ A (written sin A) = $\dfrac{a}{c}$

the cosine of ∠ A (written cos A) = $\dfrac{b}{c}$

the tangent of ∠ A (written tan A) = $\dfrac{a}{b}$.

In like manner, $\sin B = \dfrac{b}{c}$; $\cos B = \dfrac{a}{c}$;

$\tan B = \dfrac{b}{a}$.

ILLUSTRATION

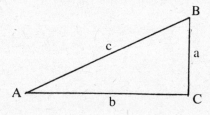

Given the **t**angent of an angle you can find the measure of an angle by consulting a "Table of Trigonometric Functions." Conversely, given the measures of an angle you can find the tangent of the angle.

Proceed the same way when given the sine of an angle or the cosine of an angle.

PART FIVE

Natural Sciences

A Verisimilar General Examination

Glossary

5

THE GENERAL EXAMINATION IN NATURAL SCIENCE

In writing this book, we examined all available announcements and official statements about the exam, and thus predict that this is what you may face. Since examiners like to experiment with various types of questions the subjects tested and times allotted may vary from test to test. However, we feel certain that if you have touched on each of the subjects covered here, you will be well on your way to scoring high.

A MINI-GENERAL EXAMINATION

This chapter presents a miniature General Examination. The "mini-exam" contains good samples of the various types of questions you may expect to encounter. Our purpose is to offer you a bird's eye view of the Natural Science Examination. The sample questions show you the subjects that will be included, the different types of questions, and the levels of difficulty you may expect.

The time limit for this test is 90 minutes, and it contains approximately 125 multiple-choice questions. The test questions are distributed in three areas.

- About 10 percent of the questions relate to information about science as a field of endeavor and its relationship to other areas of knowledge.

- About 45 percent of the test asks questions about biology and related sciences; most are based on concepts and principles applying to both animals and plants. And the rest are about equally divided between these two aspects of biology.

- The final 45 percent of the test focuses on the physical sciences. About one third of these questions focus on physics, one third on chemistry, and the final third on astronomy, geology, and meteorology.

From your score on this examination you will learn how your knowledge and understanding of scientific principles and processes compares with that of college sophomores who are not science majors. However, you do not need to have taken special science courses. You can answer many of the questions on the basis of science articles you have read in newspapers and periodicals.

Because of its importance to understanding our physical world, this examination is based on the content of college science courses. However, your score will not hinge on your memory of factual detail or your ability to recite scientific laws.

In addition to testing your knowledge in the various subject areas stated, the questions are designed to measure these skills, or desired outcomes, of your scientific knowledge:

- About 40 percent of the test measures your ability to apply scientific theories, principles, and concepts.
- About 30 percent of the questions measure the depth of your understanding of scientific information; that is, your ability to restate scientific information.
- About 15 percent of the test measures your ability to analyze and use complicated reasoning processes. For example, you will be asked to analyze parts, evaluate possibilities, and put unlike ideas together.
- About 15 percent of the questions measure your ability to a) recognize specific pieces of scientific information, b) recognize how this information is organized, and c) recognize methods of studying judging, and criticizing this information.

A MINI-EXAM IN THE NATURAL SCIENCES

TIME: 9 Minutes. 12 Questions.

Questions 1 to 5

DIRECTIONS: *In this test each question consists of five lettered graphs followed by a list of numbered situations to be graphed. For each numbered situation select the one graph that is most closely related to it and blacken the corresponding space on your answer sheet. One graph may be used once, more than once, or not at all.*

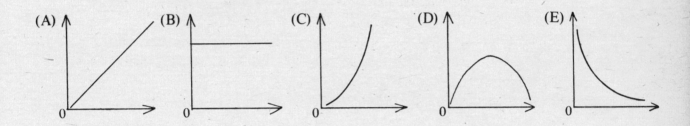

1. A sample of gas kept at constant pressure.
        Vertical axis: Average velocity of molecules
        Horizontal axis: Absolute temperature

2. A capillary tube in a beaker of water.
        Vertical axis: Height of water in capillary tube
        Horizontal axis: Diameter of capillary tube

3. A population in which the environmental resistance becomes greater than the biotic potential.
        Vertical axis: Population number
        Horizontal axis: Time

4. A string vibrating at its fundamental frequency.
        Vertical axis: Frequency of vibration
        Horizontal axis: Length of string

5. An automobile traveling along the highway.
        Vertical axis: Fluid friction of the air
        Horizontal axis: Speed of the automobile

Questions 6 to 9

DIRECTIONS: This type of question consists of the description and results of an experiment followed by questions about the experiment. Each question has five suggested answers. They are lettered (A) (B) (C) (D) and (E). Choose the answer that is best and blacken the corresponding space on the answer sheet.

An experiment was designed to test the effect of a certain *very effective* and beneficial insecticide on the shells of eggs laid by certain birds. Birds were fed varying amounts of the insecticide in their diet. When the birds laid their eggs the thickness of the shells was determined by X-ray techniques. The data obtained is presented in the table below.

AMOUNT OF INSECTICIDE IN DIET	THICKNESS OF SHELL
0.0000 %	2 millimeters
0.0010	1.9
0.0100	2.1
0.1000	2.0
1.0000	1.5
5.0000	0.1

6. According to the data presented above which of the following statements most closely describes the results of this experiment?

(A) Insecticide in the diet of the birds has no effect
(B) Insecticide in the diet of birds has a major effect at all concentrations
(C) Insecticide in the diet of birds has only a very minor effect at all concentration levels
(D) Insecticide in the diet of birds has only a very minor effect at higher levels
(E) Insecticide in the diet of birds has a major effect only at the highest levels tested

7. If the thickness of the eggshell were graphed against the amount of the insecticide in the diet which of the following examples would most closely show the data obtained?

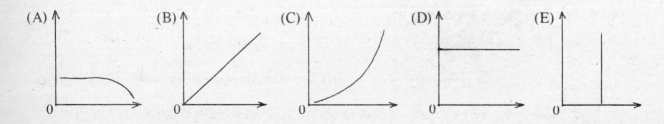

8. The term "insecticide" as used in this experiment means a substance that
   (A) may substitute for insects in the diet of birds
   (B) prevents birds from laying eggs
   (C) kills insects
   (D) fertilizes the soil
   (E) is used in small quantitites to benefit birds

9. If the amount of insecticide in the diet of the birds was increased to 25% what would be the most likely result based on the data presented?
   (A) The birds and their eggshells would be unaffected
   (B) The birds would sicken but their shells would be about 2 millimeters thick
   (C) The birds would immediately die
   (D) The shells would be extremely thin
   (E) The shells would be thicker than 2 millimeters

Questions 10 to 12

DIRECTIONS: This type of question consists of the description and results of an experiment followed by statements about the experiment. Analyze each statement solely on the basis of the experiment. From the information given about the experiment mark your answer sheet:
(A) if the experiment proves the statement is TRUE;
(B) if the experiment shows that the statement is PROBABLY TRUE;
(C) if the experiment DOES NOT SHOW whether the statement is true or false;
(D) if the experiment shows that the statement is PROBABLY FALSE;
(E) if the experiment proves that the statement is FALSE.

An experiment is done to test the activity of a particular enzyme in media of varying pH. The result of the experiment is graphed thus:

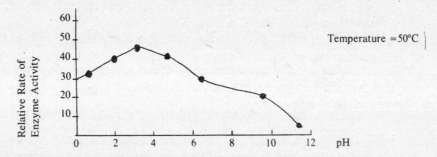

10. The enzyme graphed will be most active in an acid medium.

11. The enzyme graphed will be most active at a temperature of 50°C.

12. Enzymes are more active in alkaline media than in neutral media.

ANSWER SHEET FOR THIS MINI-EXAMINATION

CORRECT ANSWERS FOR THIS MINI-EXAMINATION

1.C	3.D	5.C	7.A	9.D	11.C
2.E	4.E	6.E	8.C	10.A	12.D

1. **(C)** As temperature rises in a sample of gas kept at constant pressure so will the average velocity of molecules.

2. **(E)** As the diameter of the capillary tube increases, the height of water in the tube decreases.

3. **(D)** If environmental resistance becomes greater than the biotic potential of a population, the population will decrease.

4. **(E)** As the length of the string grows longer, the frequency of vibration decreases.

5. **(C)** The faster an automobile moves the greater is the fluid friction of the air.

6. **(E)** There is apparently little affect on the eggshells at concentrations below one percent. At one percent and five percent there are significant changes in the thickness of the shell.

7. **(A)** The correct graph shows no real change in thickness until higher levels of insecticide are reached. Then the thickness sharply decreases.

8. **(C)** The term insecticide means a substance that kills insects.

9. **(D)** The data shows that as the amount of insecticide fed to birds increases the eggshells will decrease in thickness (at the higher levels of insecticide). It can be projected that at an extremely high level of insecticide the shells would be extremely thin. No evidence is given that the birds would sicken, die or cease to lay eggs.

10. **(A)** On the basis of the experiment, at the temperature given, the enzyme graphed was most active in an acid medium.

11. **(C)** The experiment was conducted using only one temperature. At which temperature the enzyme would show the most activity cannot be determined from the experiment.

12. **(D)** Based on the experiment with one enzyme, the statement is false. It is probably false in regard to enzymes in general.

THE NATURAL SCIENCES
FOURTH VERISIMILAR EXAMINATION

To begin your studies, test yourself now to see how you measure up. This examination is similar to the one you'll get, and is therefore a practical yardstick for charting your progress and planning your course. Adhere strictly to all test instructions. Mark yourself honestly and you'll find where your weaknesses are and where to concentrate your study.

Time allowed for the entire Examination: 1½ Hours

In order to create the climate of the actual exam, that's exactly what you should allow yourself . . . no more, no less. Use a watch to keep a record of your time, since it might suit your convenience to try this practice exam in several short takes.

ANALYSIS AND TIMETABLE: VERISIMILAR EXAMINATION IV.

This table is both an analysis of the exam that follows and a priceless preview of the actual test. Look it over carefully and use it well. Since it lists both subjects and times, it points up not only what to study, but also how much time to spend on each topic. Making the most of your study time adds valuable points to your examination score.

SUBJECT TESTED	Time Allowed	SUBJECT TESTED	Time Allowed
INTERPRETING SCIENTIFIC DATA			
Graph Selection	10 Minutes	Understanding Experiments	10 Minutes
Experiment Validity	12 Minutes		
SCIENTIFIC REASONING AND KNOWLEDGE			
Biology	30 Minutes	Chemistry	10 Minutes
Physics	15 Minutes		

ANSWER SHEET FOR VERISIMILAR EXAMINATION IV.

TEST I. GRAPH SELECTION

TEST II. EXPERIMENT VALIDITY

TEST III. UNDERSTANDING EXPERIMENTS

TEST IV. BIOLOGICAL SCIENCE

TEST V. BIOLOGY

TEST VI. PHYSICS

TEST VII. CHEMISTRY

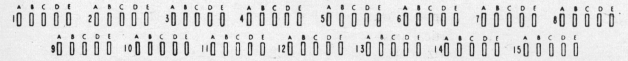

PART I. INTERPRETING SCIENTIFIC DATA

TEST I. GRAPH SELECTION

TIME: 10 Minutes. 15 Questions.

DIRECTIONS: In this test each question consists of five lettered graphs followed by a list of numbered situations to be graphed. For each numbered situation select the one graph that is most closely related to it and blacken the corresponding space on your answer sheet. One graph may be used once, more than once, or not at all.

Questions 1 to 4:

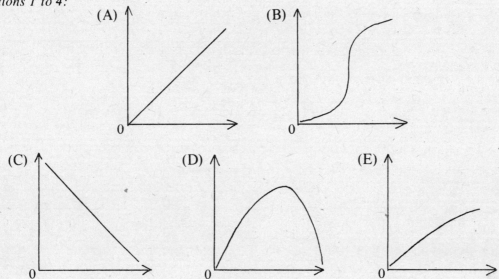

1. Change in pH as a weak acid is titrated with NaOH.

    Vertical axis: Percent of neutralization
    Horizontal axis: pH

2. Growth occurs in a colony of bacteria under ideal conditions.

    Vertical axis: Time
    Horizontal axis: Number of organisms

3. A body is under constant acceleration.

    Vertical axis: Speed
    Horizontal axis: Time

4. Force is applied to stretch a helical spring below its elastic limit.

    Vertical axis: Applied Force
    Horizontal axis: Elongation

Questions 5 to 8:

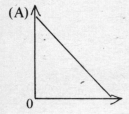

5. Rate of photosynthesis with increasing temperature when light is not a limiting factor.

    Vertical axis: Relative rate of photosynthesis
    Horizontal axis: Temperature °C

6. Variation of force during a collision.

    Vertical axis: Force
    Horizontal axis: Time

7. Effect of temperature on enzyme activity.

    Vertical axis: Rate of activity
    Horizontal axis: Temperature °C

8. Internal temperature of the earth.

    Vertical axis: Temperature °C
    Horizontal axis: Depth in miles

Questions 9 to 12:

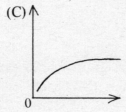
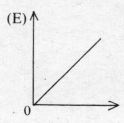

9. A sample of gas at constant volume.

    Vertical axis: Pressure
    Horizontal axis: Temperature °C

10. Human body temperature during moderate exercise.

    Vertical axis: Temperature °C
    Horizontal axis: Time

11. Adiabatic change in temperature of a descending air mass.

    Vertical axis: Altitude
    Horizontal axis: Temperature °C

12. A body falls freely from rest.

    Vertical axis: Acceleration
    Horizontal axis: Time

Questions 13 to 15

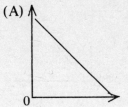 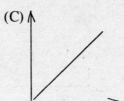 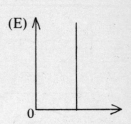

13. Density of a sample of gas as its volume increases.
    Vertical axis: Density
    Horizontal axis: Volume

14. A body is under constant acceleration.
    Vertical axis: Distance
    Horizontal axis: Time

15. The main sequence of a galactic cluster of stars.
    Vertical axis: Luminosity
    Horizontal axis: Temperature

END OF TEST

*Go on to do the following Test in this Examination, just as you would
be expected to do on the actual exam.*

TEST II. EXPERIMENT VALIDITY

TIME: 12 Minutes. 16 Questions.

DIRECTIONS: This type of question consists of the description and results of an experiment followed by statements about the experiment. Analyze each statement solely on the basis of the experiment. From the information given about the experiment mark your answer sheet:

(A) if the experiment proves the statement is TRUE;

(B) if the experiment shows that the statement is PROBABLY TRUE;

(C) if the experiment DOES NOT SHOW whether the statement is true or false;

(D) if the experiment shows that the statement is PROBABLY FALSE;

(E) if the experiment proves that the statement is FALSE.

Correct and explanatory answers are provided at the end of the exam.

Questions 1 to 5:

In a chemistry experiment five solutions were tested to determine whether they were acids or bases. The indicator used was litmus paper. The data given in the table shows the findings. Strips of litmus paper were dipped into a half liter of each solution for ten seconds.

SOLUTION	COLOR
1	red
2	red
3	blue
4	no change
5	red

1. At least one of the solutions had a pH greater than 7.

2. Solution 1 would show a higher pH than solution 4.

3. If solutions 2 and 4 were added together and tested with litmus paper the color would show no change.

4. Solution 2 would show a lower pH than solution 5.

5. Solution 3 contains a greater concentration of hydroxide ions than solution 4.

Questions 6 to 9:

An experiment is designed which permits the determination of the rates of diffusion of gases. The rate of diffusion of a gas is measured by determining the distance it travels down a tube in a specified period of time. The following table shows the results of the experiment with several gases:

GAS	MOLECULAR WEIGHT	DISTANCE TRAVELED (CM)
CO^2	44	0.20
O^2	32	0.25
H^2	2	1.00

6. An unknown gas travels 0.23 cm in the tube in a specified period of time. On the basis of the data presented the molecular weight of the gas is approximately 34.

7. The distance traveled in the tube is directly proportional to the temperature.

8. The rate of diffusion of a gas is proportional to the molecular weight of the gas as shown in the following graph:

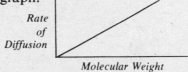

Rate of Diffusion

Molecular Weight

9. The rate of diffusion of a gas is inversely proportional to the number of atoms in the gas molecule.

Questions 10 to 13:

An experiment was designed to test the hypothesis that a certain event (E) can occur by three different avenues but will almost always occur by the way "B." The results of forty trials are presented in the table below:

WAY THE EVENT OCCURS	NUMBER OF TIMES
A	40
B	30
C	30

10. The hypothesis of this experiment has been proven.

11. The event can occur in at least three different ways.

12. The experiment was well designed.

13. The theory on which the hypothesis was based needs at least some revision.

Questions 14 to 16:

Two new compounds were tested for their weed-killing abilities. The tests consisted of adding certain amounts of each of these chemicals to a full grown weed and observing the effect on the weed. If the weed was killed, the rating for the chemical was 10. If there was no effect the rating was 0. Intermediate ratings indicated injuries of varying severity. The data obtained is presented in the table below:

CHEMICAL	WEED SPECIES TOXICITY		
	Type A	Type B	Type C
Chemical-1	10	0	9
Chemical-2	2	0	10

14. The ability to kill different types of weeds is different for chemical-1 and chemical-2.

15. Chemical-1 will kill many more types of weeds than chemical-2.

16. Type B weeds are somewhat more resistant than Types A and C to chemical-1 and chemical-2.

END OF TEST

Go on to do the following Test in this Examination, just as you would be expected to do on the actual exam.

TEST III. UNDERSTANDING EXPERIMENTS

TIME: 10 Minutes. 14 Questions.

DIRECTIONS: This type of question consists of the description and results of an experiment followed by questions about the experiment. Each question has five suggested answers. They are lettered (A) (B) (C) (D) and (E). Choose the answer that is best and blacken the corresponding space on the answer sheet.

Correct and explanatory answers are provided at the end of the exam. After you have completed the entire exam, read the explanations carefully. They'll reinforce your strengths and pinpoint your weaknesses so that you know just what to study to raise your score.

Questions 1 to 2:

The periodic table arranges the elements in order of increasing atomic number. The vertical columns consist of elements with similar properties and these groups are called families. Members of a family can be arranged in the order in which they appear in the periodic table if gradual trends in properties are noted. The following experiment involves compounds A, B, C, and D, each of which contains an element from Group II A in the periodic table. Two drops of a solution of each compound are put in four separate glass test tubes. One ml of acid #1 is added and the resulting solution is stirred. Any observable reactions are recorded. The experiment is repeated with acids #2, #3, and #4. The following chart shows the observed results.

COMPOUND	ACID #1	ACID #2	ACID #3	ACID #4
A	white opaque ppt formed (P)	white opaque ppt formed (P)	white grainy ppt formed (P)	orange opaque ppt formed (P)
B	clear no ppt (S)	white opaque ppt formed (P)	white opaque ppt formed (P)	clear orange no ppt (S)
C	clear no ppt (S)	white semi-opaque ppt formed (P)	clear no ppt (S)	clear orange no ppt (S)
D	white opaque ppt formed (P)	white opaque ppt formed (P)	white opaque ppt formed (P)	clear orange no ppt (S)

(P) = formation of precipitate
(S) = soluble, no precipitate

1. Starting with most soluble, what is the trend in solubility of the compounds in acidic solution?

   (A) Compound D, Compound A, Compound B, Compound C.
   (B) Compound A, Compound D, Compound B, Compound C.
   (C) Compound C, Compound B, Compound D, Compound A.
   (D) Compound C, Compound D, Compound B, Compound A.
   (E) Compound B, Compound C, Compound A, Compound D.

2. Which of the following is an assumption about elements that is made by the persons conducting this experiment?

   (A) An element is able to form a precipitate with at least one acid.
   (B) The relative ease with which elements form precipitates is an important property and can lead to their arrangement on the periodic chart.
   (C) The solubility of an element in an acid solution depends on the strength of the acid.
   (D) The element that is the most insoluble is the most stable and therefore would appear first in Group II A.
   (E) An element that is able to form a precipitate in one acid is also able to form a precipitate in any other acid.

Questions 3 to 7:

A classic field study in industrial melanism was carried out on the moth *Biston betularia* which is polymorphic. One form is light in color with small dark markings (giving rise to the common name—peppered moth); the other is almost uniformly black. The first dark colored peppered moth was captured in the 1840s. They were still quite rare in the 1870s. The insect feeds by night and rests during the day on tree trunks. Lichens cover the tree trunks except in industrial areas where air pollution has killed the lichens and turned the tree trunks black. Populations of moths, whose natural predators are birds, were sampled at various sites.

% MELANICS IN SAMPLE	DISTANCE FROM INDUSTRIAL SITE KILOMETERS
95	0
95	10
89	20
70	30
50	40

3. Which of the following best accounts for the fact that black peppered moths have become more numerous, especially around industrial sites?

   (A) Black color is a dominant mutation and therefore would appear more frequently in the population.

   (B) The moths have become black because the tree bark on which they rest has blackened due to air pollution.

   (C) Black peppered moths are more resistant to air pollution therefore more of them have survived to breed.

   (D) Sampling techniques have improved greatly in the past hundred years making a more accurate count possible.

   (E) Black moths have a selective advantage in that their coloring blends with the blackened bark making them less visible to predators, thus more have survived to breed.

4. Which of the following graphs best plots the distribution of black *Biston betularia*?

   Vertical axis: Percent of black moths in sample
   Horizontal axis: Distance from industrial site

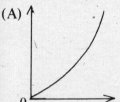 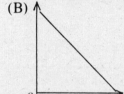 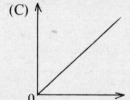 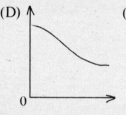 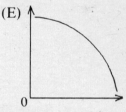

5. The term "industrial melanism" implies that

   (A) air pollution has caused the number of moths to decrease

   (B) a large percent of the population of moths near industrial sights are white

   (C) air pollution is a possible cause of the evolutionary change observed in the color of *Biston betularia*

   (D) dark colored moths are an easier prey for predators in industrial areas

   (E) black moths were first caught in industrial areas

6. What is the main purpose of this experiment?

   (A) To see if color changes in the population of a certain kind of moth vary with the degree of air pollution

   (B) To see if more black moths are now present than was true ten years ago

   (C) To find out different ways black moths are different from white moths

   (D) To ascertain what is happening to light colored moths that reside in areas of high air pollution

   (E) To control the population of moths at sites with varying degrees of air pollution

7. Which of the following best states the hypothesis this experiment was designed to test?

(A) Black *Biston betularia* have arisen due to a dominant genetic mutation.

(B) There is a geographic difference in the distribution of black *Biston betularia*.

(C) Black *Biston betularia* have a survival advantage in industrialized areas.

(D) The absence of lichens due to industrial air pollution has led to the decline of the light colored *Biston betularia*.

(E) Black *Biston betularia* migrate to the cities where they are better camouflaged on the black tree trunks.

Questions 8 to 9:

A leaf from a green and white variegated coleus which was placed in the sun for several hours was treated in the following manner: 1) placed in hot alcohol until colorless, 2) placed in a clean Petri dish and flooded with Lugol's iodine, 3) washed in distilled water, 4) spread out on clean white paper. The same procedure was followed with the leaf from a green and white variegated plant that was stored without light for twelve hours. The following chart shows the results.

TREATMENT	WHITE AREA OF LEAF		GREEN AREA OF LEAF	
	without light	with light	without light	with light
alcohol	white	white	white	white
Lugol's	brown	brown	brown	blue-black
water	no change	no change	no change	no change

8. Which of the following statements best explains the observed results of the experiment?

(A) In green plants, light plus the green pigment chlorophyll result in the presence of starch.

(B) Plants must have chlorophyll in order to synthesize organic nutrients.

(C) Plants cannot grow without light.

(D) The green chlorophyll molecule uses light energy to split one molecule of water.

(E) Enzymes convert the sugar produced during photosynthesis into starch.

9. Which of the following is the best explanation for keeping the control plant in the dark for twelve hours before sampling?

(A) Plants show prominent cycles that are known to be directly related to the photoperiod.

(B) It has been shown that plants are able to fix only a minute portion of the energy they receive from the sun.

(C) In higher plants, starch synthesis does not occur within the chloroplasts and therefore light is not necessary.

(D) Sufficient time was necessary to allow all starch formed from the previous period of photosynthesis to be transported to other tissues or utilized during cellular respiration.

(E) Time was necessary to allow the captured radiant energy to be utilized in the formation of ATP.

Questions 10 to 12:

A standard biochemical test determines the amount of organic matter in a given sample of water. The results are stated as the amount of O_2 (ppm) disappearing from the sample during an incubation period of five days (in the dark at 20°C). This test of biochemical oxygen demand was carried out on water samples taken from two locations: Site #1—.25 miles downstream from a sewage treatment plant, Site #2—.25 miles downstream from a pulp mill. At both these sites, effluent from the operations was being dumped into the river. The chart below shows the results obtained from the testing.

Site	OXYGEN (ppm) Before Incubation	After Incubation	B.O.D.
#1	8.8	6.0	2.8
#2	9.2	1.4	7.8

10. It is possible to estimate the amount of organic matter present in a sample of water by determining the amount of oxygen which disappears from the sample because

(A) the amount of oxygen present in the sample depends on the amount of organic matter the sample contains

(B) the sample is taken directly from a larger body of water which is being studied

(C) decomposers (bacteria and other organisms) oxidize organic matter, converting it to CO_2 and simple inorganic compounds

(D) the exact quantity of water originally taken is known

(E) appropriate chemicals have fixed the original amount of oxygen in the water and no more can be added

11. Which of the following best states why it is necessary to place the incubating sample in the dark?

(A) Microorganisms utilize more oxygen during conditions of daylight

(B) Photosynthetic organisms produce oxygen when exposed to light

(C) Accurate results depend upon keeping the number of organisms constant and cell division is enhanced by light

(D) Oxygen is bound into the glucose molecule during the dark phase of photosynthesis and cannot return to the water

(E) Anaerobic organisms function better during periods of darkness

12. What is the main purpose of this experiment?

(A) Determine whether the amounts of organic matter being added to fresh water at two locations were exceeding the decomposition capacity of the water

(B) Determine whether the sewage treatment plant was adequately treating the amount of waste it received

(C) Monitor the effluent from the pulp mill to determine the amount of organic matter being added to the river system

(D) Monitor the input of toxic materials at two well chosen sites along a river system

(E) Separate the biodegradable pollutants from the water and ascertain their effect on the ecosystem

Questions 13 to 14:

The results of some of the early experiments on plant hormones can be easily reproduced by the following experiment. The tips of four oat seedlings are cut off. One tip is placed on a small block of agar for two hours and is then discarded. The four plants are then treated in the following manner: 1) the first plant is left without a tip, 2) the tip is replaced on the second plant, 3) the agar cube that was in contact with a cut tip is placed on the third plant, 4) an agar cube that has not been in contact with a tip is placed on the fourth plant. The plants are then observed for one or two days.

PLANT	GROWTH
#1	no
#2	yes
#3	yes
#4	no

13. The results of the experiment on plants #1 and #2 *only* imply that

(A) the shock of decapitation temporarily stopped growth of plant #1
(B) something within the tips of oat seedlings is responsible for their growth
(C) decapitating the plants caused irreparable injury to their cells
(D) growth would have resumed in both plants, given enough time
(E) toxic substances are produced in the tips of oat seedlings

14. From the data obtained from all four plants, it is apparent that

(A) there is a chemical substance present in agar that causes oat seedlings to grow
(B) negative geotropism causes oat seedlings to grow
(C) it is possible to stop growth in oat seedlings because the tissues are not differentiated
(D) the growth inducing element in oat seedlings is probably a chemical which can diffuse into agar from the tip of the seedling
(E) the substance produced in the tips of oat seedlings acts as an inhibitor to root growth

END OF PART

Go on to the following Test in the next Part of this Examination, just as you would be expected to do on the actual exam. If you have any available time use it to make sure that you have marked your Answer Sheet properly for this Part. Correct Answers for all Parts of this Exam follow the last question. Derive your scores only after completing the entire Exam.

PART II. SCIENTIFIC REASONING AND KNOWLEDGE

TEST IV. BIOLOGICAL SCIENCE

TIME: 10 Minutes. 15 Questions.

DIRECTIONS: For each question in this test, read carefully the stem and the five lettered choices that follow. Choose the answer which you consider correct or most nearly correct. Mark the answer sheet for the letter you have chosen: A, B, C, D, or E.

Correct and explanatory answers are provided at the end of the exam. After you have completed the entire exam, read the explanations carefully. They'll reinforce your strengths and pinpoint your weaknesses so that you know just what to study to raise your score.

1. The halving of the chromosome complement during meiotic division of the sex cells lends credence to the Darwinian theory of evolution because

   (A) it prevents doubling the chromosome complement during fertilization
   (B) it separates like chromosomes
   (C) it provides a means of genetic variation
   (D) sex cells differ
   (E) mutations may be lost

2. Organisms in temperate zones are able to time their activites by cues given by the photoperiod, since

   (A) all organisms need time to rest
   (B) light is a limiting factor
   (C) all organisms have a biological clock
   (D) day length is always constant for a specific locality and season
   (E) some plants need long days in order to bloom

3. Which of the following properties make water indispensable to life as we know it?

   (A) Water expands at temperatures below 4°C.
   (B) Water has an extremely high surface tension.
   (C) Water has a very high heat capacity, heat of vaporization and heat of fusion.
   (D) Water has a high dielectric constant.
   (E) All of the above.

S 3265

4. Which of the following statements characterize the field of biology?

    I. Biology relates organic structures and activity to underlying chemical and physical activities.
    II. Biology relates organic structure and activity to their functions in and for organisms.
    III. Biology relates organic structure and activity to their evolutionary origin.

    (A) I only
    (B) II only
    (C) I and II only
    (D) II and III only
    (E) I, II, and III

5. Which of the following is true of enzyme catalysis but is not true of inorganic catalysis?

    (A) The catalyst speeds up the reaction.
    (B) The catalyst itself undergoes no change in the reaction.
    (C) The catalyst is subject to cellular controls.
    (D) Only a small amount of the catalyst is necessary.
    (E) The effect of the catalyst is similar to an increase in temperature, pressure or concentration.

6. The cell seems to be the basic unit of life for the following reason(s).

    I. All cells are self-reproductive without a host.
    II. All cells have the same general size and shape.
    III. All cells are self-regulating.

    (A) I only
    (B) II only
    (C) III only
    (D) I and II only
    (E) I and III only

7. Final cellular differentiation within a developing embryo is

    (A) determined by the physical and chemical environment surrounding the cell
    (B) entirely dependent upon the germ layer from which the cell is derived
    (C) dependent upon the specific chromosomes the cell receives
    (D) controlled by the cytoplasm of the unfertilized egg
    (E) determined before gastrulation of the embryo

8. Sharks and porpoises have a remarkably similar appearance and both give birth to live young, yet the shark is a fish and the porpoise is a mammal. This phenomenon can be attributed to which of the following?

    (A) Divergence, as two subdivisions of the same species ceased to interbreed; resulting in speciation and eventual separation.

(B) Adaptation, as the porpoise, which was originally a fish, developed mammalian characteristics to insure survival of the young.

(C) Convergence, as animals of different origins became adapted to similar environments and habits.

(D) Parallelism, as closely related organisms evolved along similar lines.

(E) Cryptic speciation, as two parts of a population have ceased interbreeding without developing any discernable differences.

9. The living material comprising the bulk of a cell is called the

(A) chloroplast
(B) protoplasm
(C) cytochrome
(D) genes
(E) hormones

10. The condition known as goiter is best described by which of the following statements?

(A) It is caused by a deficiency of iron.
(B) It is an enlarged thyroid gland.
(C) It is caused by a deficiency of insulin.
(D) It is caused by an excess of sugar.
(E) It is an abnormally small pineal gland.

11. Which of the following parts of the human eye regulates the amount of light admitted to the eye?

(A) The vitreous humor
(B) The retina
(C) The iris
(D) The optic nerve
(E) The cornea

12. Which of the following statements best describes the method used by female moths to attract male moths?

(A) The female moths use certain sound frequencies.
(B) The female moths fly in certain patterns.
(C) The female moths fly in the vicinity of certain flowers.
(D) The female moths send out certain chemical sex attractants.
(E) The female moths reflect light from their wings.

13. Which of the following items could best be called biodegradable?

(A) Phosphate detergents
(B) Polystyrene cups
(C) Polyvinylchloride pipes
(D) Cellulose
(E) Aluminum

14. Animals pass on traits to their offspring through which of the following units?

    (A) Genes
    (B) Proteins
    (C) Plasmas
    (D) Polysaccharides
    (E) Corpuscles

15. The existence of microorganisms in the human gastric system is an example of

    (A) symbiosis
    (B) parisititis
    (C) meiosis
    (D) phylesis
    (E) variance

END OF TEST

Go on to do the following Test in this Examination, just as you would
be expected to do on the actual exam.

TEST V. BIOLOGY KNOWLEDGE

TIME: 20 Minutes. 25 Questions.

DIRECTIONS: For each question in this test, read carefully the stem and the five lettered choices that follow. Choose the answer which you consider correct or most nearly correct. Mark the answer sheet for the letter you have chosen: A, B, C, D, or E.

1. Pollination characteristically occurs among which one of the following pairs?

   (A) angiosperms and psilopsids
   (B) angiosperms and gymnosperms
   (C) pteridophytes and bryophytes
   (D) bryophytes and angiosperms
   (E) angiosperms and fungi

2. A nerve impulse results in

   (A) the cessation of an electric current
   (B) a chemical flow throughout the nerve fiber
   (C) synaptic secretion of acetylcholine
   (D) a wave of electrical depolarization
   (E) a wave of electrical polarization

3. Much of the phenomena of tropistic responses of plants to light were first observed by which one of the following?

   (A) Charles Darwin
   (B) Hugo DeVries
   (C) Ivan Pavlov
   (D) Lloyd Morgan
   (E) Jacques Loeb

4. Ferns, conifers, and flowering plants are classified as

   (A) bryophyta
   (B) spermatophyta
   (C) psilophyta
   (D) chlorophyta
   (E) tracheophyta

5. Cellulose is digested in the rumen of cattle by the enzyme cellulase secreted by

   (A) protozoa   (D) the esophagus
   (B) bacteria   (E) windpipe
   (C) the rumen

6. An organism lacking chlorophyll, but nevertheless able to carry out photosynthesis has been found among which one of the following?

   (A) bacteria   (D) zoophytes
   (B) viruses   (E) protozoa
   (C) phaeophytes

7. Of the following, which one best describes phenylketonuria?

   (A) a vitamin deficiency resulting in abnormal metabolism of proteins
   (B) an inherited metabolic disorder resulting in a lack of an enzyme
   (C) a mineral deficiency resulting in abnormal bone formation
   (D) an abnormal shape in red blood cells
   (E) a chronic disease of unknown causes

8. Of the following characteristics, the one relevant to trace elements is that they

   (A) are radioactive and can be located with a Geiger Counter
   (B) exist in minute amounts in protoplasm
   (C) are not readily absorbed into protoplasm
   (D) act as inhibitors of enzymatic reactions
   (E) control the passage of materials through the pores in the cell membrane

9. Solutions of crystal violet, iodine and alcohol are used in a staining procedure known as

    (A) acid-fast stain (D) Gram stain
    (B) Wright's stain (E) spore stain
    (C) Giemsa's stain

10. The fossil, Hesperornis, is significant because it

    (A) had claws on its hind limbs
    (B) had feathers and teeth
    (C) was a link between birds and mammals
    (D) was a link between amphibia and reptiles
    (E) was a link between fish and amphibia

11. Colonies of coelenterates with individuals of more than one body form are said to exhibit

    (A) polymorphism
    (B) radial symmetry
    (C) orthogenesis
    (D) divergence
    (E) neotony

12. To which one of the following is the Haversian system related?

    (A) endocrine system
    (B) skeletal system
    (C) reproductive system
    (D) respiratory system
    (E) nervous system

13. A section of the circulatory system which plays an important role in fishes, but which disappears in higher land animals is the

    (A) hepatic portal system
    (B) renal portal system
    (C) renal arteries
    (D) hepatic arteries
    (E) hepatic veins

14. Of the following organisms, the one that has an incomplete, but functional, digestive system is

    (A) lumbricus
    (B) lobster
    (C) clam
    (D) grasshopper
    (E) planaria

15. Sodium citrate is added to bottles of donor blood to prevent clotting because it removes the

    (A) serum
    (B) plasma
    (C) calcium
    (D) prothrombin
    (E) fibrinogen

16. Protective mimicry is illustrated by

    (A) aphids and ants
    (B) hermit crab and sea anemone
    (C) monarch and viceroy butterflies
    (D) pilot fish and shark
    (E) termite and trichonympha

17. The evolutionary development of the animal kingdom can best be represented as which one of the following?

    (A) ladder
    (B) web
    (C) circle
    (D) chain
    (E) tree

18. It is probable that a mammal smaller than a shrew could not exist because it would

    (A) not get sufficient oxygen
    (B) reproduce too rapidly
    (C) have to eat at too tremendous a rate
    (D) not be able to defend itself
    (E) be unable to bear live young

19. The fruit composed of a hard endocarp and usually one seed is classified as which one of the following?

    (A) capsule
    (B) drupe
    (C) achene
    (D) samara
    (E) none of these

20. Of the following, the important fossil that was intermediate between mammals and reptiles is

    (A) Dipterus
    (B) Cynognathus
    (C) Seymouria
    (D) Smilodon
    (E) Amphioxus

21. The skin color of the earliest men was probably

    (A) white
    (B) yellow
    (C) black
    (D) red
    (E) variable

22. The *vagus substance* discovered by Loewi later turned out to be

    (A) choline esterase
    (B) adrenaline
    (C) 5-hydroxytryptamine
    (D) acetylcholine
    (E) ATP

23. A characteristic of all chordates is the presence of a

    (A) chorda tympanum
    (B) chorda tendonae
    (C) mammary gland
    (D) vertebral column
    (E) notochord

24. Of the following, the pairs which are examples of complex organic compounds with high energy bonds are

    (A) DNA, ATP
    (B) DDT, 2, 4-D
    (C) RNA, DNA
    (D) 2, 4-D, DNA
    (E) ATP, ADP

25. The center for temperature regulation in the human is the

    (A) skin
    (B) lungs
    (C) thalamus
    (D) medulla
    (E) cerebellum

END OF TEST

Go on to do the following Test in this Examination, just as you would be expected to do on the actual exam.

TEST VI. PHYSICS

TIME: 15 Minutes. 20 Questions.

DIRECTIONS: For each question in this test, read carefully the stem and the five lettered choices that follow. Choose the answer which you consider correct or most nearly correct. Mark the answer sheet for the letter you have chosen: A, B, C, D, or E.

1. A sub-atomic particle moving at a constant speed of 6×10^6 m/sec enters a region of an electric field where it is decelerated at the rate of 1.2×10^{14} m/sec^2. The linear distance the particle travels before coming to rest is, in cm, equal to
   (A) 5×10^{-6}
   (B) 30×10^{-2}
   (C) 2
   (D) 15
   (E) 15×10^{-2}

2. A 180 lb man stands in an elevator. The force, in lbs that the floor exerts on the man when the elevator is moving upward, but decelerating at 8 ft/sec^2, is closest to which one of the following?
   (A) 23 (B) 90 (C) 180
   (D) 225 (E) 135

3. According to Kepler's third law, the period of a planet is proportional to some power of its mean distance from the sun. Which is the correct statement of this law?
   (A) $T \approx R^2$
   (B) $T \approx R^{2/3}$
   (C) $T \approx R^{1/3}$
   (D) $T \approx R^{3/2}$
   (E) $T \approx R^3$

4. Young's modulus of a material is equal to
   (A) tensile stress/compressive stress
   (B) compressive strain/tensile strain
   (C) tensile stress/tensile strain
   (D) compressive stress/tensile stress
   (E) shear stress/shear strain

5. The speed of a wave traveling through a stretched string is directly proportional to the
   (A) density per unit length of the string
   (B) square of the tension
   (C) square root of the tension
   (D) square of the density per unit length
   (E) square root of the density per unit length

6. A sphere and a cylinder start from rest at the same position and roll down the same incline.
   (A) The cylinder will reach the bottom first and is independent of the mass and radius of the two objects.
   (B) Which one reaches the bottom first will depend on the mass of the object.
   (C) They will reach the bottom at the same time and are independent of the mass and radius of the two objects.
   (D) Which one reaches the bottom first will depend on the radius of the object.
   (E) The sphere will reach the bottom first and is independent of the mass and radius of the two objects.

7. A gravitational field is a conservative field. The work done in this field by transporting an object from one point to another
   (A) depends on the end points only
   (B) depends on the path along which the object is transported.
   (C) depends on both the end points and the path between these points.
   (D) is not zero when the object is brought back to its initial position
   (E) is a function of velocity.

8. Ball I, mass = 1 Kg, moves at a speed of 5 m/sec and strikes a glancing blow, in an elastic collision, on another mass, ball II, which was initially at rest. Ball I then moves off at right angles to its initial direction at a speed of 4 m/sec. After the collision, the momentum of ball II has a magnitude, in Kg-m/sec, closest to which one of the following?

(A) 1 (B) 2 (C) 4

(D) 6 — (E) 7

9. Two particles of mass m and M are initially at rest and infinitely separated from each other. At any later instant, their relative velocity of approach attributable to gravitational attraction, given in terms of their separation d, is

(A) $v_r = [2Gd/(M+m)]^{\frac{1}{2}}$

— (B) $v_r = [2G(M+m)/d]^{\frac{1}{2}}$

(C) $v_r = 2G(M+m)/d$

(D) $v_r = 2Gd/(M+m)$

(E) $v_r = 2G[(M+m)]^{\frac{1}{2}}$

10. A block of mass m at the end of a string is whirled around in a vertical circle of radius R. Find the critical speed of the block at the top of its swing below which the string would become slack as the block reaches the top of its swing.

— (A) $(Rg)^{\frac{1}{2}}$

(B) Rg

(C) $(Rg)^{1/3}$

(D) $(Rg)^2$

(E) R/g

11. Let G be the universal constant of gravitation. To escape from the atmosphere of a planet of mass M and radius R, the necessary condition for a molecule of mass is that it have a speed such that

— (A) $v^2 \geqq (2GM)/R$

(B) $v \geqq (2GMm)/R$

(C) $v \geqq (2GM)/R$

(D) $v^2 \geqq (2GMm)/R^2$

(E) $v^2 \geqq (GM)/R$

Questions 12 *and* 13 *refer to the following statement*: A small object of mass m is attached to a light string which passes through a hollow tube. The tube is held by one hand and the string by the other. The object is set into rotation in a circle of radius r_1 with a speed v_1. The string is then pulled down, shortening the radius of the path to r_2.

12. Neglecting gravity, the relation of the new angular speed ω_2 and the original one ω_1 is

(A) $\omega_2 = (r_1/r_2)\omega_1$

— (B) $\omega_2 = (r_1/r_2)^2\omega_1$

(C) $\omega_2 = (r_2/r_1)\omega_1$

(D) $\omega_2 = (r_2/r_1)^2\omega_1$

(E) $\omega_2 = \omega_1$

13. The ratio of the new kinetic energy to the original kinetic energy is

— (A) $(r_1/r_2)^2$

(B) r_1/r_2

(C) 1

(D) r_2/r_1

(E) $(r_2/r_1)^2$

14. A current of 5 amp exists in a 10-ohm resistance for 4 min. How many coulombs pass through any cross section of the resistor in this time?

(A) 1.2 coul

(B) 12 coul

(C) 120 coul

— (D) 1200 coul

(E) 12,000 coul

15. What is the flux ϕ of E through a hemisphere of radius R, if the field of E is uniform and is parallel to the axis of the hemisphere?

—(A) $\pi R^2 E$

(B) $2\pi R E$

(C) $\pi R^2 \frac{1}{2} E$

(D) $\sqrt{2}\pi R^2 E$

(E) $\pi R^2 (E/\sqrt{2})$ —

16. A parallel-plate capacitor is charged and then disconnected from the charging battery. If the plates of the capacitor are then moved farther apart by the use of insulated handles, which one of the following results?
    (A) The charge on the capacitor increases.
    (B) The charge on the capacitor decreases.
    (C) The capacitance of the capacitor increases.
    (D) The voltage across the capacitor remains the same.
    (E) The voltage across the capacitor increases.

17. A piece of copper wire is cut into ten equal parts. These parts are connected in parallel. The joint resistance of the parallel combination will be equal to the original resistance of the single wire, multiplied by a factor of
    (A) .01   (D) 100
    (B) .10   (E) .20
    (C) 10

18. The effective value of a sinusoidal alternating emf is equal to its maximum value multiplied by
    (A) 1.41   (D) 0.50
    (B) 1.732   (E) 0.707
    (C) 0.623

19. If it requires two joules of work to move 20 coulombs from point A to point B, a distance of 0.2 meter, the potential difference between points A and B, in volts, is
    (A) 2×10^{-2} (D) 8
    (B) 4×10^{-2} (E) 1×10^{-1}
    (C) 4×10^{-1}

20. A parallel plate capacitor with 0.3 cm thickness of air between its two plates has a capacitance of 15 $\mu\mu f$. When the air is replaced by mica (dielectric constant = 6) the capacitance, in $\mu\mu f$, becomes
    (A) 5   (D) 300
    (B) 15   (E) 2.5
    (C) 90

END OF TEST

Go on to do the following Test in this Examination, just as you would be expected to do on the actual exam.

TEST VII. CHEMISTRY

TIME: 10 Minutes. 15 Questions.

DIRECTIONS: For each question in this test, read carefully the stem and the five lettered choices that follow. Choose the answer which you consider correct or most nearly correct. Mark the answer sheet for the letter you have chosen: A, B, C, D, or E.

Correct and explanatory answers are provided at the end of the exam. After you have completed the entire exam, read the explanations carefully. They'll reinforce your strengths and pinpoint your weaknesses so that you know just what to study to raise your score.

1. The process of adding a basic solution to an acidic solution until the resulting solution is neither basic nor acidic is called

   (A) oxidation
   (B) reduction
   (C) nucleation
   — (D) neutralization
   (E) precipitation

2. If water is electrolyzed which of the following best describes the products obtained?

   (A) H^+ and OH^-
   (B) H_2 and OH
   — (C) H_2 and O_2
   (D) H_2O_2 and H_2
   (E) H_2O_2

3. Which of the following statements best describes the action of catalysts?

   (A) They alter the ratio of products.
   — (B) They change the rate of reactions.
   (C) They change the ratio of products and the rate of reaction.
   (D) They change the products.
   (E) They change neither the products nor the rate of reaction.

4. When a beam of light is passed through a beaker filled with a clear liquid the beam can be seen in the solution. This describes a characteristic of what type of system?

   (A) A true solution
   — (B) A colloidal system
   (C) A thermally unstable system
   (D) A mixture
   (E) A system in the process of being heated

5. Which of the following statements best distinguishes electrolytes from non-electrolytes?

   (A) Electrolytes are always ionic compounds while non-electrolytes are always covalent compounds.
   (B) Electrolytes are usually covalent compounds while non-electrolytes are usually ionic compounds.
   (C) Electrolytes and non-electrolytes are really both covalent compounds.
   (D) Non-electrolytes are usually insoluble in water while electrolytes are usually soluble.
   _ (E) Electrolytes can be covalent or ionic compounds but must be ionic in solution.

6. When small particles are added to a liquid they can often be seen to be undergoing very rapid motion on the surface of the liquid. The explanation for this motion is best described by which of the following statements?

   (A) The electrical interactions between the liquid and the suspended particles.
   (B) The molecular vibrations of the liquid causing collisions with the suspended particles.
   (C) The low density of the particles causing them to try to rise above the surface of the liquid.
   (D) Air currents above the liquid moving the particles.
   (E) The heat rising causing the particles to move.

7. Consider the following chemical formulae: CH_4, CCl_4, $CHCl_3$. These formulae show that

   (A) the carbon atom has four combining sites
   (B) many compounds contain carbon
   (C) carbon is important to living things
   (D) ionic bonds have been formed
   (E) carbon is a very complex element

8. Which of the following is a balanced chemical equation?

   (A) $H_2 + Br_2 \longrightarrow HBr$
   (B) $P_4 + O_2 \longrightarrow P_4O_{10}$
   (C) $C_3H_8 + 5O_2 \longrightarrow 3CO_2 + 4H_2O$
   (D) $H_2 + O_2 \longrightarrow 2H_2O$
   (E) $H_2O + CO_3 \longrightarrow H_2CO_3 + 2OH$

Questions 9 to 11

DIRECTIONS: Five chemical formulas are given below. For each of the questions following, you are to choose the most suitable formula.

(A)
$$\begin{array}{c} CH_3 \\ | \\ CH-C-OH \\ | \\ CH_3 \end{array}$$

(B)
$$\begin{array}{c} CH_3 \\ \diagdown CH-OH \\ CH_3 \diagup \end{array}$$

(C) $CH_3CH_2CH_2CH_2-OH$

(D) CH_4

(E) C_5H_8-OH

9. The isomer for
$$\begin{array}{c} CH_3 \\ | \\ CH_3-C-CH_3 \\ | \\ CH_3 \end{array}$$

10. Formula that is not an alcohol.

11. The adjacent homolog to CH_3CH_2-OH

Questions 12 to 15

Directions: Five options are given below. For each question, choose one of the options and blacken its letter in the corresponding space on your answer sheet.

(A) H : Ö : H   (B) $\left[: \overset{..}{C}l : \right]^-$ (C) (H ·)

(D) H : C : : : C : H   (E) H ·

C 12. Orbital diagram of the hydrogen atom.

A 13. A covalent bond representation.

D 14. A multiple bonded compound.

E 15. Lewis diagram of the hydrogen atom.

END OF EXAMINATION

If you finish before the allotted time is up, check your work on this test only. Do not go back to earlier tests. When time runs out, compare your answers for this test and all the other tests in the examination with the correct key answers that follow.

CORRECT ANSWERS FOR VERISIMILAR EXAMINATION IV.

TEST I. GRAPH SELECTION

1.B	4.A	7.D	10.C	13.A
2.E	5.D	8.A	11.A	14.B
3.A	6.B	9.E	12.D	15.D

TEST I. EXPLANATORY ANSWERS

1. **(B)** When equal amounts of a weak acid and a weak base are combined, a buffered solution is obtained. This means that large amounts of acid or base are necessary in order to change the pH of the solution appreciably. However, outside this buffered region, pH changes rapidly with the addition of small amounts of acid or base. When pH is graphed over the entire course of a titration, a sigmoid or S shaped curve is obtained since pH changes slowly within the buffered region. (B) is the only graph which demonstrates this relationship.

2. **(E)** Under ideal conditions, bacteria divide about every 20 minutes. (If this rate were maintained for three days, their volume would be greater than that of the earth!) The rate of growth is a geometrical progression with a common multiple of two. Graphs (A) and (E) show both properties increasing, however (A) shows a proportional increase. Graph (E) shows one property increasing faster than the other which is the situation in this instance; therefore (E) is the correct answer.

3. **(A)** In a body under constant acceleration, speed increases in direct proportion to time. Only in graph (A) does one property increase in direct proportion to the other.

4. **(A)** Question 4 is based on Hooke's law which states that elastic deformation is proportional to the force producing it. Graph (A) is the only one that illustrates a direct proportionality.

5. **(D)** Given sufficient light, an increase in temperature results in an increase in the rate of photosynthesis—up to a point. Once that point is exceeded photosynthesis slows down rapidly then ceases altogether as the proteins making up chlorophyll and enzymes become denatured. Choices (B) and (D) show one of the properties increasing and decreasing in a bell shaped curve. However only (D) shows a rapid decrease in the property and it best illustrates the rapid decline in the rate of photosynthesis at temperatures above 30° C.

6. **(B)** During a collision, force reaches a peak at the time of closest approach. It is zero before the first contact and after the objects have separated. Since the magnitude of the force does not decrease more rapidly than it increases the correct choice is the simple bell shaped curve, graph (B).

7. **(D)** This situation is almost identical to that in question 5. Enzymes, being proteins, are denatured by high temperatures; therefore, beyond a certain temperature the rate of enzyme activity decreases rapidly.

8. **(A)** Present thinking is that the temperature of the earth does not increase directly with depth, but that the greatest rate of increase is near the surface. Since depth is plotted on the horizontal axis, only graph (A) shows the correct relationship.

9. **(E)** This question is based on Gay-Lussac's law, at constant volume, the pressure of a given mass of gas varies directly with the absolute temperature. Choices (B), (C), and (E) show both properties rising, but only (E) represents a direct proportionality.

10. **(C)** During moderate exercise, body temperature may rise as much as one or two degrees. After this initial rise, regulatory mechanisms go into effect which keep the temperature stable. Since temperature is plotted on the vertical axis, only graph (C) illustrates an initial rise up to the point at which a constant temperature is maintained.

11. **(A)** Pressure is greater at lower altitudes. This causes the air mass to contract, thus increasing temperature. Only graph (A) illustrates one property rising as the other falls.

12. **(D)** A body falling freely from rest is under constant acceleration. Only graph (D) shows one property remaining constant.

13. **(A)** The density of a gas varies inversely with its volume. (A) is the only graph that illustrates an inverse relationship.

14. **(B)** The distance covered by a body under constant acceleration is proportional to the square of the time. (B) depicts one quantity increasing faster than the other quantity.

15. **(D)** Luminosity and temperature increase proportionally, however neither quantity reaches zero. (D) is the only graph which satisfies both requirements.

TEST II. EXPERIMENT VALIDITY

1.A	3.D	5.A	7.C	9.E	11.A	13.A	15.B
2.E	4.C	6.B	8.E	10.E	12.C	14.A	16.A

TEST II. EXPLANATORY ANSWERS

1. **(A)** Knowledge that an acid turns litmus paper red, a base turns it blue, and a neutral solution shows no change is necessary to solve this problem. From the data given, each solution can be determined to be an acid, base or neutral. A base has a pH greater than seven.

2. **(E)** In the experiment, solution one is an acid. Solution four is neutral. An acid does not show a higher pH than a neutral solution.

3. **(D)** Unless the acid is extremely weak so that the concentration of hydrogen ions when placed in a neutral solution is no longer sufficient to react with the indicator, the indicator will probably turn red.

4. **(C)** Litmus paper will not show relative acidity.

5. **(A)** The definition of a base is a substance containing OH⁻ or hydroxide ions. This question is essentially stating that solution three is more of a base than solution four. According to the table, three is a base and four is neutral.

6. **(B)** We observe that as the molecular weight of the gas *decreases* the distance traveled *increases*. Therefore a gas which travels 0.23 cm should have a molecular weight slightly greater than 32. However this statement is not definitely proved but only probably true. Therefore the correct answer is (B).

7. **(C)** Since the temperature of the gases was not specified, the correct answer is (C).

8. **(E)** The data presented indicates that the rate of diffusion *decreases* with increasing molecular weight. The graph shows the opposite situation and is therefore false. The correct answer is (E).

9. **(E)** The data presented shows that although H^2 and O^2 have the same number of atoms their rates of diffusion are quite different. Therefore this statement is also false and the correct answer is (E).

10. **(E)** Since the hypothesis of this experiment was that the event will almost always occur in way "B," the hypothesis has definitely not been proven. Therefore the correct answer is (E).

11. **(A)** The data obtained shows that the event can occur three different ways, thus the answer is (A).

12. **(C)** There is no information regarding how well the experiment was designed. The correct answer is therefore (C).

13. **(A)** The theory upon which the hypothesis was based is obviously wrong in at least one respect so that it does need some revision. The answer is therefore (A).

14. **(A)** Chemical-1 will kill Type A completely and almost kill Type C. Chemical-2 slightly harms Type A and kills Type C. Since they do not have the exact same action on weeds they do have different toxicities.

15. **(B)** Since chemical-1 kills two types and chemical-2 only one type of weed, it is probably true that chemical-1 kills more types of weeds.

16. **(A)** Type B weeds are not affected by either of the chemicals so it is demonstrated that they are more resistant.

TEST III. UNDERSTANDING EXPERIMENTS

1.C	3.E	5.C	7.B	9.D	11.B	13.B
2.B	4.D	6.A	8.A	10.C	12.A	14.D

TEST III. EXPLANATORY ANSWERS

1. **(C)** The first two questions require that a person be able to organize information contained in a chart and to evaluate this information in light of information contained in the description of the experiment. By referring to the chart one should be able to pick (C) as the correct choice.

2. **(B)** The trend in solubility coupled with the information that one can arrange members of a family by noting trends in properties leads to the correct choice (B).

3. **(E)** This question requires a knowledge of evolutionary theory. Organisms can do nothing about their genetic makeup. However, this genetic makeup renders some organisms more viable under given circumstances and they survive to breed more organisms which contain the genetic advantage under consideration.

4. **(D)** This is a straightforward question requiring the translation of information from a table to a graph. By referring to the table one can see that the percent of melanics decreases with increasing distance from the city. Graphs (A) and (C) can be disregarded since they show both properties increasing. The percent of melanics never reaches zero and graph (D) is the only one which illustrates this finding.

5. **(C)** This question requires the selection of the most logical and scientifically accurate definition of a term using the information contained in the description of the experiment. The term 'industrial melanism' implies causation. Of the choices only (C) presents the idea of industrialization being a causative factor in the observed change.

6. **(A)** Choice (B) makes no mention of geography, therefore it does not include all aspects of the study. Choices (C), (D) and (E) are not consistent with the data or description of the experiment.

7. **(B)** This question tests a general understanding of scientific principles. It determines not only whether a person can define the word hypothesis but also whether he can relate this abstraction to the concrete. (A), (C), (D), and (E) all seek to explain the results of the experiment. They could not have been stated prior to obtaining the results. Only (B) is consistent with the description of the experiment.

8. **(A)** This question requires knowledge of the process of photosynthesis in which sugar is produced from $CO_2 + H_2O$, and of the fact that the sugar is then changed into starch. One must also be familiar with an elementary chemical test for starch. This experiment has a double purpose: testing the effects of both the presence and absence of light and the presence and absence of chlorophyll. In question 8 only choice (A) relates all these factors and it is the correct answer.

9. **(D)** This question requires the ability to reason and to apply a knowledge of cellular metabolism and transportation. The presence of starch in the plant tissues was used as an indicator of photosynthetic activity. In order to assure the validity of the observed data, it was necessary to allow the nutrients produced during a previous period of photosynthesis to be eliminated.

10. **(C)** This question requires knowledge of the ecological importance of decomposers plus knowledge of the chemical process of oxidation and the ability to relate this knowledge to an experimental process. The disappearance of O_2 must be related to the presence of organic matter since it is used as an indicator. Only choice (C) outlines this relationship.

11. **(B)** To answer this correctly one must be familiar with the process of photosynthesis whereby green plants utilize solar energy to convert $CO_2 + H_2O$ into sugar + O_2 which is released into the environment. One must also know that small unicellular algae, phytoplankton, are of major importance as food producers (through photosynthesis). As the basis of the food chain they are present in nearly all bodies of water. With this knowledge one can choose (B) as the correct answer.

12. **(A)** As samples were only collected once, there was no monitoring and (C) and (D) can be eliminated. Choice (B) only refers to one of the sites sampled and choice (E) is not consistent with the information given. Choice (A) is consistent with all data and is the correct answer.

13. **(B)** Plant 1 did not resume growth during the period of observation. No indication was given that growth would have resumed at any later time so choice (A) is not supported by the data. There is no evidence given in support of (C), (D) or (E). However, growth did resume in the seedling which had its tip replaced. It follows from this that something within the tips of oat seedlings promotes growth as in choice (B).

14. **(D)** No growth was observed in Plant 4 therefore choice (A) can be eliminated. There is no evidence given that would support (B), (C) or (E). However, when the agar which was in contact with a cut tip is placed on a seedling the seedling grows as if the tip itself had been replaced. Something within the tip must have diffused into the agar and this can only occur if the substance is a chemical.

TEST IV. BIOLOGICAL SCIENCE

1.C	3.E	5.C	7.A	9.B	11.C	13.D	15.A
2.D	4.E	6.E	8.C	10.B	12.D	14.A	

TEST IV. EXPLANATORY ANSWERS

1. **(C)** Hereditary variation provides for adaptation to differing environmental conditions. Adaptation and resultant natural selection are basic to evolutionary theories proposed by Darwin. Answer (C) is the only one which expresses this idea.

2. **(D)** Only answers (D) and (E) are directly related to cues which are given by the photoperiod. However, answer (E) is too limited while (D) encompasses all activities in all plants. Thus, (D) is the correct choice.

3. **(E)** Water just below the freezing point (A) is denser than ice, therefore, it sinks, protecting bottom dwelling organisms from freezing. High surface tension (B) causes water to rise unusually high in capillary tubes, which is very important in plant physiology. High heat capacity (C) causes water to act as a thermal buffer. High heats of vaporization and fusion also help in keeping environmental temperatures stable. A high dielectric constant (D) makes water a solvent for a large variety of molecules which are necessary for the chemical functioning of organisms. Since all the properties mentioned are indispensable to life, the correct answer is (E).

4. **(E)** There are three types of explanations in biology: 1) the physiological, (I); 2) the teleonomic, (II); 3) the historical, (III). Therefore the correct answer includes all three.

5. **(C)** Enzyme catalysis takes place in living systems and therefore is subject to cellular controls. This is not true of inorganic catalysis which is a laboratory procedure. Therefore (C) is the correct choice.

6. **(E)** There are many one-celled organisms which are self regulating and self reproductive but one need only compare the yolk of a chicken egg and a rod-shaped bacteria to realize that cells come in many sizes and shapes. The correct answer, (E), only includes the first two possibilities.

7. **(A)** Experiments with the embryos of animals such as frogs have shown that final cellular differentiation depends upon the milieu of the cell. In early stages of gastrulation, cells which are in the location of the cell mass from which the eye arises have been transplanted to the region behind the mouth and there they develop into gills. These experiments have been widely published and familiarity with these ideas will lead to a correct answer of (A).

8. **(C)** Sharks and porpoises are not closely related. One would have to go back to the Paleozoic Era to find a common ancestor. This leads to choice (C) as the correct one.

9. **(B)** This question concerns the biology of all living organisms. Options (A), (C) and (D) are specific entities which are located in the cell. Option (E) concerns certain chemicals found in the body. The correct answer is option (B) the protoplasm, which is common to both plant and animal cells.

10. **(B)** A goiter is a large lump in the area below the neck and is caused by a deficiency of iodine. The iodine deficiency causes the enlargement of the thyroid gland. The correct answer is therefore option (B).

11. **(C)** This is a question from the field of human physiology. Option (A), the vitreous humor, is the fluid material which fills the eye. Option (B), the retina, is at the rear of the eye and option (E), the cornea, is the protective lens at the front of the eye. Neither of these parts functions to regulate the amount of light admitted to the eye. The optic nerve, option (D), transmits the light signal to the brain. Therefore the correct answer is option (C), the iris.

12. **(D)** This question from the field of insect behavior can be answered if the candidate realizes that insects communicate via certain chemical scents (*pheromones*). This type of communication is also true of sex attraction which is accomplished by a class of materials known as insect sex attractants. The correct answer is option (D).

13. **(D)** A biodegradable substance is one that can be recycled by nature. Options (A) and (B) will not be recycled by the environment but remain to pollute it. This is also true for options (C) and (E). The correct answer is option (D). As a general rule artificial materials such as plastics are not biodegradable while natural materials, such as starch or wood, are.

14. **(A)** This question concerns the science of heredity. Genes are individual chemical units which determine how tall we are or what color hair and eyes we have. Each gene has a different job to perform. The correct answer is (A).

15. **(A)** This question from biology can be answered by knowing that options (C) (disease), (D) (hormonal deficiency) and (E) (genetic throwback) are not pertinent to the existence of microorganisms in the human gastric system since this is not only a normal situation but a necessary one. When two organisms exist together and each derives a benefit from the relationship the situation is called *symbiosis*. If one suffers at the expense of the other the situation is called *parasitisis*. The correct answer is therefore (A).

TEST V. BIOLOGY

1.B	5.B	8.B	11.A	14.E	17.E	20.B	23.E
2.D	6.A	9.D	12.B	15.E	18.C	21.E	24.E
3.E	7.B	10.B	13.B	16.C	19.C	22.D	25.C
4.E							

TEST V. EXPLANATORY ANSWERS

1. **(B)** Pollination occurs only in plants that produce seeds. In order for seed formation to take place, pollen grains must come into effective contact with ovules. Pollination transfers the pollen from the anther to the stigma of a plant. Among the choices listed, only Angiosperms and Gymnosperms produce seeds, and as such exhibit the vital process of pollination.

2. **(D)** Normally, a "resting" nerve exhibits polarization with positive charges on the outside of the nerve fiber and negative charges on the inside. When an outside stimulus comes into contact with the nerve, sodium (positive) ions are permitted to infiltrate the fiber, leading to a wave of depolarization — becoming positively charged on the inside and negatively charged on the outside.

3. **(E)** Jacques Loeb compared the tropistic movements of plants to light with a behavioral pattern similar to that of the pill bug.

4. **(E)** Ferns, Gymnosperms and Angiosperms possess conducting tubes for transporting vital materials to all parts of the plant. This characteristic distinguishes a member of the Tracheophyta.

5. **(B)** Symbiotic bacteria inhabiting the alimentary canal secrete the enzyme cellulose, converting the polysaccharide cellulose into sugar, which is absorbed and utilized.

6. **(A)** Photosynthetic bacteria possess an enzyme, different from chlorophyll, but still capable of enabling them to produce their own food.

7. **(B)** Phenylketonuria is caused by a lack of a single gene responsible for initiating the production of an enzyme that normally converts phenylalanine to tyrosine.

8. **(B)** Trace elements (copper, sulfur, iron, etc.) are present in protoplasm in very minute quantities — fractions of a per cent. However, even though present in trace quantity, their presence is vital to the normal functioning of the organism.

9. **(D)** The gram stain, routinely utilized in bacteriology, employs crystal violet, Lugol's iodine, 95% alcohol and safranin as part of its technique.

10. **(B)** *Hesperornis regalis* was found during the Cretaceous period and exhibited feathers and teeth. It is classified as a bird, but was wingless and inhabited coastal areas, diving for its food.

11. **(A)** Obelia and other colonial coelenterates include many specialized individuals who help the colony to function as a unit. These unusual members display polymorphism, or many body shapes.

12. **(B)** Bone tissue is composed of many Haversian systems, which comprise such parts as lamellae, lacunae and bone canals.

13. **(B)** The renal portal system gathers blood from the hind fin and posterior body wall, dividing into capillaries within the kidneys. The blood is then collected by renal veins and returned to the heart. Amphibians also possess a renal portal system, functioning in much the same manner.

14. **(E)** The planaria do not have complete digestive systems — that is, a separate mouth and anal opening. However, the digestive system does secrete enzymes which digest food sucked in through the proboscis. There are no specialized digestive organs like stomach, liver, esophagus, etc., but rather a diverse, branching intestine.

15. **(E)** Fibrinogen, a plasma protein, is vital for the clotting of blood. When acted upon by thrombin, fibrinogen causes threads of fibrin to be formed. It is this interlocking network of fibrin which traps red blood corpuscles, etc. and prevents the blood from flowing out of the wound.

16. **(C)** Protective mimicry is exhibited by several animals that inhabit the same environment. The monarch butterfly produces a chemical that does not appeal to most birds. Because the viceroy butterfly resembles it so perfectly, birds do not prey upon them. This evolutionary achievement has proved most beneficial to the survival and continuance of these insects.

17. **(E)** All animals evolved from a common ancestry. If we think of the trunk, or main part of a tree, as representing this original main line, the branches are all divisions or groupings from this origination point. Smaller branches and twigs are subgroups and constitute specific lines of evolutionary development from the aforesaid larger groupings.

18. **(C)** The shrew is the smallest mammal in the world. Each day it must consume several times its own body weight in order to survive, insects supplying most of these demands. The great frequency of hunting, killing and feeding would make it almost impossible for any smaller mammal to exist.

19. **(C)** The achene dry fruit contains an individual seed attached at one point to the wall of the fruit, which does not split open. The dandelion is an example.

20. **(B)** In the Permian period, a group of reptiles possessing a few mammalian characteristics (therapsids) appeared. One representative member, *Cynognathus,* possessed teeth differentiated into incisors, canines and molars. In addition, the skull size was intermediate between that of a reptile and a mammal.

21. **(E)** There is sufficient evidence that all the present races evolved from a common ancestor, and that there is no such term as a "pure" race. Skin color also varies within a race, exhibiting a very wide array of shades.

22. **(D)** Loewi established that transmission of an impulse at a nerve-muscle junction is by chemical means. Acetylcholine, a neuro-humor, is released by terminal dendrites of motor neurons when stimulated by an impulse.

23. **(E)** All chordates possess a notochord at some time during their life span.

24. **(E)** Adenosine triphosphate and adenosine diphosphate possess high energy bonds among their phosphate groups. They are vital to all cells, providing the needed energy for cellular reactions.

25. **(C)** The body temperature is controlled and regulated by the thalamus of the brain. It is not understood how this region functions.

TEST VI. PHYSICS

1.D	4.C	7.A	10.A	13.A	15.A	17.A	19.E
2.E	5.C	8.E	11.A	14.D	16.E	18.E	20.C
3.D	6.E	9.B	12.B				

TEST VI. EXPLANATORY ANSWERS

1. **(D)** Since 6×10^6 m/sec is much less than the speed of light, we may treat this problem classically.

$dv/dt = a$

Upon integration: $v - v_0 = at$

$dx/dt = v$

Upon a second integration: $x - x_0 = v_0 t + \frac{1}{2} at^2$

$a = -1.2 \times 10^{14}$ m/sec²

$v_0 = 6 \times 10^6$ m/sec $\qquad v_f = 0$

$0 - 6 \times 10^6$ m/sec $= (-1.2 \times 10^{14}$ m/sec²$)t$

$\therefore \quad t = 5 \times 10^{-8}$ sec

$x_f - x_0 = (6 \times 10^6$ m/sec$)$ $(5 \times 10^{-8}$ sec$)$
$\qquad - \frac{1}{2}(1.2 \times 10^{14}$ m/sec²$)$ $(5 \times 10^{-8}$ sec$)^2$

$\therefore \quad x_f - x_0 = .15$ m $= 15$ cm.

2. **(E)** The force the floor will exert upon the man will be the force due to gravity, 180 lb, minus the imaginary force due to the deceleration of the elevator.

$F^* = F_g - ma^* \qquad m = F_g/g$

$g = 32$ ft/sec² $\qquad F_g = 180$ lb

$a^* = 8$ ft/sec²

$\therefore F^* = 180$ lb $- [(180$ lb$)/(32$ ft/sec²$)]$
$\qquad \times (8$ ft/sec²$)$

$F^* = 135$ lb.

3. **(D)** Kepler's Laws of Planetary Motion are the following:
1. Each planet moves in an elliptical orbit with the Sun at one focus of the ellipse.
2. The line from the Sun to any planet sweeps out equal areas in equal times.
3. The squares of the sidereal periods of the several planets are proportional to the cubes of their mean distances from the Sun.
Therefore, by Law 3, above, T^2 is proportional to R^3 or $T \propto R^{3/2}$.

4. **(C)** By Hooke's Law (supplied in terms of Young's modulus), $F = -EA\frac{\Delta l}{l_0}$ where E is Young's modulus. Therefore, Young's modulus must have units equal to tensile strength divided by tensile strain.

5. **(C)**

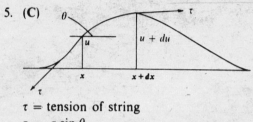

$\tau =$ tension of string

$\tau_u = \tau \sin \theta$

$\sin \theta \doteq \tan \theta = \partial u / \partial x$

$dF = [\tau_u]_{x+dx} - [\tau_u]_x$

$\qquad \doteq \frac{\partial}{\partial x} \left(\tau \frac{\partial u}{\partial x} \right) dx$

Thus $\theta dx \frac{\partial^2 u}{\partial t^2} = \frac{\partial}{\partial x} \left(\tau \frac{\partial u}{\partial x} \right)$

For a horizontal string and small amplitude τ is constant

$\theta (\partial 2u/\partial t^2) = \tau (\partial^2 u/\partial x^2)$

$\partial^2 u/\partial x^2 - 1c^2(\partial^2 u(\partial t^2) = 0$

$\therefore c = (\tau/\sigma)^{1/2}$.

6. **(E)** The velocity at which these two objects will roll depends upon how much of the potential energy will be transformed into rotational energy and how much into translational

$\frac{1}{2} Mv^2 + \frac{1}{2} I\omega^2 = Mgh$

where h is the height the bodies have dropped and v is the angular velocity of the object. For both $\omega = v/R$, where R is the radius. The moments of inertia are $\frac{2}{5} MR^2$ for a sphere of uniform density and $\frac{1}{2} MR^2$ for a cylinder of uniform density rolling along its axis.

Sphere: $\frac{1}{2} Mv^2 + \frac{1}{2}(\frac{2}{5} MR^2)(v/R)^2 = Mgh$

$$v = \sqrt{\frac{10}{7} gh}$$

Cylinder: $\frac{1}{2} Mv^2 + \frac{1}{2}(\frac{1}{2} MR^2)(v/R)^2 = Mgh$

$$v = \sqrt{\frac{4}{3} gh}$$

Therefore, the sphere is rolling faster than the cylinder and will reach the bottom first, independent of the mass and radius.

7. **(A)** By definition, a conservative field is one in which energy is conserved. That is, if you return to the same point you have the same energy at that point. This implies that the work done must be independent of the paths and dependent only upon the end points.

8. **(E)**

By conservation of momentum

$5 \text{kg-m/sec} = P \cos \theta$

$4 \text{kg-m/sec} = P \sin \theta$

$P^2 = 25 \,(\text{kg-m/sec})^2 + 16 \,(\text{kg-m/sec})^2$

$\therefore P = \sqrt{41} \text{ kg-m/sec}.$

9. **(B)** By universal gravitation the force between the two particles is GMm/r^2. Thus, the total kinetic energy available is GMm/d. Also, momentum must be conserved.

$mv_m = Mv_M$

$\frac{1}{2}(mv_m^2 + Mv_M^2) = GMm/d$

By manipulation

$v_M^2(1 + M/m) = 2Gm/d$

$v_m^2(1 + m/M) = 2GM/d$

$v_M^2 + v_m^2 + \frac{m}{M} v_m^2 + \frac{M}{m} v_M^2 = \frac{2G}{d}(M + m)$

$(v_M + v_m)^2 = \frac{2G}{d}(M + m).$

10. **(A)** The critical speed would be that speed such that the centrifugal force is equal to the gravitational force exerted on the block.

$mv^2/R = mg$

$v = \sqrt{Rg}.$

11. **(A)** To escape the velocity would have to be such that the kinetic energy would be greater than or equal to the change in potential energy between the surface and infinity.

$\frac{1}{2} mv^2 \geq GMm/R$

$v \geq \sqrt{2GM/R}.$

12. **(B)** If there is no external torque on the system, there must be conservation of angular momentum.

$m\omega_1 r_1^2 = m\omega_2 r_2^2$

$\omega_2 = \omega_1 (r_1/r_2)^2.$

13. **(A)** The kinetic energy of a body moving in a circle is

$T = \frac{1}{2} mr^2\omega^2$

$T_1 = \frac{1}{2} mr_1^2\omega_1^2$

$T_2 = \frac{1}{2} mr_2^2\omega_2^2$

$\dfrac{T_2}{T_1} = \dfrac{r_2^2\omega_2^2}{r_1^2\omega_1^2} = \dfrac{r_2^2[\omega_1(r_1/r_2)^2]^2}{r_1^2}$

$T_2/T_1 = (r_1/r_2)^2$

14. **(D)** Current is defined as the rate at which the charge is flowing. Thus, $Q = I\Delta t$.
$I = 5$ amp $= 5$ coulomb/sec. $\Delta t = 240$ sec. Therefore, $Q = 1200$ coulomb.

15. **(A)** ϕ is equal to the component of E normal to a surface times the area of the surface; that is, ϕ is equal to E times the cross-sectional area it passes through.

Cross-sectional area $= \pi R^2$

$\phi = \pi R^2 E$.

16. **(E)** Since the plates are moved apart by the use of insulated handles, the charge on the capacitor must remain constant. For a parallel plate capacitor C is proportional to A/l, where A is the area of the plate and l is the distance between the plates. Therefore, C must decrease. By definition, $C = Q/V$. Therefore, the voltage must increase.

17. **(A)** If the original resistance of the single wire is R, each piece will have a resistance $0.1R$. If these are then connected in parallel, the total resistance is

$1/R_t = 10(1/0.1\,R)$
$R_t = 0.01R$
$R_t/R = 0.01$.

18. **(E)** The effective value of a sinusoidal emf is its root mean square value.

$$v_{\text{eff}}^2 = \frac{\int_0^T v_m^2 \sin^2 \omega t \, dt}{T} = \tfrac{1}{2} v_m^2$$

$$v_{\text{eff}} = \frac{\sqrt{2}}{2} v_m.$$

19. **(E)** The potential difference is the work required to move a test charge from point A to B divided by the magnitude of the test charge.

$V = 2$ joules/20 coulomb
$V = 0.1$ joule/coulomb
one volt = one joule/coulomb
$V = 1 \times 10^{-1}$ volt.

20. **(C)** For a parallel plate capacitor $C = \varepsilon\varepsilon_0 A/l$, where ε is the relative dielectric constant.

$\varepsilon = 1$ for air. Thus,

$C_{\text{air}} = \varepsilon_0 A/l$

$C_{\text{mica}} = \varepsilon_{\text{mica}}\varepsilon_0 A/l = \varepsilon_{\text{mica}} C_{\text{air}}$

$= 6(15\,\mu\mu\text{f})$

$C_{\text{mica}} = 90\,\mu\mu\text{f}$.

TEST VII. CHEMISTRY

1.D	3.B	5.E	7.A	9.C	11.B	13.A	15.E
2.C	4.B	6.B	8.C	10.D	12.C	14.D	

TEST VII. EXPLANATORY ANSWERS

1. **(D)** This question is from basic chemistry. When an acidic solution is made *neutral* by the addition of base, the process is called neutralization. Options (A) and (B) involve changes in the oxidation-state of the chemicals while options (C) and (E) involve the formation of precipitates from solution.

2. **(C)** When a sample of water is placed in an electrical circuit the water is said to be *electrolyzed*. The action of the electricity converts water to hydrogen (H_2) and oxygen (O_2). These two molecules can then be reconverted to water.

3. **(B)** The candidate may remember that the action of a catalyst is *only to change the rate of a reaction*. Catalysts do not affect the products or the distribution of products at all.

4. **(B)** This is a question from the field of chemistry and concerns a type of behavior characteristic of *colloidal solutions*. These are not true solutions but dispersions of very very fine particles in a liquid so that the liquid appears clear but in actuality contains solid material. The effect described in the question is called the *Tyndall* effect.

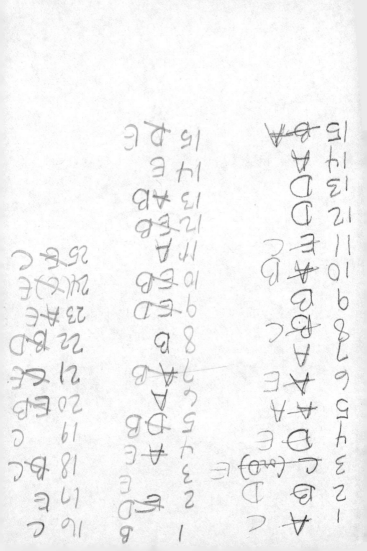

5. **(E)**   An electrolyte is a substance that when added to water will conduct an electric current (very pure water will not do this). In order to conduct the current it must: 1) dissolve and 2) carry an electrical charge (i.e., be ionic). Therefore the prime characteristic for an electrolyte is that it be ionic in solution.

6. **(B)**   This question is from chemistry and can be answered when one pictures the actions of molecules on a molecular level. They are continually vibrating and colliding. The addition of very fine particles will cause collisions between these particles and the molecules of the liquid resulting in the movement of the particles. This behavior is called *Brownian motion.*

7. **(A)**   All the formulae show four other atoms bound to the carbon atom. One can only deduce from this information that carbon has four combining sites.

8. **(C)**   A balanced chemical equation must have the same amount of each element on both sides. In choice (C) there are 3C, 8H, and 10 O on both sides of the equation.

9. **(C)**   Isomers are compounds having the same molecular formula, but a different structural and/or spatial arrangement. Options (B), (D), and (E) do not have the same formula. Option (A) has the same formula and the same structure.

10. **(D)**   This formula is not an alcohol. Alcohols are characterized by the presence of a carbinol group (C OH). The only formula which does not contain this group is the formula for methane.

11. **(B)**   Homologs are defined as members of a series of one type of compound, each adjacent member being increased in this case by an increment of CH_2.

12. **(C)**   A Lewis diagram is a convenient method for representing the number of electrons in the outer shell of an atom. The chemical symbol stands for the nucleus and all inner electrons. Orbital diagrams show something of the spatial arrangement of the electrons.

13. **(A)**   The only orbital diagram shown is that of the hydrogen atom. The hydrogen atom is also shown in a Lewis diagram.

14. **(D)**   Two dots between chemical symbols indicate covalent bonds.

15. **(E)**   More than two dots indicates multiple bonding.

SCORE YOURSELF

Compare your answers to the Correct Key Answers at the end of the Examination. To determine your score, count the number of correct answers in each test. Then count the number of incorrect answers. Subtract ¼ of the number of incorrect answers from the number of correct answers. Plot the resulting figure on the graph below by blackening the bar under each test to the point of your score. Plan your study to strengthen the weaknesses indicated on your scoring graph.

EXAM IV NATURAL SCIENCES	Very Poor	Poor	Average	Good	Excellent
GRAPH SELECTION 15 Questions	1-2	3-6	7-10	11-13	14-15
EXPERIMENT VALIDITY 16 Questions	1-3	4-6	7-11	12-14	15-16
UNDERSTANDING EXPERIMENTS 14 Questions	1-2	3-5	6-9	10-12	13-14
BIOLOGICAL SCIENCE 15 Questions	1-2	3-6	7-10	11-13	14-15
BIOLOGY 25 Questions	1-4	5-10	11-17	18-22	23-25
PHYSICS 20 Questions	1-3	4-8	9-14	15-17	18-20
CHEMISTRY 15 Questions	1-2	3-6	7-10	11-13	14-15

NATURAL SCIENCE GLOSSARY

This is some of the language you're likely to see on your examination. You may not need to know all the words in this carefully prepared glossary, but if even a few appear, you'll be that much ahead of your competitors. Perhaps the greater benefit from this list is the frame of mind it can create for you. Without reading a lot of technical text you'll steep yourself in just the right atmosphere for high test marks.

This glossary was created to help you master some of the key words you will meet in the Natural Science section of the test. You should know that astronomy is the study of celestial bodies, biology the study of living things, chemistry the study of the composition of different kinds of matter and the changes that happen to them, and physics the study of the actions of objects and the reasons behind their actions.

In the glossary, you will usually find a science in parenthesis after the word. This means that the word is by and large identified with that science. That does not mean that the word might not be used in other sciences, though. The word *element* refers to a chemical element and is used, of course, in connection with chemistry. But uranium is an element which is most important in nuclear fission, which is usually considered part of the field of physics.

You will notice that certain words or phrases have been italicized. These italicized words are defined in the glossary.

[A]

absolute zero (physics) The lowest temperature to which a gas can get. This is 460 degrees below zero on the *Fahrenheit* scale and 273 degrees below zero on the *centigrade* scale.

acceleration (physics) A change in the speed of an object. If the object goes faster, this is called positive acceleration. If the object goes slower, it is called negative acceleration.

acid (chemistry) A *compound* that dissolves in water, has a sour taste, and changes blue *litmus paper* to red.

alchemy (chemistry) The *theory* that less valuable metals can be transformed into gold or silver. This idea, popular during the Middle Ages, was false, but the *experiments* of alchemists laid the foundation of modern *chemistry*.

alkali (chemistry) A *base* that dissolves in water, has a bitter taste, and changes red *litmus paper* to blue.

alkaline (chemistry) The adjective form of *alkali*.

ampere (physics) A measurement of the *velocity* of electric current. It was named after a French scientist, Andre Marie Ampère.

Ampère, Andre Marie (physics) A French scientist (1775–1836) whose work and *theory* laid the foundation for the science of electrodynamics. His name lives on in the electrical measurement *ampere*, and its abbreviation, amp.

amphipods (biology) A *crustacean* group that includes sand fleas.

anatomy (biology) The study of the structure of living things. Usually anatomy refers to the structure of the human body.

anemone (biology) A sea animal that resembles the flower of the same name.

aphid (biology) A small insect which is destructive to crops. A fluid produced by aphids is eaten by ants.

aquatic (biology) An adjective referring to water, such as "aquatic sports" (diving, swimming, etc.)

Aristotle (biology) An ancient Greek philosopher whose active mind pondered all aspects of life and its processes. He is often called the "Father of Biology."

asteroids (astronomy) Small *planet*-like bodies that orbit around the sun.

astrology (astronomy) A false *theory* that the position of the stars, sun, moon and planets influence people's lives. Although this is false, the study of astrology was most helpful to the development of *astronomy*.

astronomer (astronomy) A person who studies the movements of *celestial* bodies.

astronomy The study of the movements of *celestial* bodies. This is a major science.

atmosphere (general) The air mass surrounding the earth.

atom (physics and chemistry) A small particle of matter. See *atomic energy*. Once it was thought that the atom was the smallest particle of matter that existed, but now it is known that atoms are made up of *protons*, *neutrons* and *electrons*.

atomic energy (physics) Power released when *atoms* are split or united. This is also called *nuclear* energy. Also see *nuclear fission* and *nuclear fusion*.

[B]

bacteria (biology) Tiny *organisms* with one *cell*.

bacteriology (biology) The study of *bacteria*. Bacteriology is a branch of *biology*.

base (chemistry) A compound that can combine with an *acid* to make a *salt*.

biochemistry (biology and chemistry) The study of the chemical makeup of *organisms*. This science is a branch of both *chemistry* and *biology*.

biology The study of living things. This is a major science.

botany (biology) The study of plant life. Botany is a branch of *biology*.

Brahe, Tycho (astronomy) A Danish *astronomer* (1546–1601) who made the first systematic study of the movement of *celestial* bodies. He is often referred to only as Tycho.

[C]

carbohydrate (biology) A food substance made up of *carbon*, *hydrogen* and *oxygen*.

carbon (chemistry) An important chemical *element*.

carbon dioxide (chemistry) A gas made up of *carbon* and *oxygen*.

celestial (astronomy) An adjective referring to the sky.

cell (biology) The basic and smallest part of living things.

centigrade (physics) A system of measurement of temperature. On the centigrade scale, the freezing point of water is zero degrees. The boiling point of water is 100 degrees. Another generally used temperature measurement is the *Fahrenheit* scale.

chemistry The study of the composition of different kinds of matter and the changes that happen to them. This is a major science.

chlorophyll (biology) The green coloring matter in the cells of living plants, caused by sunlight. Chlorophyll is the means by which all regular absorption and digestion of plant food is made.

chromosome (biology) The part of *cells* that determines heredity. Chromosomes contain *genes*.

colloid (chemistry) A substance that does not pass through *membranes* very quickly and may not pass through them at all.

compound (chemistry) The combining of two or more *elements* into a single unit.

conduction (physics) The process by which heat is carried from *molecule* to molecule.

conservation of energy (chemistry) The idea that *energy* changes its form but cannot be created or destroyed.

conservation of matter (chemistry) The idea that matter can change its form but cannot be created or destroyed.

constellation (astronomy) A particular grouping of stars.

copepod (biology) A small *crustacean* which is in the *plankton* family.

Copernicus, Nicholas (astronomy) A Polish astronomer (1473–1543) who put forth the idea that the earth moved through space. It was generally believed in this time that the earth was the center of the *universe* and did not move through space at all.

cosmic year (astronomy) The time it takes the sun to go around its *galaxy*.

crop rotation (biology) A method by which crops in an area are changed each year. This helps maintain the *fertility* of the soil.

crustacean (biology) A group of *aquatic* animals with a hard covering. They are often called ''shellfish.''

crystal (chemistry) The form many inanimate objects take.

[D]

Dalton, John (physics) An English scientist (1766–1844) who set forth the idea that matter was made up of *atoms*.

Darwin, Charles (biology) The English scientist (1809–1883) who developed a *theory* of *evolution*.

deforestation (biology) The process by which land is cleared of forests.

dorso-ventral (biology) An adjective referring to the dorsal vertebrae. These are a set of bones which are found in the spinal column of the human body near the chest.

[E]

eclipse (astronomy) The blotting out of light when one *celestial* object moves in front of another celestial object. When the moon comes between the earth and the sun it casts a shadow or an eclipse on part of the earth. During this time, the sun cannot be seen on that part of the earth. This is known as a *solar eclipse*. When the earth comes between the sun and the moon, it casts a shadow on the moon. The moon cannot be seen during this time. This is a *lunar eclipse*.

Einstein, Albert (physics) A German scientist (1879–1955) who lived the last years of his life in the United States. His *theories* changed the field of *physics*. He, more than any other scientist, was responsible for *nuclear fission*.

electron (physics) The smallest electrical charge known. It is part of every *atom*. See *proton* and *neutron*.

electronics (physics) The study of the motion of *electrons*.

element (chemistry) One of 102 known basic substances. These substances, or combinations of them, make up all matter as far as is known.

embryology (biology) The study of the early development of *organisms*, usually plant and animal.

energy (physics) The capacity to do *work*.

enzyme (biology) An *organic* substance that acts as an agent of change within cells.

eugenics (biology) A system it is thought will improve the human race by mating so-called superior men and women.

evolution, theory of   (biology) Usually refers to *Darwin's theory* that living things change from generation to generation. Furthermore, the living things that survive, according to Darwin, manage to do so because they have acquired certain characteristics that make them more powerful or adaptable than others of their kind.

evaporation   (biology and chemistry) The process by which liquids and solids change to gases.

experiment   (general) A test to see if an idea is true or false.

[F]

Fahrenheit   (physics) The system of measurement of temperature which is generally used in the United States. It was developed by Gabriel Fahrenheit (1686–1736), a German scientist. On the Fahrenheit scale, 32 degrees is the freezing point of water and 98.6 degrees is the average temperature of the human body. Another widely used temperature measurement is the *centigrade* scale.

Faraday, Michael   (physics) An English scientist (1791–1867) who discovered electricity could move through metal by the use of a magnet.

fertility   (biology) The ability to reproduce. See *reproduction*.

force   (physics) That which stops or creates motion, or changes the *velocity* of motion.

friction   (physics) The resistance objects have when they are moved across other objects.

fungi   (biology) A group of simple plants. Fungi do not have any leaves, flowers or color. Because they have no *chlorophyll*, they must feed on plants, animals or decaying matter.

fungicides   (biology) Chemicals which kill *fungi*.

[G]

galaxy   (astronomy) A grouping of stars. Our sun is a star in the galaxy called the Milky Way.

Galileo   (astronomy and physics) An Italian scientist (1564–1642) who made many contributions to science. He discovered that objects of different weights and shapes fall to the ground at the same rate of speed, attracted by *gravity*. He was a strong believer in *Copernicus'* theory that the earth moved in space and was persecuted for this belief.

gene   (biology) A part of the *cell* found in the chromosome. Genes determine the traits of *heredity*.

genetics   (biology) The study of the differences and similarities between living things and those living things that have reproduced them. See *reproduction*.

geology (general) The study of how the earth has changed since its beginning.

gravitation (physics and astronomy) The tendency of objects in space to move towards each other.

gravity (physics and astronomy) Usually the tendency of smaller objects to move towards the earth.

[H]

Harvey, William (biology) An English scientist (1578–1657) who discovered the way blood moves through the body.

heat (physics) The measurement of *kinetic energy*.

hemoglobin (biology) A substance that gives blood its red color.

heredity (biology) The way traits are carried from generation to generation.

hormone (biology) An *organic* substance produced by the body. Hormones are responsible for many bodily functions.

hydrogen (chemistry) One of the most important chemical *elements*.

hypothesis (general) An unproved explanation of something that has happened or might happen.

[I]

inorganic (biology) An adjective meaning "not organic." See *organic*.

insecticides (biology) Chemical combinations used to destroy harmful insects.

interstellar (astronomy) An adjective meaning "between the stars."

isotopes (physics) Atoms that belong to the same chemical element, but are different in weight or mass.

[K]

Kepler, Johannes (astronomy) A German *astronomer* (1571–1630) who made important discoveries about the *orbits* of *planets*.

kinetic energy (physics) *Energy* that is in motion. The motion of the baseball between the pitcher's hand and the catcher's glove is an example of kinetic energy. See *potential energy*.

Koch, Robert (biology) A German doctor (1843–1910) who studied bacteria. He and *Louis Pasteur* are considered the founders of the science of *bacteriology*.

[L]

Lamarck, Chevalier de (biology) A French scientist (1744–1829) who developed a *theory* of *evolution*. See *Darwin*.

Lavoisier, Antoine (chemistry) A French scientist (1743–1794) who made important discoveries concerning fire and *conservation of matter*.

light year (astronomy) The distance it takes light to travel through *interstellar* space in one year.

Linnaeus, Carolus (biology) A Swedish scientist (1707–1778) best-known for developing a system to name animals and plants.

litmus paper (chemistry) A special paper used by chemists to test for *acid* and *alkalies*.

lunar (astronomy) An adjective referring to the moon. A lunar *eclipse* is an eclipse of the moon. See *solar*.

[M]

marine (biology) An adjective meaning ''of the sea.'' Example: ''Fish are a form of marine life.''

molecule (physics and chemistry) A basic unit of matter made up of *atoms*.

mechanics (physics) The study of the effect force has on moving or motionless bodies. This is a branch of *physics*.

membrane (biology) Soft, thin sheet of tissue in an *organism*. A membrane acts as a wall between two different parts of the organism, or it covers a particular part of the organism.

Mendel, Gregor Johann (biology) An Austrian monk and scientist (1822–1844) who made important discoveries concerning *heredity*.

metabolism (biology) The process used by all living *organisms* to change food into tissue and *energy*.

mercury (chemistry) An important chemical *element*.

meteorology (general) A science that studies the weather and the *atmosphere*.

mollusks (biology) A family of animals usually found in water. Mollusks have no bones. Examples of mollusks are snails, oysters, and octopuses.

mutation (biology) A change from the parents in an offspring. If a rat was born with no tail although its parents had tails, this change would be a mutation.

[N]

nebula (astronomy) A cloudy and gaseous mass found in *interstellar* space.

neutron (physics and chemistry) A small particle that is part of the *atom* and has no electrical charge. See *electron* and *proton*.

Newton, Isaac (physics and astronomy) An English scientist (1642–1727) who made major discoveries in *astronomy* and *physics*. His most important work was in his study of *gravitation* and *optics*.

nuclear (physics) An adjective referring to the *nucleus* of the *atom*.

nuclear fission (physics) The splitting of an *atom* in order to produce *energy*.

nuclear fusion (physics) The joining together of light-weight *atoms* resulting in the releasing of *energy*.

nucleus (physics and chemistry) The center or core of an object, necessary to maintain human life.

[O]

observatory (astronomy) A specially constructed building containing one or more telescopes for observation of the heavens.

optics (physics) The study of light and its effect. Optics is a branch of *physics*.

orbit (astronomy) The route that an object in space (such as the moon) takes around another body (such as the earth).

organic (biology) An adjective referring to living things. See *inorganic*.

organism (biology) Living things, such as people, plants or animals.

oxide (chemistry) A compound made up of *oxygen* and another *element*. Water, for example, is a compound made up of 2 *atoms* of *hydrogen* for each atom of oxygen.

oxygen (chemistry) A very important chemical element. Oxygen, a gaseous element, makes up about 20% of air and is the supporter of ordinary combustion.

[P]

Pasteur, Louis (biology) A French scientist (1822–1895) who made major discoveries in *chemistry* and *biology*, especially in the control of many diseases. He and Robert Koch were the founders of the science of *bacteriology*.

physics The study of the action of objects and the reasons behind these actions.

phytogeographic map (biology) A map showing plant life.

Planck, Max (physics) A German scientist (1858–1947) who did notable work in *thermodynamics*.

planet (astronomy) A large body that moves around the sun. The earth is a planet.

plankton (biology) A group of sea life—both plant and animal—which drifts with tides and currents. Jellyfish are an example of plankton.

potential energy (physics) *Energy* that is available for use. The baseball in the pitcher's hand is an example of potential energy. It becomes *kinetic energy* when it is thrown.

Priestley, Joseph   (chemistry) The English chemist (1738–1804) who discovered *oxygen*.

primeval   (general) An adjective meaning "the first" or "early."

protein   (biology) A class of food necessary for life. Proteins build tissues and provide *energy*.

proton   (physics) An electrically charged particle found in all *atoms*. See *electron* and *neutrons*.

protoplasm   (biology) A substance necessary for life found in the *cells* of all *organisms*.

[R]

radio astronomy   (astronomy) The study of radio waves received from outer space.

regeneration   (biology) The capacity of an *organism* to create new parts of itself.

reproduction   (biology) The process by which *organisms* create offspring of their own species.

[S]

salinity   (chemistry) The degree of salt present. Usually refers to the amount of salt in a fluid.

salt   (biology) A substance that is formed when an *acid* is mixed with a *base*.

satellite   (astronomy) An object that *orbits* around a *planet*, such as a moon. In recent years, the earth has had man-made satellites.

soluble   (chemistry) Able to be dissolved in a fluid. See *solute, solvent* and *solution*.

solar   (astronomy) An adjective referring to the sun. A solar *eclipse* is an eclipse of the sun. See *lunar*.

solar system   (astronomy) The sun, the *planets*, *satellites*, and the *asteroids*.

solute   (chemistry) What is dissolved in a fluid to form a *solution*. See *solution*, *soluble*, and *solvent*.

solution   (chemistry) A solution occurs when a liquid, solvent or gas mixes completely in a fluid. For example, when sugar is completely dissolved in hot water, the result is a solution. See *solute*, *solvent*, and *soluble*.

solvent   (chemistry) The fluid in which a *solute* is dissolved to form a *solution*. Also see *soluble*.

sonic   (physics) An adjective referring to sound.

spawn   (biology) A noun referring to the eggs of certain *aquatic* animals, such as fish. Also a verb meaning to lay eggs, usually used in connection with fish.

stimulus   (general) That which brings a response. If a person is hungry, the sight of food might make his mouth water. The stimulus is food, and the response, the watering of the mouth.

substratum   (geology) A layer lying beneath the top layer.

supersonic   (physics) An adjective meaning "faster than sound."

[T, U]

theory (general) An unproved explanation of something that has happened or might happen.

thermodynamics (physics) The study of the actions of *heat*.

ultrasonic (physics) An adjective referring to sound no person can hear because of its high frequency.

unicellular (biology) An adjective meaning "one-celled." See *cell*.

universe (astronomy) All things that exist in space taken as a whole.

[V]

velocity (physics) The rate of motion.

Vesalius, Andreas (biology) An Italian scientist (1514–1564) who studied the body. His discoveries were so important that he is often referred to as "The Father of Anatomy." See *anatomy*.

virus (biology) A tiny germ that attacks body *cells* and causes disease.

vitamins (biology) Name for many special substances found in food which are necessary for the operation of particular functions of the body and to maintain health.

[W, X, Y, Z]

water table (general) The level nearest to the surface of the ground where water is found.

work (physics) In science, work is what occurs when a *force* moves an object.

zoology (biology) The study of animals. This science is a branch of *biology*.

PART SIX

Social Sciences - History

A Verisimilar Examination

Glossary

6

THE GENERAL EXAMINATION IN SOCIAL SCIENCES-HISTORY

If you want a preview of your exam, look these questions over carefully. We did ... as we compiled them from official announcements and various other sources. First try the "mini-exam," then the complete Verisimilar Exam that follows.

A MINI- GENERAL EXAMINATION

This chapter presents a miniature General Examination. The "mini-exam" contains good samples of the various types of questions you may expect to encounter. Our purpose is to offer you a bird's eye view of the Social Sciences-History Examination. The sample questions show you the subjects that will be included, the different types of questions, and the levels of difficulty you may expect.

This examination is designed to test your knowledge of the subject matter of history, geography, economics, government, anthropology, sociology, and social psychology. You will not be questioned on the content of any specific course of study, so your knowledge could have been acquired from many other sources. If you have read widely, seen films, watched educational television, made observations of our culture and discussed these things with others, you have been preparing yourself for this examination. The time limit for this exam is 90 minutes and it contains about 150 questions. About two-thirds of the questions deal with the social sciences. The remaining one-third deal with history: United States history, European history since the Renaissance, and contemporary world history.

ANALYSIS OF TYPICAL QUESTIONS

Many of the questions merely test your factual knowledge. Others supply information and ask you to interpret it. You might be given an excerpt from a speech or a document, a statement summarizing a point of view, or a description of a movement or a period of history. Then you will be asked to interpret its meaning or significance by making reasonable inferences from the facts supplied. Here's a rather difficult question of this type, followed by a reasonable interpretation.

"He has forbidden the Governors to pass laws of immediate and pressing importance, unless suspended in their operation till his assent should be obtained; and when so suspended, he has utterly neglected to attend to them."

This quotation was most probably taken from the

(A) Constitution of British Commonwealth of Nations
(B) American Declaration of Independence
(C) French Declaration of Rights of Man
(D) Proclamation of Kerensky Government of Russia
(E) Manchu Revolutionary Proclamation

The purpose of the question is not to test your memory of specific items in documents, but to determine whether you can read a quotation carefully, evaluate it in terms of information you have, and apply these skills to arrive at the correct answer. First, you should determine the key ideas expressed in the quotation:
(1) the ruler's suspension of the rights of the Governors to enact legislation,
(2) the ruler's neglect when, after attaining suspension, he neglected to act.

Next, you must bring into play what you know about the five documents listed as choices. Hence, by deduction and the process of elimination, you should discern the correct answer, the document to which all of the key ideas apply. Of the five choices, (A) must be eliminated, since no constitution would be likely to contain such inflammatory statements. Choice (C) would be incorrect, since the France of that period had no Governors. Choice (E) is clearly incorrect because China had an Empress at the time the proclamation was issued. Therefore, the proclamation could not possibly use the pronoun "he" in referring to the ruler. Choices (B) and (D) are both possible; but (B) is the correct answer.

You can expect to find, in addition to the example just given, questions based on the statements of several speakers, or on a longer excerpt. You will be tested on your ability to apply the knowledge you possess.

Other questions may ask you to define a term or demonstrate your understanding of a concept. Question 8, for example, asks if you understand the term "conditioned reflex," and question 4 measures your grasp of the tenets of the socialist movement. Question 3, on the contrary, requires you to identify the term that defines a particular government action, and question 9 tests your knowledge of a method employed by social scientists.

This examination tests your knowledge in many other ways as well. Questions like number 5 measure your grasp of theories or bodies of work. Also, some questions are based on visual materials, such as cartoons. Other visuals you might encounter are maps, tables and graphs.

SUMMARY OF SOCIAL SCIENCES–HISTORY EXAMINATION

The questions in this test are based on the contents of many subject areas, including history, geography, economics, government, anthropology, and social psychology. Because of this wide coverage, you should not expect to make a perfect score. The purpose of the examination is to let you show your understanding of history and the social sciences; questions can be answered with knowledge gained from general reading and observation.

A MINI-EXAM IN HISTORY

TIME: 8 Minutes . 10 Questions.

DIRECTIONS: For each question in this test, read carefully the stem and the five lettered choices that follow. Choose the answer which you consider correct or most nearly correct. Mark the answer sheet for the letter you have chosen: A, B, C, D, or E.

Correct and explanatory answers are provided at the end of the exam.

1. In the transfer of power in 1800 from Federalists to Republicans, the Federalists still maintained their control over the

   (A) Senate
   (B) State governments
   (C) House of Representatives
   (D) Presidency
   (E) federal courts

2. One reason why the United States declared war on England rather than on France in 1812 was that

   (A) Napoleon held us to the Treaty of Alliance of 1778
   (B) Napoleon had scrupulously respected our rights as neutrals
   (C) New England shipowners and merchants clamored for war with England
   (D) western expansionists wanted to annex Canada
   (E) French naval power in the Caribbean was too great for us to overcome

3. Which one of the following was the primary issue in the decision in Marbury vs. Madison?

   (A) Could the Supreme Court hear an appeal from a state court?
   (B) Could a defeated President appoint "midnight judges"?
   (C) Could the federal government tax a state agency?
   (D) Was Section 13 of the Judiciary Act of 1789 constitutional?
   (E) Could a justice participate in a case in which he was an interested party?

4. Which one of the following statements is true of the Monroe Doctrine?

   (A) It was of long range rather than immediate significance.
   (B) It forestalled a planned intervention by the Concert of Europe.
   (C) It received the formal assent of Congress.
   (D) It led to the abandonment by the European powers of their colonies in the Western Hemisphere.
   (E) Its basic outlines had been opposed by the British whom Monroe had consulted in 1823.

5. The Treaty of Guadalupe-Hidalgo was concerned with the

   (A) land ceded by Mexico to the United States
   (B) Panama Canal Zone
   (C) intervention of the United States in Cuba
   (D) Venezuelan boundary question
   (E) building of the Southern Pacific Railroad

6. Which one of the following statements is *not* true of American foreign relations in the post-Civil War period?

   (A) The activities of Fenians along the Canadian border embarrassed our relations with Canada.
   (B) The outbreak of a Cuban rebellion in 1868 threatened to involve the United States in war with Spain.
   (C) Secretary of State Seward pursued a vigorous expansionist policy.
   (D) President Grant showed no interest in an expansionist policy.
   (E) President Cleveland strongly supported a unilateral interpretation of the Monroe Doctrine.

7. President Cleveland dealt with the question of the annexation of Hawaii by

   (A) restoring Queen Liliuokalani to the throne
   (B) urging the Senate to ratfiy the treaty of annexation
   (C) offering to buy Hawaii from the Queen
   (D) withdrawing the treaty of annexation from the Senate
   (E) ordering fleet units to oppose European landings

8. Which one of the following statements regarding the Domesday Book is correct?

   (A) It was similar to our census taken every ten years.
   (B) It recorded the names of those who bound themselves to William by the Salisbury Oath.
   (C) It perpetuated the literary heritage begun by the authors of the Anglo-Saxon Chronicle.
   (D) It provided the vehicle through which the subject of the Mystery Plays was handed down to the learned populace.
   (E) It was a key to deciphering Middle English.

9. Which one of the following occurred after the fall of Constantinople?

   (A) The Battle of Tours
   (B) The Crusades
   (C) The Model Parliament
   (D) The Hegira
   (E) The expulsion of the Moors from Spain

10. Which one of the following statements regarding the position of the serf in 16th century western Europe is correct?

    (A) He was required to work for his lord at all times.
    (B) He could not be deprived of the right to cultivate land for his own benefit.
    (C) He lacked security because he could be sold to another master.
    (D) He was like a tenant farmer in his relationship to the lord.
    (E) He was without standing in the Church courts.

ANSWER SHEET FOR THIS MINI-EXAMINATION

CORRECT ANSWERS FOR THIS MINI-EXAMINATION

Now compare your answers with these Correct Key Answers. If your answers differ from these, go back and study the Practice Questions to see where and how you made your mistakes. In doing this, the following Explanatory Answers should prove helpful. They provide concise clarifications of the basic points behind the Key Answers. Even where your Key Answers are the same as ours, go over the explanations carefully because they may be quite useful in helping you pick up extra points on the exam.

| 1.E | 3.D | 5.A | 7.D | 9.E |
| 2.D | 4.A | 6.D | 8.B | 10.D |

EXPLANATORY ANSWERS FOR THIS MINI-EXAMINATION

1. *(E)* The federal courts were staffed by Federalist judges who received their lifetime appointments prior to 1800. After the Federalist defeat in the election of 1800, but before Jefferson's inauguration, President John Adams appointed many Federalists to the federal bench. These were the so-called "midnight judges."

2. *(D)* In 1811-12 a group of Congressmen representing the West gained control of the House of Representatives. Their two most important leaders were Henry Clay and John C. Calhoun. They advocated a war with England so as to have an opportunity to annex Canada and to punish England for encouraging Indian raids along the frontier.

3. *(D)* In his decision in Marbury vs. Madison, Chief Justice John Marshall held that the Supreme Court had the power to pass on the constitutionality of Congressional legislation. This is the doctrine of judicial review.

4. *(A)* The Monroe Doctrine first became a significant factor in American foreign policy when it was applied by President James K. Polk to justify his expansionist policies.

5. *(A)* The Treaty of Guadalupe-Hidalgo (1848) ended the Mexican War. Under the terms of the treaty, Mexico was compelled to cede vast territories to the United States.

6. *(D)* President Ulysses S. Grant attempted to annex the Dominican Republic.

7. *(D)* When he took office, President Grover Cleveland followed his anti-imperialist tendencies by withdrawing the Treaty of Annexation from the Senate. The Treaty was not ratified until the administration of William McKinley.

8. *(B)* The Domesday Book was a survey of all the land and population in England. William I had it prepared so that he would be able to govern more effectively. William also compelled all large landholders to take an oath to support him. This was the Salisbury Oath.

9. *(E)* The Moors were expelled from Spain in 1492. Constantinople fell to the Turks in 1453. The dates of the other events follow: The Hegira, 622; The Battle of Tours, 732; The Crusades, 1096-1291; and the Model Parliament, 1282,

10. *(D)* With the development of a cash economy, the status of the peasant changed from that of serf to tenant farmer.

SOCIAL SCIENCES - HISTORY
FIFTH VERISIMILAR EXAMINATION

This professionally-written Examination enables you to display and exercise the important test-taking abilities leading to high scores . . . judgment, coolness, and flexibility. The various Tests fairly represent the actual exam. They should help in jogging your memory for all kinds of useful and relevant information which might otherwise be lost to you in achieving the highest exam rating possible.

Time allowed for the entire Examination: 1½ Hours

In order to create the climate of the actual exam, that's exactly what you should allow yourself . . . no more, no less. Use a watch to keep a record of your time, since it might suit your convenience to try this practice exam in several short takes.

ANALYSIS AND TIMETABLE: VERISIMILAR EXAMINATION V.			
It is well known that examiners like to experiment with various types of questions, so the test you take may be slightly different in form or content. However, we feel certain that if you have mastered each subject covered here, you will be well on your way to scoring high.			
SUBJECT TESTED	*Time Allowed*	*SUBJECT TESTED*	*Time Allowed*
SOCIAL SCIENCE			
Government	15 Minutes	Sociology	30 Minutes
Economics	15 Minutes		
HISTORY			
American History	20 Minutes	World History	10 Minutes

ANSWER SHEET FOR VERISIMILAR EXAMINATION V.

TEST I. GOVERNMENT

TEST II. ECONOMICS

TEST III. SOCIOLOGY

TEST IV. AMERICAN HISTORY

TEST V. WORLD HISTORY

PART I. SOCIAL SCIENCE

TEST I. GOVERNMENT

TIME: 15 Minutes. 22 Questions.

DIRECTIONS: For each of the following questions, select the choice which best answers the question or completes the statement.

1. Which one of the following is *incorrect* with regard to congressional organization and procedure?

   (A) In each House, one-fifth of the members present are guaranteed the right to demand a record vote on any question.
   (B) The only congressional officers that are mentioned in the Constitution are the Speaker of the House of Representatives, the Vice-President, and the President Pro-Tempore.
   (C) There is not a word in the Constitution about the committee structure of Congress.
   (D) The seniority system determines committee chairmanships.
   (E) Each House may punish its members for disorderly behavior or may, by a majority vote, expel a member.

2. Under the United States Constitution no state may, without the consent of Congress,

   (A) tax business enterprise
   (B) regulate public utilities
   (C) enter into agreements or compacts with another state
   (D) establish a militia
   (E) determine administrative personnel for its educational system

3. Under existing budgetary procedures, the President of the United States of America

   (A) may veto items in appropriation bills
   (B) may reduce but not eliminate items from appropriation bills
   (C) must accept or reject appropriation bills in their entirety
   (D) may veto items in appropriation bills for expenditures other than military purposes

   (E) may veto only congressional additions to his programs

4. Which one of the following is *incorrectly* matched with a political principle he espoused?

   (A) Rousseau—Popular Sovereignty
   (B) Hegel—Totalitarianism
   (C) Hobbes—War of All vs. All
   (D) Nietzsche—Superiority of the Elite
   (E) Locke—Proletarianism

5. In which one of the following are the items regarding the United Nations *incorrectly* paired?

   (A) Uniting for Peace Resolution—Right of the General Assembly to act because of a Security Council veto
   (B) UNESCO—Rehabilitation of Korea following the Korean War
   (C) Procedural Matters—Vote of any seven members of the Security Council
   (D) Trusteeship Council — Supervision of designated territories whose peoples have not attained self-government
   (E) International Development Association —Assist backward countries in their economic growth

6. Which of the following decisions of the Supreme Court during the incumbency of Chief Justice John Marshall declared an Act of Congress to be unconstitutional?

   (A) Fletcher v. Peek
   (B) McCulloch v. Maryland
   (C) Dartmouth College v. Woodward
   (D) Marbury v. Madison
   (E) Gibbons v. Ogden

7. The Smith Act of 1940

   (A) requires registration as alien representatives by those who are in the employ of a foreign country
   (B) compels American Communists to renounce their U.S. citizenship
   (C) requires Communist and Communist-front organizations to register with the government
   (D) forbids the use of government mediation services to organizations whose officials do not sign the oath of allegiance
   (E) makes it a criminal offense to advocate or teach the overthrow of the government by force or violence

8. Which one of the following was the first official step taken by the United States in support of resistance to Communist aggression?

   (A) Joint action with the Allies in support of Italy's claims against Yugoslavia
   (B) Secretary of State Marshall's plan to strengthen Western Europe
   (C) President Truman's plan to aid Greece and Turkey
   (D) The signing of the North Atlantic Alliance
   (E) The breaking of the Berlin blockade

9. With respect to the nomination and election of presidential candidates, the United States Constitution

   (A) directs that the convention system be used for nomination
   (B) provides for direct popular election of presidential electors
   (C) provides that nominations be made by either party conventions or primaries
   (D) makes no provision other than the electoral system
   (E) forbids popular election of the President

10. The Constitution of the United States forbids any amendment which would

    (A) deprive a state, without its consent, of equal suffrage in the Senate
    (B) permit the formation of a new state within the jurisdiction of another state without the consent of its legislature
    (C) authorize a state to enter into a treaty with a foreign power

    (D) change the procedure for amendment set forth in the Constitution
    (E) affect interstate contracts

11. Which one was *not* a result of the British-French-Israeli action against Egypt in October 1956?

    (A) It resulted in a deadlock in the U.N. because of the Soviet veto.
    (B) It caused a drastic decline in British influence in the Middle East.
    (C) It increased United States and Soviet influence in the area.
    (D) It increased the influence of President Nasser with the Arab masses.
    (E) It temporarily exacerbated relations between the United States and Britain.

12. Which one of the following does *not* require the President's signature?

    (A) a joint resolution
    (B) a pardon
    (C) a private bill
    (D) a public bill
    (E) a proposed amendment to the Constitution

13. Presidential electors in the United States must vote for their party's presidential candidate

    (A) because of recent federal legislation
    (B) as the result of a Supreme Court decision
    (C) if legislation of their state so prescribes
    (D) since the adoption of the 12th Amendment
    (E) at all times

14. Which of the following was *least* in accord with Communist principles?

    (A) Gosplan
    (B) NEP
    (C) Comintern
    (D) Five-Year Plan
    (E) Collectivization

15. New Deal economic policies most closely reflected the principles of

    (A) Arthur F. Burns
    (B) Alfred Hayek
    (C) John M. Keynes
    (D) Ludwig von Mises
    (E) Paul Samuelson

16. Which one of the following is generally characteristic of modern underdeveloped countries?

    (A) Rising nationalism, population problems, middle class philosophy
    (B) Low savings rate, inequality of wealth, need for land reform
    (C) Poor endowment of natural resources, failure of the wealthy to invest in manufacturing, security of foreign investments
    (D) Desire for Western material goods, large role of government investment, full utilization of manpower
    (E) Overpopulation, full utilization of manpower, security of foreign investments

17. The Rules Committee of the House of Representatives is the most powerful committee of that branch of Congress by virtue of the fact that

    (A) the Speaker of the House is chairman of the Rules Committee
    (B) it is the only committee of Congress composed exclusively of members of the majority party
    (C) it ordinarily decides when to call up or to reject bills for consideration by the House
    (D) it includes the floor leaders of both major parties
    (E) it has unlimited delaying power

18. Two international agencies of the United Nations which did not exist under the League of Nations are

    (A) a Trusteeship Council and an International Labor Office
    (B) an Economic and Social Council and an International Court of Justice
    (C) an International Court of Justice and a Trusteeship Council
    (D) an International Labor Office and an Educational, Scientific and Cultural Council
    (E) an Educational, Scientific and Cultural Council and an Economic and Social Council

19. The Supreme Court of the United States

    (A) has the right to reverse decisions previously handed down by the Court

    (B) may deal directly with a problem even before it is faced with it in the tangible form of a legal controversy
    (C) must avoid passing judgment on federal laws that state courts have declared contrary to the Constitution
    (D) must muster a two-thirds vote of its membership to declare a law unconstitutional
    (E) has no original jurisdiction in cases with a state as parties

20. The British government differs from that of the United States in that its powers cannot be expanded by

    (A) laws passed by Parliament
    (B) customs and practices
    (C) judicial decisions
    (D) a specific process of amending the Constitution
    (E) administrative usage

21. The following problems were common to the post-war settlements of World War I and World War II *except*

    (A) the Italo-Yugoslav boundary
    (B) the Polish boundaries
    (C) Russian intransigence at post–war conferences
    (D) reparations from the defeated countries
    (E) realization of nationalistic sentiment

22. Which one of the following statements is *incorrect* concerning the process of amending the United States Constitution?

    (A) Of the two methods of proposing amendments to the Constitution, only one, proposal by Congress, has ever been employed.
    (B) If a state rejects an amendment it cannot reverse its action.
    (C) Congress may fix a time limit of seven years in which the necessary number of states must ratify an amendment if it is to go into effect.
    (D) Of the two methods of ratifying amendments, ratification by conventions has been employed but once.
    (E) Petition of two-thirds of the state legislatures is necessary.

END OF TEST

TEST II. ECONOMICS

TIME: 15 Minutes. 23 Questions.

DIRECTIONS: For each of the following questions, select the choice which best answers the question or completes the statement.

1. The most fundamental fact that economics is concerned about is
   (A) the problems of poverty
   (B) the control of goods and services produced
   (C) the reality of scarcity
   (D) the taxation of recipients of income
   (E) the market structure of an economy

2. If we assume that price decreases as total expenditures increase, we may conclude that
   (A) elasticity of demand is greater than one
   (B) elasticity of demand is less than one
   (C) elasticity of demand is equal to one
   (D) all of the above are true
   (E) none of the above is true

3. Microeconomics is concerned about
   (A) an overall view of the functioning of an economic system
   (B) determination of distribution of income
   (C) the aggregate levels of income, employment, and output
   (D) the prediction of specific demands in a sector of the economy
   (E) an examination of specific economic units that constitute an economic system

4. The law of increasing costs states which one of the following?
   (A) If the prices of other resources used in the production of goods increases, the price of the production of a specific good will increase at the same rate.
   (B) If the economy wants to produce more of a specific good, it must sacrifice larger quantities of other goods to do so.
   (C) The total of the costs of producing a specific good will be increased to the point of surpassing the current market price of such a good.
   (D) The sum of the costs of producing a specific good will rise relative to the price of all other goods
   (E) None of the above.

5. Of the following, which is not one of the market models viewed from the seller's side of the market?
   (A) pure competition
   (B) monopoly
   (C) capitalism
   (D) monopolistic competition
   (E) oligopsony

6. Of the following, which one is a characteristic of monopolistic competition?
   (A) standardized product
   (B) strong feeling of mutual interdependence
   (C) paucity of firms
   (D) comparatively easy entry
   (E) little non-price competition

Questions 7-8 are based on the diagram below.

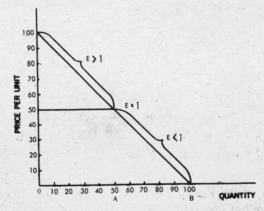

Letter E represents the elasticity of demand.

7. Assuming there is no cost of production, in order to obtain the greatest total revenue the seller will try to sell
   (A) at the highest possible price
   (B) the largest possible quantity
   (C) where e is greater than one
   (D) where e is less than one
   (E) where e is equal to one

8. The maximum possible total revenue is
   (A) 240
   (B) 100
   (C) 1,000

(D) 120
(E) 250

9. In which one of the following cases will the effect upon equilibrium price be indeterminable?

   (A) Demand rises and supply remains constant
   (B) Supply rises and demand falls
   (C) Demand rises and supply also rises
   (D) Demand rises and supply falls
   (E) Supply falls and demand is constant

Questions 10-12 are based on the following data for cotton:

QUANTITY DEMANDED (Bales)	PRICE $	QUANTITY SUPPLIED
450	50	770
500	40	730
560	30	680
610	20	610
670	10	570

10. Equilibrium price is

    (A) 10
    (B) 30
    (C) 40
    (D) 20
    (E) indeterminable from given data

11. Assume that the government imposes a minimum price of $40 per bale.

    (A) A shortage of cotton will result.
    (B) Producers of the cotton will not be able to sell all of their cotton.
    (C) Purchasers would prefer to buy more cotton than is being supplied.
    (D) Producers of the cotton will make a reduction in the factors of production employed in the production of cotton.
    (E) Either A or C will be true.

12. If the government withdraws the $40 price support, then

    (A) the price of cotton will increase
    (B) the quantity demanded will fall
    (C) the producers will continue to sell at $40
    (D) supply will continue to exceed demand
    (E) the quantity supplied will decrease

13. In the following diagram, if the supply curve moves from S to S¹, there has occurred

(A) an increase in supply
(B) a decrease in supply
(C) a decrease in quantity supplied
(D) an increase in quantity supplied
(E) a decrease in the quality of the good

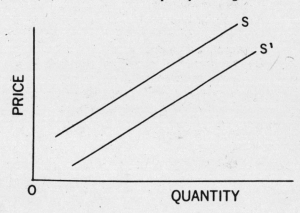

14. A consumer will be maximizing his utility if he allocated his money income so that
    (A) the marginal utility of the last unit of each product consumed is equal
    (B) the gained marginal utility from the last dollar spent on each purchased product is the same
    (C) elasticity of demand is the same for all purchased products
    (D) total utility gained from each product consumed is the same
    (E) total utility gained from all products consumed is the same

15. The substitution effect works to encourage a consumer to purchase more of a product when the price of that good is falling because
    (A) the consumer's real income has increased
    (B) the consumer's real income has decreased
    (C) the product is now less expensive than before
    (D) other products are now less expensive than before
    (E) the consumer's taste has changed

16. Of the following, which is *not* an essential assumption of the marginal utility theory of consumer demand?
    (A) Small income of the consumer
    (B) Rationality of the consumer
    (C) The fact that goods and services have a price
    (D) The fact that as more goods and services are purchased by the consumer, these goods and services yield decreasing amounts of marginal utility
    (E) Either D or C

17. Assume that as the price of product A decreases, the demand for product B increases. It can then be concluded that
    (A) A and B are substitute goods
    (B) A and B are complementary goods
    (C) A is an inferior good
    (D) B is an inferior good
    (E) Both A and B are superior goods

Questions 18-20 are based on the following diagram:

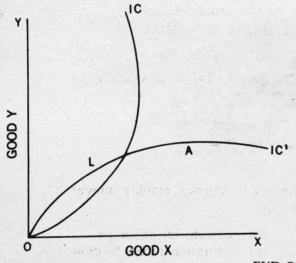

18. If curve IC represents the income consumption curve, then we can conclude that
    (A) X only is an inferior good
    (B) Y only is an inferior good
    (C) both X and Y are inferior goods
    (D) X is superior good
    (E) no conclusions are possible

19. If we assume that curve IC′ is the income consumption curve, it can be concluded that
    (A) only Y is an inferior good
    (B) neither Y nor X is an inferior good
    (C) only X is an inferior good
    (D) X is inferior but Y is a superior good
    (E) both Y and X are inferior goods

20. On curve IC′, there is a negative income effect
    (A) beyond point L
    (B) between points O and L
    (C) beyond point A
    (D) between LA only
    (E) between all points from O to A

21. Elasticity of demand depends on
    (A) income elasticity of demand
    (B) the elasticity of substitution
    (C) A together with B
    (D) cost of the goods on market
    (E) none of the above

22. The average revenue curve of a firm is
    (A) the curve representing the cost per unit of output
    (B) the same as the demand curve of consumers for the firm's product
    (C) total receipts realized by the firm
    (D) A and B
    (E) B and C

23. Of the following, which one constitutes an implicit cost to a firm?
    (A) Profits realized from current production
    (B) Payments made on leased equipment
    (C) Taxes paid to a local municipality for real estate
    (D) Salaries paid to its legal consultants
    (E) Depreciation charges on company-owned equipment

END OF TEST

TEST III. SOCIOLOGY

TIME: 30 Minutes. 50 Questions.

DIRECTIONS: For each of the following questions, select the choice which best answers the question or completes the statement.

Correct and explanatory answers are provided at the end of the exam. After you have completed the entire exam, read the explanations carefully. They'll reinforce your strengths and pinpoint your weaknesses so that you know just what to study to raise your score.

1. Avoiding conflict by recruiting potential or existing leaders of the opposition is a technique known as

   (A) premption
   (B) co-optation
   (C) foreclosure
   (D) isolation
   (E) assignation

2. Which one of the following is not generally considered a form of social sanction?

   (A) taxes
   (B) imprisonment
   (C) Presidential citations
   (D) "black ball"
   (E) ostracism

3. In sociometric studies, the correspondence between ego's perceptions of the choices and actual choices of others could be best employed as a measure of which of the following?

   (A) group cohesion
   (B) identification with the group
   (C) social empathy
   (D) social distance
   (E) discrimination

4. Which of the following is the *second* largest religious grouping in the world?

   (A) Islam
   (B) Taoism
   (C) Buddhism
   (D) Hinduism
   (E) Judaism

5. Gerhard Lenski and others maintain that, in America, ethnic groups as primary reference groups give way to

   (A) social class identification
   (B) urban or rural identification
   (C) occupational identification
   (D) religious identification
   (E) generational identification

6. As compared to medieval times which one of the following functions of the church has remained most constant today?

    (A) artistic functions
    (B) scholarly functions
    (C) governmental functions
    (D) educational functions
    (E) ethical functions

7. Which one of the following single indicators would give the best prediction of a person's reputational social class position in the United States?

    (A) religion
    (B) neighborhood of residence
    (C) interests
    (D) occupation
    (E) ancestry

8. Which one of the following culture-groups displays the most matriarchal authority structure?

    (A) traditional Chinese
    (B) Iroquois
    (C) ancient Hebrew
    (D) suburban middle-class American
    (E) lower-class American Negro

9. Which one of the following would NOT constitute ''cross-pressures'' on an American voter?

    (A) working-class occupation; rural background
    (B) Democratic voting history; anti-labor attitudes
    (C) white-collar job; Catholic church-goer
    (D) Jewish religion; Democratic spouse
    (E) friends Democratic; family Republican

10. The Calvinists Weber wrote of were in Riesman's terminology

    (A) tradition-directed
    (B) outer-directed
    (C) inner-directed
    (D) other-directed
    (E) self-directed

11. A society's resistance to social change is likely to be negatively related to its

    (A) integration
    (B) tightness of structure
    (C) isolation
    (D) stress on conformity
    (E) cultural base

12. The turn-of-the-century Prohibitionists and pre-Civil War abolitionists exemplify which type of social movement below?

    (A) Expressive
    (B) Reform
    (C) Utopian
    (D) Revolutionary
    (E) Resistance

13. Ethology can best be described as

    (A) a branch of comparative psychology
    (B) a branch of anthropology devoted to comparative and descriptive studies of different cultures
    (C) the idealistic (as opposed to materialist) branch of the sociology of knowledge
    (D) the field of social history which attempts to study the *ethos* of a particular era
    (E) the branch of sociology concerned with ethnic relations

14. Family dissolution by divorce is relatively——————for Protestants as compared to Catholics; dissolution by desertion or separation relatively ——————

    (A) frequent-frequent   (D) infrequent-infrequent
    (B) frequent-infrequent   (E) frequent-equal
    (C) infrequent-frequent

15. When Hefner catalogues *ad tedium* discrepancies between American sex practices and state laws, we have examples of the conflict between

    (A) virtue and hypocrisy   (D) folkways and mores
    (B) law and sociology   (E) nature and nurture
    (C) ideal culture and real culture

16. The divorce rate in the United States was highest in which one of the following years?

    (A) 1895   (B) 1920   (C) 1936   (D) 1944   (E) 1953

17. Which one of the following was not among the positive checks on population control listed by Malthus?

    (A) famine   (D) plague
    (B) contraception   (E) great towns
    (C) war

18. The region of the United States with the highest murder rate is the

    (A) West   (D) Midwest
    (B) Southwest   (E) Northeast
    (C) Southeast

19. In a society with a high sex ratio, possession of multiple wives is probably a

    (A) functional adaptation to an excess of females
    (B) functional alternative to male infanticide
    (C) form of conspicuous consumption, in Veblen's sense
    (D) mark of low status
    (E) widespread phenomenon

20. According to Max Weber, the Calvinist ethic gave rise to

    (A) persecution of heretics
    (B) autocratic political institutions
    (C) empirical science
    (D) capitalistic economic institutions
    (E) rigidity of thought

21. Which one of the following is *not* related to marital happiness?

    (A) financial status *per se*
    (B) church membership
    (C) higher education
    (D) early sex instruction
    (E) small town or rural background

22. Culture lag refers to

    (A) the temporal gap between acceptance of a trend by elite culture and its acceptance by mass culture
    (B) the difference between the content, at any one time, of the elite and mass cultures
    (C) the gap at any one time between material culture and non-material culture, caused by more rapid change in the former
    (D) the gap between culture's aspirations and its accomplishments at a given time
    (E) the gap at any one time between material culture and non-material culture, caused by more rapid change in the latter

23. An authoritarian personality is characterized in part by condemnation of

    (A) primary groups
    (B) minority groups
    (C) secondary groups
    (D) in-groups
    (E) out-groups

24. The opposite of the underdog effect of preelection polls on election results is

    (A) the halo effect
    (B) the bandwagon effect
    (C) the Doppler effect
    (D) the serendipity effect
    (E) the top-dog effect

25. Which one of the following is almost always present in marital discord?

    (A) alcoholism
    (B) physiologically-based sexual difficulties
    (C) psychologically- and culturally-based sexual difficulties
    (D) in-law problems
    (E) financial difficulties

26. The process in which one cultural group takes over and incorporates selected cultural elements from another group with which it is in contact is called

    (A) acculturation
    (B) assimilation
    (C) amalgamation
    (D) invasion
    (E) adoption

27. The phrase *marginal man* refers to
    (A) an inadequately socialized individual
    (B) an individual who shares in two distinct cultures
    (C) a homosexual
    (D) an individual without group affiliations
    (E) an individual ostracized by his cultural group

28. Relative deprivation refers to
    (A) the tendency of industrialization to strengthen the nuclear family
    (B) the tendency of urbanization to weaken the consanguine family
    (C) deprivation relative to one's reference group
    (D) deprivation relative to one's peers
    (E) deprivation relative to those in one's immediate environment

29. The family composed specifically of *ego*, his wife, and children, if any, is ego's
    (A) consanguine family
    (B) conjugal family
    (C) family of orientation
    (D) family of procreation
    (E) extended family

30. Most members of delinquent juvenile gangs are
    (A) mentally retarded
    (B) neurotic
    (C) psychopaths
    (D) paranoid
    (E) normal except for their delinquency

31. Of the following, the most comprehensive study of illegal sexual behavior was made by
    (A) Reckless
    (B) Bonger
    (C) Kinsey
    (D) Krafft-Ebing
    (E) Merton

32. Of the following which one sanction is NOT available to inmates?
    (A) blackmail
    (B) ostracism
    (C) violence
    (D) transfer
    (E) abasement

33. An individual who tends to withdraw from association with others is called
    (A) very suggestible
    (B) well socialized
    (C) poorly socialized
    (D) psychotic
    (E) hysterical

34. The process of acting in awareness of others and adjusting responses to the way others repond is called
    (A) role awareness
    (B) social awareness
    (C) social organization
    (D) social interaction
    (E) role response

35. According to David Riesman, the main psychological mechanism of conformity for an *inner-directed* person is

(A) egoism   (D) love
(B) ostracism   (E) fear
(C) guilt

36. "Other-directed" means that a person

(A) is an extrovert
(B) is an introvert
(C) looks to his immediate associates for his standards
(D) looks to tradition for his standards
(E) has no standards

37. The method of studying stratification which asks people how they classify each other is called

(A) reputational approach
(B) subjective approach
(C) objective approach
(D) objective-subjective approach
(E) self classification approach

38. Which is NOT generally an important factor in choosing a marriage partner?

(A) race   (D) number of siblings
(B) religion   (E) education
(C) age

39. One's place in a closed-class system is usually determined by the

(A) males in the society
(B) individual
(C) family
(D) government
(E) females in the society

40. The "Hawthorne effect" is

(A) an experimental effect derived from the experiments of James Hawthorne
(B) an experimental effect that affects different parts of the experimental group in different ways
(C) an experimental effect that affects different parts of the control group in different ways
(D) an experimental effect in which the experimental group reacts because they know they are part of an experiment
(E) a case where the experiment does not produce any new results

41. One who leaves a social group or a culture without adjusting in another group or culture can best be described as

    (A) an autonomous man
    (B) inner directed
    (C) psychotic
    (D) a marginal man
    (E) a radical

42. The institution that is both instrumental and evaluative is

    (A) art
    (B) polity
    (C) religion
    (D) economy
    (E) family

43. A latent function of a primitive rain dance is to

    (A) aid the rainfall
    (B) provide a prelude to puberty rites
    (C) provide a *rite de passage*
    (D) solidify the group
    (E) appease the gods

44. Influence that is considered legitimate by a group is called

    (A) power
    (B) authority
    (C) dominance
    (D) force
    (E) prestige

45. Which question is worded in a clear and unslanted way?

    (A) "Have you stopped beating your wife?"
    (B) "Do you get your information from books, magazines, newspapers, or textbooks?"
    (C) "Do you agree that Red China should be admitted to the U.N.?"
    (D) "Are you in favor of higher taxes for education?"
    (E) "Is that the best you can do?"

46. Using rates of groups to draw conclusions about individuals is an example of

    (A) misplaced concreteness
    (B) ecological fallacy
    (C) fallacy of composition
    (D) poor statistical calculations
    (E) false analogy

47. The idea that social change comes about as a result of contradictions and incompatibilities in the existing social system was stated by

    (A) Moore
    (B) Spengler
    (C) Marx
    (D) Smelser
    (E) Davis

48. Ideally, the doctor-patient relationship should be characterized by all the following EXCEPT

    (A) affective neutrality
    (B) diffuseness
    (C) universalism
    (D) performance orientation
    (E) collectivity-orientation

49. Which one of the following is not a correlate of technological growth?

   (A) population growth
   (B) stratification into working and middle classes
   (C) an increase in status relations as opposed to contractual relations
   (D) commercialization
   (E) industrialization

50. Class-oriented political parties will tend to emerge

   (A) during times of crisis
   (B) in a society that emphasizes religion
   (C) during times of calm
   (D) in a society that is rigidly stratified
   (E) when the country is industrializing

END OF PART

Go on to the following Test in the next Part of this Examination, just as you would be expected to do on the actual exam. If you have any available time use it to make sure that you have marked your Answer Sheet properly for this Part. Correct Answers for all Parts of this Exam follow the last question. Derive your scores only after completing the entire Exam.

PART II. HISTORY

TEST IV. AMERICAN HISTORY

TIME: 20 Minutes. 35 Questions.

DIRECTIONS: For each question in this test, read carefully the stem and the five lettered choices that follow. Choose the answer which you consider correct or most nearly correct. Mark the answer sheet for the letter you have chosen: A, B, C, D, or E.

(1)

Which event occurred in the United States during the Critical Period (1781-1789)?

(A) Whiskey Rebellion
(B) Shay's Rebellion
(C) Hartford Convention
(D) Closing of the port of Boston
(E) Meeting of the Second Continental Congress

(2)

One reason for the importance of the Northwest Ordinance (1787) was that it provided for

(A) the government of Texas
(B) the sale of western lands
(C) free navigation on the Great Lakes
(D) the eventual admission of territories as equal states
(E) the judicial system of the United States

(3)

Some of the best arguments in support of the adoption of the United States Constitution are found in

(A) *Common Sense*
(B) the Articles of Confederation
(C) *The New Freedom*
(D) the Freeport Doctrine
(E) *The Federalist*

(4)

Which of the following was a result of the other three?

(A) Alien and Sedition Acts
(B) Disappearance of the Federalist Party
(C) Hartford Convention
(D) Increase in democratic spirit in the United States
(E) None of these

(5)

The idea that the federal government was a compact or contract among the states was expressed in

(A) Lee's Resolutions
(B) the theory of "manifest destiny"
(C) South Carolina's "Exposition and Protest"
(D) Webster's reply to Hayne
(E) the Freeport Doctrine

(6)

The Treaty of 1795 with Spain was most popular with

(A) western farmers using the Mississippi River for shopping
(B) northern fur trappers seeking the removal of British troops from the Northwest Territory
(C) patriotic Americans attempting to stop the impressment of seamen
(D) New England merchants seeking to reopen triangular trade
(E) southerners seeking new markets for tobacco

(7)

Which statement best describes the reaction of many American colonists toward British colonial policy following the French and Indian War?

(A) They refused to accept the idea of Parliament's right to manage their internal affairs.
(B) They petitioned the British Parliament for immediate independence.
(C) They urged the colonial legislatures to enforce the taxation program of the British Parliament.
(D) They opposed the withdrawal of British troops from the Ohio Territory.
(E) They advocated higher taxes to cover the costs of the war.

S1339

8

The friendship between the United States and France can be traced back to

(A) the Alliance of 1778
(B) the activities of Citizen Genêt
(C) French aid during the War of 1812
(D) French support of the North during the Civil War
(E) the gift of the Statue of Liberty

9

On which issue did Thomas Jefferson reverse his opinion as to strict construction of the Constitution?

(A) The Bank of the United States
(B) The purchase of the Louisiana Territory
(C) The moving of the capital to Washington, D.C.
(D) The appointment of the "midnight judges"
(E) The election of 1800

10

One reason why Great Britain supported the Monroe Doctrine in 1823 was that she

(A) had declared war on Spain
(B) wished to support the Holy Alliance
(C) had developed trade with the Latin American countries
(D) followed a policy of supporting democratic revolutions
(E) wished to curry favor with the United States

11

An important result of the Napoleonic Wars in Europe was the

(A) spread of the Industrial Revolution
(B) success of the Continental system
(C) rise of a spirit of nationalism
(D) elimination of monarchies
(E) military supremacy of France

Base your answers to questions **12** - **13** *on information given in the graph below.*

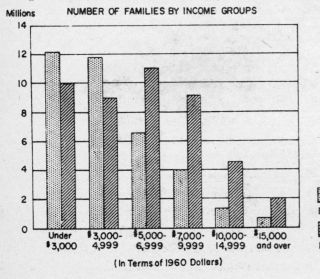

NUMBER OF FAMILIES BY INCOME GROUPS

Millions

14
12
10
8
6
4
2
0

Under $3,000 | $3,000-4,999 | $5,000-6,999 | $7,000-9,999 | $10,000-14,999 | $15,000 and over

1947

1960

(In Terms of 1960 Dollars)

12

Which trend is indicated during the period 1947-1960?

(A) The average family income increased.
(B) The number of families with incomes over $15,000 declined.
(C) The number of families earning between $3,000 and $4,999 increased.
(D) In 1960, 35 percent of the families in the United States earned $10,000-$15,000 per year.
(E) In 1947, more than half of United States families earned less than $3,000.

13

In which income group was there the greatest increase in the number of families?

(A) $3,000-$4,999   (B) $5,000-$6,999
(C) $7,000-$9,999   (D) $10,000-$14,999
              (E) $15,000 and over

Questions **14** - **16**

Directions: Match each of the numbered quotations below with the appropriate lettered document.

(A) Albany Plan of Union
(B) Gettysburg Address
(C) Declaration of Independence
(D) Mayflower Compact
(E) United States Bill of Rights

14

"We hold these truths to be self-evident, that all men are created equal, that they are endowed by their Creator with certain inalienable rights..."

15

"It is for us the living, rather, to be dedicated here to the unfinished work which they who fought here have thus far so nobly advanced."

16

"No Soldier shall, in time of peace be quartered in any house, without the consent of the Owner, nor in time of war, but in a manner to be prescribed by law."

17

The theory of "manifest destiny" is best illustrated in the

(A) Good Neighbor Policy
(B) slogan "Fifty-four forty or fight"
(C) selection of the parallel 36° 30' in the Missouri Compromise
(D) granting of independence to the Philippines
(E) Emancipation Proclamation

(18)

One direct result of the passage of the Kansas-Nebraska Act was the

(A) rise of the abolition movement
(B) migration of settlers from the Kansas-Nebraska territory
(C) formation of the Republican party
(D) organizing of the first "underground railroad"
(E) Missouri Compromise

(19)

The chief reason for the opposition of the South to the election of Abraham Lincoln in 1860 was his

(A) resistance to secession
(B) demand for the immediate abolition of slavery
(C) hostility to the extension of slavery
(D) insistence on equal education for Negroes and whites
(E) unsophisticated appearance

(20)

The presidential candidacies of John C. Breckinridge in 1860 and Theodore Roosevelt in 1912 were similar in that

(A) both men were Republicans
(B) their campaigns split their parties and allowed the election of President by a minority vote
(C) both men announced support for high protective tariffs for industry
(D) both failed to gain any electoral votes
(E) both were opposed by agrarian interests

(21)

In which pair is the first item an *immediate* cause of the second?

(A) Assassination of James Garfield—Pendleton Act
(B) Election of John Quincy Adams—Twelfth Amendment
(C) Assassination of Alexander Hamilton—End of the Federalist Party
(D) Sinking of the *Lusitania*—Entry of the United States into World War I
(E) Hitler's attack on Poland—United States' entry into World War II

Questions **(22)** - **(26)** *are concerned with the following discussion on Imperialism.*

Speaker I: It is our duty to extend the blessings of Christianity and civilization to backward peoples. If we are to fulfill our duty, we must govern them.

Speaker II: The United States must be a major power in the world. Therefore, we will have to have a powerful navy and merchant fleet. To service these fleets, we need to acquire naval bases in various parts of the world.

Speaker III: We need overseas areas where American businessmen can safely invest surplus capital and find new markets as well as raw materials.

Speaker IV: If we should become involved in creating a world empire, we might find that in the process, democracy at home has been hurt.

(22)

Which speaker would have been most apt to support the Open Door Policy?

(A) I   (B) II
(C) III   (D) IV

(23)

Before the Spanish-American War, most Americans shared the views of Speaker

(A) I   (B) II
(C) III   (D) IV

(24)

Alfred T. Mahan's views are best expressed by Speaker

(A) I   (B) II
(C) III   (D) IV

(25)

The objectives of "dollar diplomacy" in the Caribbean are best expressed by Speaker

(A) I   (B) II
(C) III   (D) IV

(26)

After a brief revolution in 1893, Americans who shared the ideas of Speakers I and III urged Congress to annex

(A) Hawaii   (B) Jamaica
(C) Bermuda   (D) the Virgin Islands

(27)

Which of the following statements about the North Atlantic Treaty Organization (NATO) are true?

I. Originally, it was an outgrowth of the Brussels Treaty organization for defense against Soviet encroachment.
II: It had the effect of bringing the United States and a number of additional nations—(not all European)—into association for the purpose of Western European defense.
III. For the United States, membership was a drastic reversal of foreign policy in that, for the first time in history, the United States entered into a European military alliance in peacetime.

IV. Aside from its military implications, NATO has also been intended as a major means for the advancement of European political unity.

(A) I, II, III, and IV
(B) II, III, and IV
(C) I, II, and IV
(D) I, II, and III
(E) I, III, and IV

(28)

Samuel Gompers attempted to win gains for labor by

(A) uniting skilled and unskilled workers into one union
(B) organizing industrial or vertical unions
(C) forming craft unions of skilled workers
(D) campaigning actively for the election of AFL members to public office
(E) urging civil disobedience as a means to win public support

(29)

In the period 1887-1890, Congress passed major legislation to regulate abuses in

(A) local governments
(B) industrial combinations
(C) union methods
(D) farm credit
(E) governmental hiring practices

(30)

The Embargo and Non-Intercourse Acts passed by the United States in the early nineteenth century illustrate the

(A) unsuccessful attempt of the United States to isolate itself from a European conflict
(B) success of the United States in obtaining recognition of neutral rights
(C) temporary submergence of sectionalism as an issue
(D) overwhelming support given by members of Congress to President Jefferson's policy
(E) desire of the United States to ally itself with Napoleon

Questions (31) - (34)

Directions: Match each numbered statement with the appropriate map projection.

(A) Mercator   (B) Sinusoidal
(C) Goode's Interrupted   (D) Azimuthal Equidistant
          (E) Orthographic

(31)

This projection is most favored for aircraft navigation.

(32)

This projection cannot be used for a world map.

(33)

This is the most favored projection for marine charts because all compass directions appear as straight lines.

(34)

This projection is excellent for land areas but poor for oceans.

(35)

The pre-Civil War South objected to protective tariffs because they

(A) increased the cost of slaves
(B) kept the price of cotton low
(C) increased the prices of manufactured goods
(D) aided western farmers at the planters' expense
(E) destroyed the market for tobacco

END OF TEST

Go on to do the following Test in this Examination, just as you would be expected to do on the actual exam.

TEST V. WORLD HISTORY

TIME: 10 Minutes. 20 Questions.

DIRECTIONS: For each of the following questions, select the choice which best answers the question or completes the statement.

Answer questions 1-3 with reference to the map below:

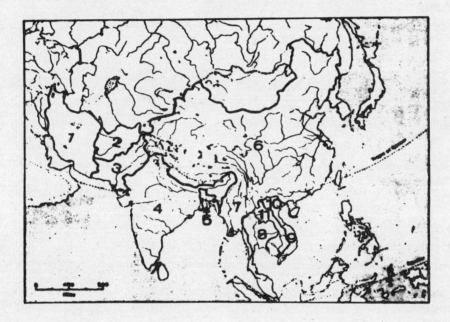

1. The Tashkent Agreement signalled at least a temporary truce in the long series of border disputes between

   (A) 4 and 6
   (B) 3 and 4
   (C) 2 and 3
   (D) 3-5 and 4
   (E) 3-5 and 6

2. The Battle of Dien Bien Phu meant the end of direct French influence in

   (A) 8
   (B) 9 and 10
   (C) 7 and 8
   (D) 1
   (E) 5

3. Which of the following nations has not been under colonial rule in modern times?

   (A) 4
   (B) 5
   (C) 7
   (D) 8
   (E) 11

4. In which labor dispute did government interference, either federal or local, result in a solution generally satisfactory to labor?

   (A) Homestead strike of 1892
   (B) Railroad strikes of 1877
   (C) Pullman strike of 1894
   (D) Steel strike of 1919
   (E) Anthracite coal strike of 1902

5. Which group contains a list of names of foreign heads of state, all of whom Theodore Roosevelt had to deal with while he occupied the office of President?

   (A) Sun Yat Sen; Tsar Alexander III; Pancho Villa
   (B) Emperor Mutsuhito; Emperor Francis Joseph; Joseph Pilsudski
   (C) Mustapha Kemal; Yuan Shih-kai; Emperor Louis Napoleon
   (D) Porfirio Diaz; Kaiser William II; Tsar Nicholas II
   (E) Herbert Asquith; Porfirio Diaz; Alexander III

6. The Gentlemen's Agreement of 1907 between the United States and Japan provided for

   (A) mutual recognition of the Open Door policy in China
   (B) establishment of a specific quota for Japanese immigration to the United States
   (C) restrictions on the naval armaments of the two nations
   (D) United States restrictions on Japanese immigration
   (E) Japanese restriction of Japanese emigrato the United States

7. Which one of the following was *not* a cause of controversy between the United States and England in the period immediately following the Treaty of Paris of 1783?

   (A) Debts owed to English merchants
   (B) The impressment of American seamen
   (C) The treatment of Loyalists
   (D) The presence of British garrisons on United States soil
   (E) The northern boundary of the new nation

8. Which one of the following did *not* lead to conflict between France and the United States?

   (A) XYZ Affair
   (B) Ostend Manifesto
   (C) Genêt Affair
   (D) Maximilian Affair
   (E) Multilateral Nuclear Force

9. Which one of the following was *not* a cause for rivalry between England and the Netherlands in the 17th century?

   (A) Competition for fisheries in the North Sea
   (B) Rivalry for commercial posts in the East Indies
   (C) Control of settlements in America
   (D) Antagonism arising from religious differences
   (E) Selection of a monarch after the Glorious Revolution

10. Which one of the following was *not* a result of the Commercial Revolution?

    (A) The domestic system of production was introduced.
    (B) Europe started on her career of world conquest.
    (C) Some European merchants became wealthy enough to live like princes.
    (D) The power of the absolute monarchs decreased.
    (E) Feudalism continued to disintegrate on the Continent.

11. Which one of the following is *incorrectly* associated with his contribution to the Agricultural Revolution?

    (A) Arthur Bakewell—organization of agricultural societies
    (B) Justus von Liebig—chemical fertilizers
    (C) Lord Townshend—crop rotation
    (D) Jethro Tull—seed-drill
    (E) John Deere—steel plow

12. Which one of the following is paired correctly with the work which he wrote?

    (A) Galileo Galilei—Principia
    (B) John Milton—Areopagitica
    (C) Michel de Montaigne—The Praise of Folly
    (D) Thomas More—England's Treasure by Foreign Trade
    (E) John Locke—On Liberty

13. Which one of the following 19th century scientists is paired correctly with the field in which he made his major contributions?

    (A) Agassiz—Chemistry
    (B) Dalton—Mathematics
    (C) Lamarck—Biology
    (D) Lyell—Zoology
    (E) Roentgen—Botany

14. Which one of the following did *not* break with the Roman Catholic Church during the Protestant Reformation?

    (A) John Calvin
    (B) Desiderius Erasmus
    (C) John Knox
    (D) Huldreich Zwingli
    (E) Henry Tudor

15. "Man is born free, and everywhere he is in irons" is a quotation from the writings of

    (A) Denis Diderot
    (B) John Locke
    (C) Jean Jacques Rousseau
    (D) Francois Voltaire
    (E) Karl Marx

16. Which one of the following monarchs was *not* considered an enlightened or benevolent despot in the eighteenth century?

    (A) Catherine the Great of Russia
    (B) Frederick the Great of Prussia
    (C) Joseph II of Austria
    (D) Louis XV of France
    (E) Peter the Great of Russia

17. Which one of the following statements does *not* apply to the Revolution of 1789 in France and to the Revolutions of 1848 in Europe?

    (A) In both cases serfdom was abolished.
    (B) In both cases an immediate economic crisis helped to crystallize discontent into revolution.
    (C) In both cases a new industrial working class put forth an essentially identical social and economic program.
    (D) In both cases constitutional monarchies were established.
    (E) In both cases the revolution in France was a signal for a European tidal wave of disturbances.

18. Which one of the following was championed by the supporters of democratic principles during the period 1815 to 1848?

    (A) Carlsbad Decrees
    (B) Policies of the Quadruple Alliance
    (C) Chartist Movement
    (D) Six Acts of Parliament of 1819
    (E) Organic Articles

19. Critics of the Beard thesis maintain that at the Philadelphia Convention

    (A) the desire for a strong central government was in part an effort to obtain a favored position under the new government for the propertied classes
    (B) large numbers of adult males were unrepresented because they did not own property
    (C) patriotic motivations of the delegates were not present to the degree cited by Beard
    (D) a number of delegates supported federalism because they expected that under a strong central government the depreciated Continental debt would be funded at par
    (E) there was no correlation between the delegates' property holdings and the position they took on constitutional issues

20. The outcome of the Whiskey Rebellion demonstrated the

    (A) effectiveness of the doctrine of nullification
    (B) authority of the central government
    (C) popular acceptance of excise taxes
    (D) growing approval of Federalist Party policies
    (E) persuasive ability of Hamilton

END OF EXAMINATION

Now that you have completed the last Test in this Examination, use your available time to make sure that you have written in your answers correctly on the Answer Sheet. Then, after your time is up, check your answers with the Correct Answers we have provided for you. Derive your scores for each Test Category and determine where you are weak so as to plan your study accordingly.

CORRECT ANSWERS FOR VERISIMILAR EXAMINATION V.

TEST I. GOVERNMENT

1.E	4.E	7.E	10.A	13.C	16.B	19.A	21.C
2.C	5.B	8.C	11.A	14.B	17.C	20.D	22.B
3.C	6.D	9.D	12.E	15.C	18.E		

TEST I. EXPLANATORY ANSWERS

1. *(E)* E is the incorrect statement since expulsion requires a two-thirds vote.

2. *(C)* Article I, Section 10, of the U.S. Constitution specifically forbids a state to "enter into any agreement or compact with another State" without the consent of Congress.

3. *(C)* The President may not veto items in any bill, but must accept or reject all bills in their entirety. The item veto has been suggested as a possible reform, but this change would require a Constitutional Amendment.

4. *(E)* Proletarianism refers to the idea that private property should be abolished and placed in the hands of the collective community. Locke felt that man possessed certain rights which could not be taken away. Among these was the right of private property.

5. *(B)* UNESCO is the United Nations Educational, Scientific, and Cultural Organization. Rehabilitation of Koreans was carried on by a United Nations Korean Reconstruction Agency.

6. *(D)* In *Marbury v. Madison*, the Supreme Court declared a part of the Judiciary Act of 1789 unconstitutional. This was the first time an Act of Congress had been declared unconstitutional by the Court, and it established the principle of Judicial Review.

7. *(E)* The major provisions of the Smith Act (The Alien Registration Act of 1940) make it unlawful to "teach, advocate, or distribute information advocating the forcible overthrow of government or to knowingly organize or join an organization that so advocates." Other requirements for aliens are also set forth. The Act is important because it was the first Act passed in peacetime, since 1789, which restricted speech and writing.

8. *(C)* Truman's Plan to aid Greece and Turkey (The Truman Doctrine) was important because it, for the first time, renounced Communist aggression and made clear U.S. intentions to support those people who were resisting such aggression.

9. *(D)* The Constitution provides only that the electoral system be used and that each state shall have electors equal to the number of Senators and Representatives it has. The method of choosing these electors is left to the legislature in each state.

10. *(A)* The Constitution in Article V sets forth the amending procedure. It also provides that "no state, without its consent, shall be deprived of its equal suffrage in the Senate." It is true that Article IV, Section 3, provides that a new state shall not be formed within the jurisdiction of another state without its consent, but there is no provision forbidding an Amendment which would change this provision. This is a restriction on the power of Congress to admit new states. Article I, Section 10, forbids states to enter into treaties with foreign nations, but Amendments are not prohibited in regard to this provision.

11. *(A)* The British-French-Israeli action against Egypt in October, 1956, did not result in a deadlock in the U.N. because of the Soviet veto. The U.N. was protesting intervention of Egypt. Russia was in agreement with this.

12. *(E)* The amending process is entirely a legislative process. The President is not involved in this procedure.

13. *(C)* There is no Constitutional provision, federal regulation, or Supreme Court decision requiring electors to vote for their party's candidate. Electors must do so only if their state laws require it. At this time, few states have this requirement.

14. *(B).* The New Economic Policy (NEP) was a retreat from Communist principles since it provided for the restoration of a free market and private shops.

15. *(C)* John M. Keynes' *The General Theory of Employment, Interest and Money* had a great influence on Roosevelt's New Deal policies.

16. *(B)* Answer B contains three characteristics of modern under-developed countries. One or more characteristics, such as middle class philosophy, poor endowment of natural resources, security of foreign investments, and full utilization of manpower, can be eliminated in answers A, C, D, and E.

17. *(C)* Since 1841 it has been possible for the rules of the House to be suspended without the normal 2/3 majority, upon receipt of a special resolution from the Rules Committee. Special resolutions are sought for most of the important legislative items. This situation gives the Rules Committee considerable power. It can keep items from the floor, or it can require that changes be made before it will release items to the floor.

18. *(E)* The United Nations Educational, Scientific, and Cultural Council was established in November, 1946. The Economic and Social Council was provided for in Chapter X of Article 61 of the U.N. Charter. No comparable agencies existed under the League of Nations.

19. *(A)* The Supreme Court may review and reverse a previous decision in connection with a similar case appearing before it. It may review any state or federal law in connection with a particular case, a simple majority being necessary to decide. The Supreme Court has original jurisdiction in cases where a state is a party.

20. *(D)* The power of the British government cannot be expanded by a specific Constitutional amending process because Britain has no single document which is its Constitution.

21. *(C)* Russia was not involved in post-World War I peace conferences.

22. *(B)* If Congress has not set a time limit on the ratification of an amendment, a state can at any time after the amendment has been placed before it, consider or reconsider, and approve it. Thus, in 1939 the Supreme Court held that a child labor amendment was still "alive" after 15 years.

TEST II. ECONOMICS

1.C	4.B	7.E	10.D	13.A	16.B	19.A	22.B
2.A	5.E	8.E	11.B	14.B	17.B	20.C	23.E
3.E	6.D	9.C	12.E	15.C	18.A	21.C	

TEST II. EXPLANATORY ANSWERS

1. **(C)** Scarcity is fundamental to economics because human demands for goods will always exceed the supply of goods available. Thus resources are scarce and must be rationally allocated to best satisfy human demands.

2. **(A)** Elasticity is always a ratio of the relative changes in two quantities. Price elasticity equals the relative change in quantity divided by the relative change in price, here greater than one.

3. **(E)** Microeconomics concerns itself with the rational allocation of capital, land, labor and entrepreneurial skill.

4. **(B)** Increasing costs are caused by external diseconomies accompanying increased production. External diseconomies or diminishing returns to scale result from higher input prices or diminishing physical input productivities.

5. **(E)** Oligopsony exists when a few large firms can control the market prices of the various factors they purchase.

6. **(D)** Monopolistic competition in an industry means that there are many different firms, each producing and selling differentiated products. This is to be distinguished from monopoly, where one seller exists, and oligopoly, where only a few sellers exist.

7. **(E)** As long as demand is elastic, the lower the price falls the greater the total revenue will be. Similarly, as long as demand is inelastic, the higher the price rises the greater total revenue will be. Total revenue will therefore be greatest where e equals one.

8. **(E)** At e equals one, price equals 50 and quantity equals 50, so total revenue is 2500.

9. **(C)** One can be certain only that the quantity will increase, but the effect on price cannot be determined.

10. **(D)** Equilibrium price exists where supply equals demand.

11. **(B)** Governmental minimum prices invariably result in a surplus, which merely means an excess supply exists at the minimum price.

12. **(E)** With the market forces again free to operate, the natural price and quantity equilibrium will reassert itself.

13. **(A)** The increased supply is manifested by the fact that at each price the quantity supplied at S1 is greater than that supplied at S.

14. **(B)** The more of a product one owns, the less important is any one unit of it. Since goods are scarce relative to one another, one must ra-

tionally balance one's purchases in order to gain the same degree of satisfaction out of the last dollar spent on any given product.

15. **(C)** When the price of a good falls, the "income effect" means that the consumer's real income has been increased. At the same time, the "substitution effect" means the consumer buys greater quantities of a given commodity after its price falls. These two effects operate independently, each accounting for a part of the total increase in demand which occurs when the price of a good falls.

16. **(B)** The rationality of men is an assumption of all economic models and thus not an assumption essential to any particular theory.

17. **(B)** Complementary goods are goods often used together — for example, hot dogs and mustard. If the price of hot dogs falls, more will be purchased and the demand for mustard will naturally increase.

18. **(A)** If, when a consumer's income increases beyond a certain level, the consumer purchases less of a certain good, that good is an inferior good.

19. **(A)** Again, as income increases beyond a certain level, less and less of Good Y is purchased.

20. **(C)** Point A is the income level at which purchases of Good Y begin to decrease.

21. **(C)** Income elasticity of demand is the ratio of the percentage change in the quantity demanded to the percentage change in income. The elasticity of substitution means? generally, that a rise in the price of a given good increases the demand for its substitutes and lessens the demand for its complements.

22. **(B)** The demand curve for a firm is always synonomous with its average revenue curve.

23. **(E)** Depreciation, while not a visible cost to a firm, must be written off during each fiscal period in order to record accurately the expense of capital deterioration.

TEST III. SOCIOLOGY

1.B	8.B	15.C	22.C	29.D	36.C	41.D	46.B
2.A	9.D	16.D	23.E	30.E	37.A	42.D	47.C
3.C	10.C	17.B	24.B	31.C	38.D	43.D	48.B
4.A	11.E	18.C	25.C	32.D	39.C	44.B	49.C
5.D	12.B	19.C	26.A	33.C	40.D	45.D	50.D
6.E	13.A	20.D	27.B	34.D			
7.D	14.B	21.A	28.C	35.C			

TEST III. EXPLANATORY ANSWERS

1. **(B)** This is the common usage of the term. (*Cf.*, *e.g.*, John T. Zadrozny, *Dictionary of Social Science*, Washington, D.C., Public Affairs Press, 1959.)

2. **(A)** The other items are clearly sanctions, in the sense of being punishments or rewards whose purpose is to obtain conformity with social norms. Of course tax considerations also influence behavior, and in acting on tax proposals legislators usually give some care to assure that the influence of any given tax program will be in directions generally regarded as socially desirable. Despite this the main purpose of taxes is usually considered to be the raising of revenue, rather than social sanction.

3. **(C)** This would be an example of "skill in taking-the-role-of-the-other," or social empathy as usually defined.

4. **(A)** The *Britannica Book of the Year* for 1976 gives 538,213,900 as the estimated world membership of Islam, second only to Christianity with 954,766,700.

5. **(D)** *Cf.* Gerhard Lenski, *The Religious Factor* (Garden City, Doubleday, 1961), p. 291 ff.

6. **(E)** As compared with, say, medieval times, all of the functions listed here have decreased in modern times, but ethical functions have clearly decreased less than others.

7. **(D)** Occupation, education, and income are usually taken as the most important objective indicators of social class. (*Cf.* Robert W. Hodge and Paul M. Siegel, "Social Stratification: The Measurement of Social Class," in *International Encyclopedia of the Social Sciences* 15:316-324.)

8. **(B)** Authority within the Iroquois household was vested in the senior matron.

9. **(D)** Cross pressures occur in social situations involving, for a given individual, incompatible motives resulting in an intra-personal conflict. (*Cf.* Frank A. Pinner, "Cross Pressure," *International Encyclopedia of the Social Sciences* 3:519.) Option D presents no such conflict, the sociological pressures associated with the Jewish religion and Democratic spouse tending very likely to point in the same general direction.

10. **(C)** For Riesman, the "inner-directed" people are those who "acquire early in life an internalized set of goals." (*The Lonely Crowd*, New Haven, Yale Univ. Press, 1950, p.9.) Weber himself used the phrase "inner-worldly asceticism" to describe the Calvinists' way of life.

11. **(E)** The more advanced, more complex society is likely to be more open to change. For one thing, the larger culture base promotes invention. Though changes in different parts of a culture (e.g., social, technological, educational) may proceed at different rates, they are interdependent. A broader culture base is likely to encourage innovation, and is likely to facilitate adaptive changes in response to these innovations.

12. **(B)** In general, they did not challenge the basic foundations of the existing social order, but sought to change by peaceful and legal means certain existing practices in such a way as to make them conform more closely to their ideals.

13. **(A)** *The Study of Instinct* by Nikolaas Tinbergen (1951) is generally considered the first modern ethology textbook. A brief overview of the field is provided by: Irenaus Eibl-Eibesfeldt and Wolfgang Wickler, "Ethology," *International Encyclopedia of the Social Sciences* 5:186-193.

14. **(B)** In other words, the divorce rate is higher for Protestants than for Catholics, while the rate of desertion and separation is higher for Catholics than for Protestants. An apparent explanation would be that divorce is less acceptable among Catholics than among Protestants, so that situations which for Protestant families would be accompanied by divorce, among Catholic families often are not.

15. **(C)** The discrepancy between a society's avowed ideals and the actual behavior of real human beings is what is involved. This is conveyed best by option C. In option D, for example, mores are not really opposed to folkways, but *are* folkways themselves.

16. **(D)** Actually, the divorce rate continued to climb until the end of the Second World War in 1946, but of the options given, D (1944) showed the highest rate. (*Cf.* U.S. Bureau of the Census, *Historical Statistics of the U.S., Colonial Times to 1957*, Washington, D.C., 1960, p. 30.)

17. **(B)** In Malthus' scheme contraception was a preventive, rather than a positive, check. The other options are listed by him as positive checks in Chapter II of Book I of his *Essay on Population*.

18. **(C)** This can be verified by checking the annual *Uniform Crime Reports* published by the Federal Bureau of Investigation.

19. **(C)** The sex ratio is usually defined as the number of males per 100 females in a given population. In a society characterized by a high sex ratio, possession of multiple wives would necessarily be limited to a relatively few individuals, and would probably be a basis for what Veblen termed "invidious comparison." As such it would probably become a form of "conspicuous consumption." (*Cf.* Thorstein Veblen, *Theory of the Leisure Class,* first published in 1899.)

20. **(D)** Weber elaborated this theory in his *The Protestant Ethic and the Spirit of Capitalism*, first published in German in 1904-05.

21. **(A)** The "*per se*" identifies this as the preferred option. Although "financial difficulties" are frequently cited as a factor contributing to family dissolution (*cf., e.g., The Encyclopedia of Social Work*, 15th ed., N.Y., National Association of Social Workers, 1965, p. 307), these are in fact apt to arise at any level of income and are not so much related to financial status, or the amount of money available, as to conflicting ideas about how the money should be handled, etc.

22. **(C)** This is clearly the way in which the expression is most frequently used by sociologists. A discussion of the phenomenon is found in most introductory sociology texts. A frequently cited discussion of cultural lag is found in W. F. Ogburn, *Social Change* (N.Y., Viking, 1950).

23. **(E)** Not all minority groups would be condemned by the typical authoritarian personality—only those which were also "out groups."

24. **(B)** Whereas the underdog effect would encourage a voter to favor a candidate with seemingly little support or chance of winning, the bandwagon effect would operate to encourage the voter to support the most favored candidate for the sake of being on the winning side.

25. **(C)** The *Encyclopedia of Social Work* (15th ed., N.Y., National Assoc. of Social Workers, 1965, p. 307) notes that "most marital dislocations are the result of a combination of factors, some deeply emotional and psychological as well as situational." Although this source cites "financial difficulties," "drinking," and "interference of relatives," as well as "sexual incompatibility" among the most prominent immediate causes of marital discord, the latter is doubtless the most common single factor.

26. **(A)** This is the common definition. *Cf.,* for example, Gould and Kolb, *A Dictionary of the Social Sciences*, p.6.

27. **(B)** The term appears to have originated with R. E. Park, who used it in 1928 to refer to a cultural hybrid sharing the traditions of two different peoples as a result of migration ("Human Migration and the Marginal Man," *American Journal of Sociology*, 33:892). *Cf.* "The Marginal Man Concept, An Analysis and Critique," *Social Forces* 30:333-9, 1951-2.

28. **(C)** A classic presentation of this concept is found in Robert K. Merton and Alice S. Kitt, "Contributions to the Theory of Reference Group Behavior," in Merton and Lazarsfeld (eds.) *Continuities in Social Research: Studies in the Scope and Method of "The American Soldier"* (Glencoe, Free Press, 1950).

29. **(D)** It is ego's family of procreation (rather than his family of orientation or the one into which he was born). It contains both consanguine elements (his children) and nonconsanguine elements (his wife). His wife also represents a conjugal element. The family described is a nuclear, rather than extended, unit.

30. **(E)** Delinquent gangs arise chiefly out of informal childhood play groups, following roughly the same dynamics as account for the development of non-delinquent gangs. These dynamics are discussed in most standard sociology texts (*e.g.,* Broom and Selznick, *Sociology,* 3rd ed., N.Y., Harper & Row, 1963, p. 557-560) and do not suggest any of the psychological abnormalities listed.

31. **(C)** While Kinsey's two best-known works—*Sexual Behavior in the Human Male* (1948) and *Sexual Behavior in the Human Female* (1953)—do not deal exclusively with illegal behavior, they probably do offer the most comprehensive sources of statistical data in this area.

32. **(D)** While ostracism can be quite effectively applied against someone who remains physically present, the option of physically transferring someone to another place is not typically available to persons to whom the term "inmates" would apply: that term being in sociological literature most characteristically applied to inmates of prisons or mental hospitals.

33. **(C)** A poorly socialized individual is typically one who has not learned adequately the social roles, group norms, etc. that would enable him to interact with others in satisfying and socially acceptable ways. Of the options given, this is doubtless the most appropriate term to apply to the individual described in the question. While some psychotics would withdraw from association with others, not all do, and certainly not all individuals who do so are psychotic. (*Cf.* the definitions of "socialization" in standard sociological dictionaries such as Zadrozny's *Dictionary of Social Science* or Gould and Kolb's *Dictionary of the Social Sciences*.)

34. **(D)** This is the standard sociological usage. (Cf. "Social Interaction" in Gould and Kolb, *Dictionary of the Social Sciences*.)

35. **(C)** *Cf.* David Riesman, *The Lonely Crowd* (New Haven, Yale Univ. Pr., 1950) pp. 14-17.

36. **(C)** *Cf.* David Riesman, *The Lonely Crowd* (New Haven, Yale Univ. Pr., 1950) pp. 19-25.

37. **(A)** The reputational method is said to have been first used by Floyd Hunter (*Community Power Structure*, Chapel Hill, Univ. of North Carolina Pr., 1953). A concise description of the method is given in: Nelson W. Polsby, "Community: The Study of Community Power," *International Encyclopedia of the Social Sciences,* v. 3, pp. 157-163.

38. **(D)** The relative importance of the factors listed has been investigated in numerous studies. The results of these studies are summarized in most of the standard "marriage and family living" texts. An article by Jacobsohn and Matheny entitled "Mate Selection in Open Marriage Systems" (*International Journal of Comparative Sociology* 3:98-123) that appeared in September, 1962, provides a good review of the literature up to that date.

39. **(C)** Since a closed-class system is based on ascribed—rather than achieved—criteria, one's place in such a society tends to be determined by the family into which one is born.

40. **(D)** This "effect" was discovered in a series of studies, begun in 1924, at the Western Electric Company's Hawthorne plant, near Chicago.

41. **(D)** This is not intended to be an adequate definition of "marginal man." "Marginal man," however, is the concept that most aptly fits this particular situation. (The term originated with R. E. Park— "Human Migration and the Marginal Man" in *American Journal of Sociology* 33:892, 1928—and was elaborated by E. V. Stonequist— *The Marginal Man*, 1937—and others).

42. **(D)** While it may be argued that the other institutions have to some smaller degree and in some more limited sense a dual character, economy is necessarily and importantly both evaluative and instrumental: evaluative, for example, in placing relative values or priorities on different kinds of goods and services; instrumental, in providing a mechanism of exchange, in establishing and maintaining effective channels of production and distribution.

43. **(D)** "Latent functions" have been defined (*e.g.,* by R. K. Merton in his *Social Theory and Social Structure*, p. 51) as those functions which are neither intended nor recognized by the participants. A, B, and C—if present as functions at all—would clearly be manifest, rather than latent.

44. **(B)** Influence exerted through power or force is seldom (if ever) considered entirely legitimate (unless justified on some other basis than brute force alone). Influence based on dominance alone would clearly be "undue influence," only a little removed from physical force. Similarly, prestige can be obtained by fraudulent means, by a deceptive display of attainments, powers, etc., not actually possessed. "Authority," on the other hand, is typically used in sociological writings to apply to that leadership or influence that is somehow legitimate or "capable of reasoned elaboration" (*cf.* Lasswell and Kaplan, *Power and Society*, New Haven, Yale Univ. Press, 1950).

45. **(D)** A is a leading question. B limits options (*i.e.*, no way to indicate, for example, television, lectures, or discussions). C slants the question a bit by the use of the word "agree," perhaps also making it somewhat unclear, possibly putting the person being questioned on the defensive. D presents its question clearly and in an unslanted way. E implies that you can do better.

46. **(B)** A frequently cited study in this area is W. S. Robinson's, "Ecological Correlations and Behavior of Individuals," *American Sociological Review*, 15:351-57, June, 1950.

47. **(C)** This view is expounded at some length in his *Capital*. A briefer statement is found in the *Communist Manifesto* written with Friedrich Engels in 1848.

48. **(B)** The alternatives refer to the various pattern variables set forth by Talcott Parsons. Some of the considerations relating to the ideal physican-patient relationship are discussed by him in *The Social System* (Glencoe, Free Press, 1951), pp. 439-454. For a physican to adopt a diffuse understanding of his relationship with his patient would be for him to have in mind obligations or "interests" lying outside the responsibilities and relationship institutionalized in his role. Under such circumstances, when the physician's conduct can no longer be predicted to fall within the institutionalized role, the patient can no longer predict what considerations will prompt his physician's conduct, and can no longer assume that the physician will act in his (*i.e.*, the patient's) best interest.

49. **(C)** An increase in status relations as opposed to contract relations would tend to impede technological growth.

50. **(D)** The rigid stratification would tend to increase the class orientation of most of the social institutions, including political parties. (*Cf.*, Max Weber, *Class, Status, Party*, 1921.)

TEST IV. AMERICAN HISTORY

1.B	6.A	11.C	16.E	21.A	26.A	31.D
2.D	7.A	12.A	17.B	22.C	27.A	32.E
3.E	8.A	13.C	18.C	23.D	28.C	33.A
4.B	9.B	14.C	19.C	24.B	29.B	34.C
5.C	10.C	15.B	20.B	25.C	30.A	35.C

TEST IV. EXPLANATORY ANSWERS

①

(B) Shays' Rebellion took place in 1786.

②

(D) The Northwest Ordinance provides for the formation of "no less than three nor more than five states" from the territory and that these states would be "on an equal footing with the original states in all respects whatever."

③

(E) *The Federalist* was a series of essays by Alexander Hamilton, James Madison, and John Jay, setting forth reasons for the adoption of the new Constitution.

④

(B) The increased spirit of democracy led to objection to the Alien and Sedition Acts and the proposals of the Hartford Convention. The cumulative effect was the demise of the Federalists as a political party.

⑤

(C) South Carolina's "Exposition and Protest" was patterned after the Virginia and Kentucky Resolutions and advocated that the Union was formed by compact among sovereign states and could be dissolved at will.

⑥

(A) The treaty provided for the "right of deposit" at New Orleans and free navigation of the Mississippi.

⑦

(A) They felt that they had earned the right to self-government by their part in the war.

⑧

(A) The Alliance of 1778 with France helped provide the margin of victory in the American Revolution.

⑨

(B) The need for prompt action to confirm the Louisiana Purchase made a constitutional amendment impractical. Therefore, Jefferson had to reverse his position and accept a loose interpretation.

⑩

(C) Britain's trade with the newly independent countries of Latin America was of even greater volume than ours. She feared that the return of Spain would mean an end to her trade.

⑪

(C) Nationalism was fostered as a device to defeat Napoleon by urging the subject peoples to demand their own government.

⑫

(A) The graph shows that in 1947 about 24 million families earned less than $5,000, and in 1960 the number had dropped to 19 million. At the same time the families earning over $5,000 increased from about 13 million to over 26 million.

⑬

(C) This group more than doubled. It had an increase of 5 million.

⑭

(C) This principle of the "natural rights of man," formulated by Locke and advocated by Rousseau in France, was written by Thomas Jefferson in the Declaration of Independence.

⑮

(B) This statement is from Lincoln's most famous short speech—the Gettysburg Address.

⑯

(E) This is the Third Amendment of the Bill of Rights.

⑰

(B) The slogan, "Fifty-four forty [54° 40'] or fight," implied that we were unwilling to settle for less than complete control of the Oregon Territory.

⑱

(C) One of the pledges in the original program of the Republican Party was to favor repeal of the Kansas-Nebraska Act.

⑲

(C) Lincoln had steadfastly maintained that he would not interfere with slavery in the states, but opposed its extension into the territories.

⑳

(B) In 1860 Lincoln was elected with about 40 percent of the vote. In 1912 Wilson received about 45 percent. Both were elected.

㉑

(A) Garfield was shot by a rejected job-seeker in 1881. The Pendleton Act of 1883 set up a fair merit system for government employees.

㉒

(C) The Open Door Policy enabled the United States to invest in other countries' spheres of influence.

㉓

(D) The United States was too busy at home to look elsewhere.

㉔

(B) Mahan was a strong advocate of sea power.

㉕

(C) "Dollar diplomacy" implies a profit motive.

㉖

(A) Americans living in Hawaii wanted United States control to protect themselves.

㉗

(A) All the statements are correct.

㉘

(C) Gompers learned from the earlier failures in union organizing and limited himself to skilled workers.

㉙

(B) In 1887 Congress passed the Interstate Commerce Act, and in 1890 the Sherman Anti-Trust Act was passed.

㉚

(A) The United States attempted to avoid both England and France. Since we (New England) existed on trade with both, we could not afford to lose the friendship of either.

㉛

(D) The Azimuthal Equidistant projection is accurate for Great Circle arcs.

㉜

(E) Since the Orthographic projection is based on visual perception of a sphere, only one side (hemisphere) can be shown at a time.

㉝

(A) Mercator projections distort land masses at the upper and lower ends of the map, but compass directions remain fixed.

㉞

(C) The interruptions in Goode's Interrupted projection occur at points that cut into the sea areas. Thus the oceans cannot be viewed in their entirety.

㉟

(C) Southern needs for manufactured goods were most usually filled by England, and protective tariffs became a burden to southern planters.

TEST V. WORLD HISTORY

1.D	4.E	7.B	10.D	13.A	15.C	17.C	19.E
2.B	5.D	8.B	11.A	14.B	16.D	18.C	20.B
3.D	6.E	9.D	12.B				

TEST V. EXPLANATORY ANSWERS

1. *(D)* The Tashkent Agreement of January 10, 1966 was between India (4) and Pakistan (3 and 5).

2. *(B)* The Battle of Dien Bien Phu meant the end of direct French influence in South Viet Nam (9) and North Viet Nam (10).

3. *(D)* Thailand (8), or Siam, is the only nation in Southeast Asia that has not been under colonial rule in modern times.

4. *(E)* President Theodore Roosevelt's intervention in the Anthracite Coal strike produced a settlement that was generally satisfactory to John Mitchell's United Mine Workers Union.

5. *(D)* President Theodore Roosevelt had to deal with President Porfirio Diaz of Mexico (1877-1911), Kaiser William II of Germany (1888-1918), and with Tsar Nicholas II of Russia (1894-1917).

6. *(E)* In response to opposition to Oriental immigration, particularly on the West Coast, President Theodore Roosevelt entered into a Gentlemen's Agreement with Japan, whereby Japan agreed to limit emmigration to the United States.

7. *(B)* The impressment of American seamen did not become a source of controversy with England until the Napoleonic Wars; when she attempted to suppress American trade with France.

8. *(B)* The Ostend Manifesto (1854) was drawn up by the American ministers to Great Britain, France, and Spain. It implied that if Spain refused to sell Cuba to the United States, the United States might have considered taking the island by force.

9. *(D)* England and the Netherlands were both Protestant nations. When the English and Dutch crowns were united after the Glorious Revolution in the person of William III (Orange), many Englishmen objected to his use of English troops and money to fight his Dutch wars.

10. *(D)* The power of the absolute monarchs increased as a result of the Commercial Revolution. The monarch and the rising merchant class found that it was to their mutual advantage to support each other against the old feudal aristocracy.

11. *(A)* Robert Bakewell began the scientific breeding of cattle and sheep for meat rather than for hides or wool.

12. *(B)* The correct pairing of authors and major works follow: Galileo Galilei, *Dialogue on Two New Sciences* and *Dialogue on the Two Chief World Systems;* Michel de Montaigne, *Essays*; Thomas More, *Utopia*; and John Locke, *Two Treatises on Government*. Additional correct pairings follow: Sir Isaac Newton, *Principia*; Desiderius Erasmus, *The Praise of Folly*; Thomas R. Malthus, *An Essay on Population;* and John Stuart Mill, *On Liberty.*

13. *(A)* The correct pairing of the other nineteenth century scientists is: Dalton, physics and atomic theory; Lamarck, naturalist and evolutionist; Lyell, Orientalist; and Roentgen, physics and discovery of the X-ray.

14. *(B)* Desiderius Erasmus believed that the Roman Catholic Church could be reformed from within; therefore, he did not break with the Church.

15. *(C)* The quotation is the opening sentence of Rousseau's *Social Contract*. Rousseau believed that government derives its authority from the people by virtue of their entering into a "contract" with government.

16. *(D)* An enlightened despot must devote considerable time and energy to governing his nation efficiently. He must also show concern for the welfare of his subjects. Louis XV was more interested in his own pleasures than in the welfare of his nation and subjects.

17. *(C)* Emphasis in the Revolution of 1789 was on political rather than on social or economic reform. By 1848, with the emergence of an industrial proletariat, there was greater demand for social and economic reforms.

18. *(C)* The Chartist Movement was championed by supporters of democratic principles. Each of the other alternatives was championed by the forces of reaction.

19. *(E)* The Beard Thesis implies that the majority of the delegates to the Philadelphia Convention were men of property and their interest in preserving that property influenced the positions they took on Constitutional issues.

20. *(B)* The Whiskey Rebellion was the first test of the federal government's power to operate directly against individual citizens within the states. President Washington used his powers under the Constitution to put down the rebels, and to provide an example for future agitators.

SCORE YOURSELF

Compare your answers to the Correct Key Answers at the end of the Examination. To determine your score, count the number of correct answers in each test. Then count the number of incorrect answers. Subtract ¼ of the number of incorrect answers from the number of correct answers. Plot the resulting figure on the graph below by blackening the bar under each test to the point of your score. Plan your study to strengthen the weaknesses indicated on your scoring graph.

EXAM V SOCIAL SCIENCES-HISTORY	Very Poor	Poor	Average	Good	Excellent
GOVERNMENT 22 Questions	1-3	4-8	9-14	15-19	20-22
ECONOMICS 23 Questions	1-3	4-8	9-15	16-20	21-23
SOCIOLOGY 50 Questions	1-7	8-18	19-33	34-44	45-50
AMERICAN HISTORY 35 Questions	1-6	7-14	15-24	25-31	32-35
WORLD HISTORY 20 Questions	1-3	4-8	9-14	15-17	18-20

SOCIAL STUDIES GLOSSARY

This is some of the language you're likely to see on your examination. You may not need to know all the words in this carefully prepared glossary, but if even a few appear, you'll be that much ahead of your competitors. Perhaps the greater benefit from this list is the frame of mind it can create for you. Without reading a lot of technical text you'll steep yourself in just the right atmosphere for high test marks.

This glossary was created to help you master some of the key words and terms you will meet in the Social Studies section of the test. You will notice that certain words or phrases have been italicized in the definitions. This means those words or phrases are defined in the glossary.

[A]

age   An historical period. The Elizabethan Age, for example, refers to the time when Queen Elizabeth I was on the throne of England. Also see *era* and *epoch*.

American Federation of Labor and Congress of Industrial Organizations (AFL-CIO)   A group of American labor *unions* joined together in a huge federation. AFL-CIO is the unification of two federations, the American Federation of Labor (AFL) with the Congress of Industrial Organizations (CIO). The AFL began in 1881. The CIO was formed in 1935. The merger of the two groups took place in 1955.

anarchist   A believer in the idea that any government is an evil institution and should be eliminated.

Antarctic Circle   An imaginary line around the earth which is about 23½ degrees from the South *Pole*. See *Arctic Circle*.

anthropology   The study of man, how he lives and his customs.

archaeology   The study of how man lived in the past. This is usually done by investigating ancient buildings, household articles, etc.

Arctic Circle   An imaginary line about 23½ degrees south of the North *Pole*. See *Antarctic Circle*.

aristocracy (1) government by a group of people who are considered to be the highest social *class*; (2) a social class with special privileges.

atomic An adjective that in social studies refers to the splitting of the atom to produce energy, as exemplified by the atomic bomb, *hydrogen bomb*, and nuclear energy.

automation The replacement of the work of people by machines.

[B]

ballot A vote in elections.

Bill of Rights The first ten amendments to the *Constitution* of the United States, in which the *rights* of citizens are specifically stated.

Bolshevik A Russian communist. This term was used in the first half of the 20th century, but is not commonly used now. See *communism*.

bureaucracy A term usually referring to the institutions and power of the federal government.

[C]

cabinet In the United States, a body of people specially chosen by the President to advise him and to manage certain branches of the government.

capitalism An *economic* system in which companies or individuals own and manage most or all of a nation's economic activity.

caucus A meeting of politicians who decide on the policies and candidates of their *political party*.

Central Intelligence Agency (CIA) An agency of the United States government which collects and evaluates secret data of other countries.

civic An adjective referring to citizenship. "Voting is a civic duty" means each citizen should vote in elections.

civics The study of citizenship, dealing especially with the *rights* and duties of citizens.

civil disobedience The doctrine that citizens do not have to obey unjust laws, and have the *right* and duty to demonstrate against them in order to have them eliminated.

civil rights The *rights* belonging to all citizens. In recent years in the United States, the term has mainly referred to the struggle of black people, especially in the South, to obtain the *right* to vote and to equal opportunities.

civilization A social system which is highly developed and complex, as opposed to primitive society which is simple and centers around a small group of people, or a tribe. *Western Civilization* refers to the *culture* of the nations of Europe and the American continents. *Eastern Civilization* refers to the culture of the nations of Asia.

class   Usually in social studies, this term refers to social class. According to some people, *society* is divided into several distinct groups, such as the working class, aristocracy, etc.

Cold War   Following World War II, hostility developed between the communistic nations led by the Soviet Union and the more democratic nations of *Western Civilization*, led by the United States. This period has been called "the Cold War."

colony   A land area owned and ruled by a nation usually separated by distance. The United States, for example, was once a colony of Great Britain.

confederation   A banding together of various groups for specific reasons, such as defense, trade, etc.

Congress of the United States   A term referring to the *House of Representatives* and the *Senate of the United States.*

Congress of Industrial Organizations (CIO)   See *American Federation of Labor and Congress of Industrial Organizations (AFL-CIO).*

conservative   A person who believes in maintaining existing social and governmental institutions with little or no change. This word is also an adjective. "A conservative person" is one with conservative views. See *radical* and *liberal.*

Continental Congress   (1) First Continental Congress: The group of American delegates from the 13 *colonies* who met before the American Revolution to discuss and protest British laws. (2) Second Continental Congress: The group of delegates from the 13 colonies that conducted the American Revolution. See *Declaration of Independence.*

constituents   Those people who are represented by a representative or representatives in a legislative body. For example, all the people living in a Congressional District are constituents of the member of the *House of Representatives* elected from that district.

Constitution   Rules that form the duties and rights of a particular social or governmental body. The Constitution of the United States sets forth the structure of the federal government, its responsibilities, limits of power, and rights of citizens.

communism   The idea that in the perfect *society* all goods will be owned commonly by all citizens. For more than one hundred years, communism has usually meant the doctrine held by Karl Marx. See *Marxism.* Certain nations, such as the Soviet Union, are referred to as communist nations.

Counter-Reformation   An *era* in the history of the Roman Catholic Church (1545–1648) in which clerical leaders reformed the church. This was done as a result of the *Reformation.*

culture   The total of the customs, beliefs, arts, skills and practices of a *society* or *civilization.*

[D]

Dark Ages   An *era* in Europe following the breakdown of the *Roman Empire* and lasting until about 1000. Government in this period was either chaotic or almost nonexistent, and barbarians looted cities at will with little resistance.

Declaration of Independence   A paper written mainly by Thomas Jefferson at the direction of the Second *Continental Congress*. It set forth the reasons that the American *colonies* decided to break away from Great Britain. It is considered one of the greatest documents stating human *rights* ever written.

deflation   A general lowering in the prices for goods and services. See *inflation*.

defranchisement   The taking away of the *right* to vote.

democracy   To the Ancient Greeks, this term meant direct rule of the people in which all governmental policies would be decided at a meeting of all citizens. This meaning has been modified to denote representative government in which elected representatives of the people decide governmental policies. The United States is a democracy in this last sense.

democrat   (1) A believer in *democracy*. (2) A member of the Democratic *political party* of the United States.

depression   In social studies, a period in which there is widespread unemployment due to an acute reduction in business activity and industrial production. See *prosperity* and *recession*.

dictator   An absolute ruler of a country, either one legally elected who declares that an emergency necessitates his absolute rule, or one who seizes power by force.

diplomacy   In social studies, the method by which nations negotiate with each other.

dynasty   A series of rulers, usually lasting for at least one hundred years, of the same family.

[E]

Eastern Civilization   See *civilization*.

Eastern Hemisphere   See *hemisphere*.

ecology   A biological science dealing with the balance of nature, or the delicate relationship between living things and their *environments*.

economics   A social science that is the study of the way man produces, distributes and uses goods.

electorate   The people who have the *right* to vote in an election.

empire   A group of different nations ruled by a single powerful nation. See *Roman Empire*.

enfranchisement   (1) The act of freeing slaves. (2) The granting of the *rights* of citizenship.

environment   Surroundings.

epoch   An historical period of importance. See *era* and *age*.

Equator   An imaginary line extending around the earth. It lies exactly halfway between the North and South *Poles*.

era   An important historical period. See *epoch* and *age*.

ethnic   An adjective referring to the identification of people with the same language, customs, etc., into one group.

[F]

Fair Deal   A social reform program of President Harry S. Truman.

fascism   A particular kind of government that controls all activities of a nation. Italy under the *dictator* Benito Mussolini and Germany under the *dictator* Adolf Hitler are examples of fascist governments. Unlike *democracy*, in a fascist government all political, social and religious opposition to the government is ruthlessly crushed.

federalism   A political union among various states or regions in which much of the political power is given to a national government.

Federalist Party   A *political party* of the United States which advocated a strong national government. It lasted until 1816.

feudalism   A social, political and economic system that flourished throughout most of Europe during the *Middle Ages*. It had a rigid *class* system. Governments were controlled by chiefs or lords. The people ruled by the lords were called vassals. Vassals owed absolute obedience to the lord who made and enforced laws and levied taxes. The lord, on the other hand, owed the vassal protection against outside invaders. In this period, nations were weak.

[G]

geography   The study of the physical world and man's relationship to it.

Gettysburg Address   A moving speech by President Abraham Lincoln at the dedication of the cemetery at Gettysburg, Pennsylvania, on November 19, 1863. The cemetery was the burial ground for Union soldiers who had been killed at the Battle of Gettysburg.

graft   The getting of money dishonestly, usually by bribery. This term specifically refers to political dishonesty.

Gross National Product   The total value of all goods produced and services rendered in a country over one year.

[H]

hemisphere   Half of the globe or earth. All the earth north of the *Equator* is called the Northern Hemisphere. All the earth south of the *Equator* is called the Southern Hemisphere. The half of the globe that contains North and South America is called the Western Hemisphere. The half of the earth containing Europe, Asia, Africa and Australia is called the Eastern Hemisphere.

House of Representatives   The more numerous legislative body of the United States, in which representation is based on the population of each state. Together with the *Senate*, it forms the *Congress* of the country.

hydrogen bomb   An extremely powerful *atomic* bomb set off by the fusion of hydrogen atoms.

[I]

ideology   A system of strongly held beliefs. *Communism* is an ideology, as is *democracy*.

immigrant   A person who has left the country of his birth to live in another country.

incumbent   A person who holds a political office.

indenture   In social studies, a contract by which one promises to work for a specified period. In colonial America, a person wishing to come to the English *colonies* would promise to work for an American for a time (usually seven years) in return for the cost of the sea voyage. The indentured servant, as such an *immigrant* was called, had few *rights*. He or she was little more than a slave. Unlike a slave, though, he or she received freedom when the contract was finished.

Industrial Revolution   A period in history beginning in the eighteenth century, and, according to some historians, still going on today. In this *era*, man has invented many machines to aid him in his work and make his life more comfortable. The *epoch* has also seen the creation of the factory system as opposed to the making of goods at home.

inflation   A general rise in the prices for goods and services. See *deflation*.

isolationism   In social studies, the belief that a nation best conducts its affairs by avoiding becoming involved in the affairs of other countries.

[L]

League of Nations   An organization of nations created in 1920 with the purpose of avoiding world war by open negotiation. The League is considered a failure since World War II broke out in 1939. It was discontinued in 1946 when the United Nations came into existence.

left In social studies, the body of people who are *liberals*, socialists, communists and *anarchists*. See *socialism* and *communism*. In other words, the left is made up of people who believe in changing national institutions. See *right*.

liberal A person who believes in modifying national institutions by peaceful methods. The word is also an adjective. A "liberal person" is one holding liberal views. See *conservative*.

[M]

Marxism Named after Karl Marx, a German, who founded this theory of *socialism*. He believed the working class was underpaid and did not get a fair share of what it produced. This would eventually lead to world revolution, after which a new communistic world *society* would be born. See *communism*. Many nations follow Marx's theories, the leader being the Soviet Union.

medieval An adjective referring to the *Middle Ages*.

metropolitan An adjective referring to the city and its surrounding area. See *urban* and *suburban*.

Middle Ages A period of stability in Europe following the *Dark Ages*. *Feudalism* prevailed in this *era* which lasted approximately from 1000 to 1450. Some historians include the Dark Ages in the Middle Ages.

militarism A view that the military forces ought to be the strongest institution in *society*, perhaps even lead the government.

monarchist A person who believes the best form of government is one headed by a king or queen.

monopoly Absolute control or ownership of a product by a single individual, a small group of people, or a corporation.

Monroe Doctrine A doctrine set forth by President James Monroe in 1823, warning European nations not to make any more colonies in the *Western Hemisphere*. See *colony*.

[N]

National Socialism Another term for *Nazism*.

nationalism A belief in the superiority of one's nation above all other nations.

Nazism The form *fascism* took in Germany from 1933 to 1945 under the *dictator* Adolf Hitler. In Nazism, all rights of dissent or mild opposition were brutally suppressed. The Nazi Party was the only *political party*. Nazis believed the "race" they belonged to was superior to all others. For this reason, they killed millions of Jews and other minority peoples during their cruel reign. Led by Hitler, Germany began World War II and was finally defeated in 1945. See *racism*, *National Socialism*.

New Deal   A program of social reform carried out by President Franklin Roosevelt during his terms of office (1933–1945).

New Frontier   A program of social reform stated as an aim of his administration by President John F. Kennedy in 1961 and partly carried out by himself and his successor, President Lyndon B. Johnson.

North Atlantic Treaty Organization (NATO)   A *confederation* of nations in Western Europe and North America, bound together in a defense pact to protect any or all of the members against an attack by the Soviet Union or any communist nation. See *communism*.

North Pole   See *poles*.

Northern Hemisphere   See *hemisphere*.

[O, P]

oligarchy   A government ruled by a very small body of people.

parliament   A legislative body. The best known is the British Parliament, consisting of a House of Commons (somewhat like our *House of Representatives)* and a House of Lords.

party (political)   A group of people bound together and dedicated to winning control of a government so they can put their ideas into force. The two leading parties in the United States are the Democratic Party and the Republican Party.

peonage   A system in which a person, usually a farm worker, is forced to work in order to pay off a debt. This system was long in use in Latin America, and was little better than slavery.

physical map   A map showing the physical features of the land. Colors usually indicate elevation.

plutocracy   Control of government by rich people.

poles   The two ends of the axis the earth revolves on. The northern axis end is called the *North Pole*. The southern axis end is called the *South Pole*.

political map   A map emphasizing political units. Usually the colors on such maps stand for different countries, states, or other political units.

political science   The study of government.

politics   (1) The management of government. (2) The contests of *political parties* for power.

primary elections   Elections held by one *political party* in various states, in which the candidates are selected to run against candidates of the other party or parties.

propaganda   The spreading of certain political ideas, usually in printed form or by TV, radio, or film.

prosperity   In social studies, a time when there is little unemployment and most people have enough money to purchase goods and services in substantial amounts. See *depression* and *recession*.

public ownership   The ownership and management by government of certain services. The postal system is an example of public ownership.

public works program   Projects run and paid for by government. This kind of program is usually begun by governments in times of *depression* or *recession* in order to reduce unemployment.

[R]

racism   A false viewpoint, which believes that one group of people are superior in all ways to other groups of peoples. For example, the Nazis believed that people of German stock were superior to all other peoples of the world. See *Nazism*.

radical   A person who holds extreme positions on either the *right* or *left*, and would like to see his views adopted without delay and possibly with violence. This word is also an adjective, as in "holding radical views."

ratify   To approve. The Senate of the United States has to approve or ratify all treaties with other nations. See *treaty*.

reactionary   A person who would like to see government or *society* in general return to methods, laws, and customs that have been discarded. This is also an adjective, as in "holding reactionary views."

recession   A limited period when unemployment rises and business activity and industrial output slow down. A period of *recession* is not as long, nor is it as devastating, as a *depression*. See *prosperity*.

Reformation   An historical *era* of the Sixteenth Century. Generally recognized as the person who began the Reformation *Age*, Martin Luther, a German monk, protested the corruption that had crept into many areas of the Roman Catholic Church. The protest led to the formation of Protestant sects throughout Europe. See *Counter-Reformation*.

Renaissance   An historical period in Europe (from about 1300 to 1600) that marked a shift from the God-centered life of the *Middle Ages* to greater emphasis upon man and his place in the universe. It was a remarkably creative *era* in all fields, including art, science, exploration, and religious thought.

republic   A type of government in which the people govern through their elected representatives. Today republic has the same meaning as *democracy*.

republican   (1) A believer in the republican form of government. (2) A member of the Republican *political party* of the United States.

right   (1) In social studies, the body of people who are *conservatives*, *reactionaries*, and *fascists*. See *reactionary* and *fascism*. In other words, the right is made up of people who wish no changes in *society*, or wish to return to discarded institutions or methods, or wish to impose a dictatorial type of government. See *left* and *dictator*. (2) A right is also used to refer to a privilege that is the property of every citizen, such as the right to vote in the United States.

Roman Empire   A period in Roman history dating from 27 B.C. to 395 A.D. during which the Romans conquered and ruled a large area of Europe as well as portions of Africa and Asia. See *empire*.

rural   An adjective referring to areas which are not part of a *metropolitan* region.

[S]

Senate   (1) The general meaning is one body of a two-body legislature, such as the Roman Senate. (2) The Senate of the United States consists of two members representing each state, or 100 members in all. See *House of Representatives*.

socialism   A social system by which all the people own or control industries and public services. Many people look upon Karl Marx as the founder of socialism, as he was of communism. However, there were advocates of socialism before Marx. Socialists in general are considered *democratic*, preferring to gain their ends by peaceful means as opposed to advocates of *communism* who would resort to violent means to impose their system if peaceful means failed. See *Marxism*.

society   The social order of a nation. See *culture*.

sociology   A science which studies man's behavior when he is in a *society*.

South Pole   See *poles*.

Southern Hemisphere   See *hemisphere*.

strike   In social studies, the refusal of employees to work until they achieve certain conditions. Usually a strike is organized by a labor *union*. A strike might be called in order to gain higher pay or better working conditions or special benefits, such as pensions for workers when they retire.

suburb   A community near a city from which many people go to the city to work. A suburb is considered to be in a metropolitan area. See *urban* and *rural*.

suburban   An adjective referring to communities near a city from which many people go to the city to work. A *suburb* is considered to be within a *metropolitan* area. See *urban* and *rural*.

[T]

tariff   A tax levied on goods entering one nation from another.

theocracy   A government ruled by members of the clergy.

topography   The physical features of the earth. See *physical map*.

totalitarianism   Any form of government which is dictatorial in nature and allows the citizen few, if any, *rights*. Communist and fascist governments are examples of totalitarian governments. See *communism*, *fascism*, and *Nazism*.

trade route   A route over which goods are sent in great numbers. Trade routes may be by water or by land.

treaty   An agreement between nations. See *diplomacy* and *ratify*.

Tropic of Cancer   An imaginary line extending around the earth at 23½ degrees north of the *Equator*. See *Tropic of Capricorn*, *Arctic Circle*, and *Antarctic Circle*.

Tropic of Capricorn   An imaginary line extending around the earth at 23½ degrees south of the *Equator*. See *Tropic of Cancer*, *Arctic Circle*, and *Antarctic Circle*.

[U, V]

union   (1) A banding together of separate political units to gain certain ends. The United States is a union of fifty states. See *federalism*. (2) A *labor* union is an organization of workers formed to protect individual *rights* and gain better working conditions. See *American Federation of Labor* and *Congress of Industrial Organizations*.

urban   An adjective referring to a city. See *rural*, *suburb*, *suburban* and *metropolitan*.

veto   A *right* to forbid a law or proposed action of a legislative body from taking effect. The President of the United States can veto a proposed law passed by the *Senate* and *House of Representatives*. However, a two-thirds vote in favor of the proposed law by the members present in the Senate and House of Representatives can overturn the veto.

[W]

welfare   A system by which poor people who are unemployed can receive assistance from government in the form of money, housing, and food.

Western Civilization   See *civilization*.

Western Hemisphere   See *hemisphere*.

Whig Party   A *political party* of the United States which opposed the Democratic Party. It started in 1832 and had disappeared by 1860.

FOR FURTHER STUDY

ARCO BOOKS FOR MORE HELP

Now what? You've read and studied the whole book, and there's still time before you take the test. You're probably better prepared than most of your competitors, but you may feel insecure about one or more of the probable test subjects. If so, you can still do something about it. Glance over this comprehensive list of books written with a view to solving your problems. One of them may be just what you need at this time . . . for the extra help that will assure your success.

EDUCATIONAL BOOKS

American College Testing Program Exams 04363-6 5.00
Arco Arithmetic Q & A Review, Turner 02351-1 4.00
Arco's Handbook of Job and Career Opportunities 04328-8 3.95
Better Business English, Classen 04287-7 2.95
Catholic High School Entrance Examination 00987-X 5.00
The College Board's Examination, McDonough & Hansen 02623-5 5.00
College By Mail, Jensen 02592-1 4.00
College Entrance Tests, Turner 01858-5 5.00
College-Level Examination Program (CLEP), Turner 04150-1 6.00
The Easy Way to Better Grades, Froe & Froe 03352-5 1.50
Elements of Debate, Klopf & McCroskey 01901-8 4.00
Encyclopedia of English, Zeiger 00655-X 2.50
English Grammar: 1,000 Steps 02012-1 5.00
English Grammar and Usage for Test-Takers, Turner 04014-9 5.00
Good English with Ease, revised edition, Beckoff 03911-6 4.00
Guide to Financial Aids for Students in Arts and Sciences
   for Graduate and Professional Study, Searles & Scott 02496-8 3.95
High School Entrance and Scholarship Tests, Turner 00666-8 5.00
High School Entrance Examinations—Special Public and
   Private High Schools 02143-8 5.00
How to Obtain Money for College, Lever 03932-9 5.00
How to Prepare Your College Application, Kussin & Kussin 01310-9 2.00
How to Use a Pocket Calculator, Mullish 04072-6 4.95
How to Write Reports, Papers, Theses, Articles, Riebel 02391-0 5.00
Mastering General Mathematics, McDonough 03732-6 5.00
New York State Regents Scholarship 00400-2 5.00
Organization and Outlining, Peirce 02425-9 4.95
Preliminary Scholastic Aptitude Tests—National Merit
   Scholarship Qualifying Tests (PSAT-NMSQT) 00413-4 4.00
Practice for Scholastic Aptitude Tests 04303-2 1.50
Scholastic Aptitude Tests 04341-5 5.00
Scoring High on Reading Tests 00731-1 5.00
Triple Your Reading Speed, Cutler 02083-0 5.00
Typing for Everyone, Levine .... 02212-4 E 3.95

GED PREPARATION

Comprehensive Math Review for the High School
   Equivalency Diploma Test, McDonough 03420-3 4.00
High School Equivalency Diploma Tests, Turner 00110-0 5.00
New High School Equivalency Diploma Tests, Turner 04451-9 4.95
Preliminary Arithmetic for the High School Equivalency
   Diploma Test 02165-9 4.00

Preliminary Practice for the High School Equivalency
   Diploma Test 01441-3 5.00
Preparation for the Spanish High School Equivalency
   Diploma (Preparacion Para El Exam De Equivalencia
   De La Escuela Superior—En Espanol) 02618-9 6.00
Step-By-Step Guide to Correct English, Pulaski 03402-5 3.95

COLLEGE BOARD ACHIEVEMENT TESTS/CBAT

American History and Social Studies Achievement Test,
   Altman 01722-8 1.45
American History and Social Studies Achievement Test 04337-7 3.95
Biology Achievement Test—Second Edition,
   Solomon & Spector 04094-7 3.95
Chemistry Achievement Test 04103-3 3.95
English Composition Achievement Test 04338-5 3.95
English Composition Achievement Test .... 01247-1 .95
French Achievement Teest, Biezunski & Boisrond 01668-X 1.45
German Achievement Test, Greiner 01698-1 1.45
Latin Achievement Test 01743-0 1.45
Mathematics: Level I Achievement Test, Bramson 03847-0 3.00
Mathematics: Level II Achievement Test, Bramson .... 01456-3 .95
Physics Achievement Test, Bruenn 01265-X 1.95
Spanish Achievement Test, Jassey 01741-4 1.45

ARCO COLLEGE CREDIT TEST-TUTORS CLEP/AP

American History: CLEP and AP Subject Examination,
   Woloch 03804-7 4.95
Advanced Placement and College Level Examinations
   in Calculus 03802-0 8.95
Advanced Placement and College Level Examinations
   in Chemistry 04484-5 4.95
Advanced Placement and College Level Examinations
   in English—Analysis and Interpretation
   of Literature 04406-3 5.95
Advanced Placement and College Board Achievement
   Tests in Physics 04493-4 5.95
Advanced Placement, College Level Examination and
   College Board Achievement Tests
   in European History 04407-1 5.95
College Level Examinations in Composition and
   Freshman English 03798-9 4.95
College Level Examinations in Mathematics 04339-3 5.95

LR—Library Reinforced Binding

GED PREPARATION

Comprehensive Math Review for the High School
  Equivalency Diploma Test, McDonough 03420-3 4.00
High School Equivalency Diploma Tests, Turner 00110-0 5.00
New High School Equivalency Diploma Tests, Turner 04451-9 4.95
Preliminary Arithmetic for the High School Equivalency
  Diploma Test 02165-9 4.00
Preliminary Practice for the High School Equivalency
  Diploma Test 01441-3 5.00
Preparation for the Spanish High School Equivalency
  Diploma (Preparacion Para El Exam De Equivalencia
  De La Escuela Superior—En Espanol) 02618-9 6.00
Step-By-Step Guide to Correct English, Pulaski 03402-5 3.95

General Education Development Series

Correctness and Effectiveness of Expression (English HSEDT),
  Castellano, Guercio & Seitz 03688-5 4.00
General Mathematical Ability (Mathematics HSEDT),
  Castellano, Guercio & Seitz 03689-3 4.00
Reading Interpretation in Social Sciences, Natural Sciences,
  and Literature (Reading HSEDT), Castellano, Guercio & Seitz 03690-7 4.00
Teacher's Manual for the GED Series, Castellano,
  Guercio & Seitz 03692-3 2.50

COLLEGE BOARD ACHIEVEMENT TESTS/CBAT

American History and Social Studies Achievement Test,
  Altman 01722-8 1.45
American History and Social Studies Achievement Test—
  Second Edition 04337-7 3.95
Biology Achievement Test—Second Edition,
  Solomon & Spector 04094-7 3.95

Chemistry Achievement Test 04103-3 3.95
English Composition Achievement Test 04338-5 3.95
English Composition Achievement Test .... 01247-1 .95
French Achievement Teest, Biezunski & Boisrond 01668-X 1.45
German Achievement Test, Greiner 01698-1 1.45
Latin Achievement Test 01743-0 1.45
Mathematics: Level I Achievement Test, Bramson 03847-0 3.00
Mathematics: Level II Achievement Test, Bramson .... 01456-3 .95
Physics Achievement Test, Bruenn 01265-X 1.95
Spanish Achievement Test, Jassey 01741-4 1.45

ARCO COLLEGE CREDIT TEST-TUTORS CLEP/AP

American History: CLEP and AP Subject Examination,
  Woloch 03804-7 4.95
Advanced Placement and College Level Examinations
  in Calculus 03802-0 8.95
Advanced Placement and College Level Examinations
  in Chemistry 04484-5 4.95
Advanced Placement and College Level Examinations
  in English—Analysis and Interpretation
  of Literature 04406-3 5.95
Advanced Placement and College Board Achievement
  Tests in Physics 04493-4 5.95
Advanced Placement, College Level Examination and
  College Board Achievement Tests
  in European History 04407-1 5.95
College Level Examinations in Composition and
  Freshman English 03798-9 4.95
College Level Examinations in Mathematics 04339-3 5.95

PROFESSIONAL CAREER EXAM SERIES

Action Guide for Executive Job Seekers and Employers, Uris ... 01787-2 3.95
Automobile Mechanic Certification Tests, Sharp 03809-8 6.00
Bar Exams 01124-6 5.00
The C.P.A. Exam: Accounting by the "Parallel Point"
  Method, Lipscomb 02020-2 15.00
Certificate in Data Processing Examination, Morrison 04032-7 12.00
Certified General Automobile Mechanic, Turner 02900-5 6.00
Computer Programmer, Luftig 01232-3 6.00
Computers and Automation, Brown 01745-7 5.00
Dental Admission Test, Arco Editorial Board 04293-1 6.00
Graduate Management Admission Test 04360-1 6.00
Graduate Record Examination Aptitude Test 00824-5 5.00
Health Insurance Agent (Hospital, Accident, Health, Life) 02153-5 5.00
How a Computer System Works, Brown & Workman 03424-6 5.95
How to Become a Successful Model—
  Second Edition, Krem 04508-6 2.95
How to Get Into Medical and Dental School, revised edition,
  Shugar, Shugar & Bauman 04095-5 4.00
How to Make Money in Music, Harris & Farrar 04089-0 5.95
How to Remember Anything, Markoff, Dubin & Carcel 03929-9 5.00
The Installation and Servicing of Domestic
  Oil Burners, Mitchell & Mitchell 00437-1 10.00
Insurance Agent and Broker 02149-7 8.00
Law School Admission Test, Turner 00840-7 5.00
Life Insurance Agent 02343-0 6.00
Life Insurance Agent, Snouffer 04306-7 8.00
Medical College Admission Test, Turner 04289-3 6.00
Miller Analogies Test—1400 Analogy Questions 01114-9 4.00

Notary Public 00180-1 6.00
Nursing School Entrance Examinations, Turner 01202-1 6.00
Oil Burner Installer 00096-1 6.00
The Official 1977-78 Guide to Airline Careers, Morton 03955-8 5.95
Playground and Recreation Director's Handbook 01096-7 6.00
Principles of Data Processing, Morrison 04268-0 7.50
Quizzer for Students of Education, Walton 01447-4 4.00
Real Estate License Examination, Gladstone 03755-5 6.00
Refrigeration License Manual, Harfenist 02726-6 10.00
Resumes for Job Hunters, Shykind 03961-2 5.00
Resumes That Get Jobs, revised edition, Resume Service 03909-4 3.00
Security Representatives' Examinations, Stefano 01934-4 5.00
Simplify Legal Writing, Biskind 03801-2 5.00
Spanish for Nurses and Allied Health Science Students,
  Hernandez-Miyares & Alba 04127-7 10.00
Stationary Engineer and Fireman 00070-8 8.00
The Test of English as a Foreign
  Language (TOEFL), Moreno, Babin & Scallon 04450-0 8.00
Veterinary College Admissions 04147-1 10.00
Your Resume—Key to a Better Job, Corwen 03733-4 4.00

ADVANCED GRE SERIES

Biology: Advanced Test for the G.R.E., Solomon 04310-5 4.95
Business: Advanced Test for the G.R.E., Berman.
  Malea & Yearwood 01599-3 4.95
Chemistry: Advanced Test for the G.R.E., Weiss 01069-X 4.95
Economics: Advanced Test for the G.R.E., Zabrenski &
  Heydari-Darafshian 01557-8 4.95

S3693

MEDICAL TEXTBOOKS

The Basis of Clinical Diagnosis, Parkins & Pegrum 03660-5 12.00
Differential Diagnosis, Beck, Francis & Souhami 03495-5 12.00
Differential Diagnosis in Gynecology, Vonter & Gamette 04129-3 12.00
Differential Diagnosis in Otolaryngology, Lee 04017-3 14.00
Differential Diagnosis of Renal and Electrolyte Disorders 04063-7 14.00
Modern Medicine, Read et al. 04124-2 14.75
Psychiatry: A Concise Textbook for Primary
  Care Practitioners, Kraft et al. 03924-8 12.00

NURSING REVIEW BOOKS

Child Health Nursing Review, Porter 03468-8 6.00
Maternal Health Nursing Review, Sagebeer 03456-4 6.00
Medical-Surgical Nursing Review, Hazzard 03645-1 6.00
Nutrition/Diet Therapy Nursing Review, Boykin 03382-7 6.00
Practical Nursing Review, Redempta 03488-2 6.00
Psychiatric/Mental Health Nursing Review,
  Rodgers & McGovern 03374-6 6.00
How to Talk to Doctors, Verby & Verby 03956-6 1.75

ARCO'S CAREER GUIDANCE SERIES

Your Future

in Air Conditioning and Refrigeration 02224-8 2.95
in Animal Services 04259-1 2.95
in Art and Design 04141-2 2.95
in Automotive Service 02226-4 2.95
in Banking 02233-7 2.95
in Beauty Culture 02235-3 2.95
in Broadcasting 03427-0 2.95
in Construction 04435-7 2.95
as a Dental Assistant 02238-8 2.95
in Dentistry 02239-6 2.95
as a Dietician 02240-X 2.95
in the Electronic Computer Field 02241-8 2.95
as an Electronic Technician 02228-0 2.95
in Forestry 02245-0 2.95
in the High Fidelity Industry 02246-9 2.95
as a Home Economist 02247-7 2.95
in Hospital Work 02230-2 2.95
in Hotel Management 02248-5 2.95
in Insurance 02249-3 2.95
in Jobs Abroad 02251-5 2.95
as a Job Applicant 03861-6 2.95

Your Future

in Law Enforcement 02252-3 2.95
in Library Careers 03913-2 2.95
in Medical Assisting 02253-1 2.95
in Medical Technology 02254-X 2.95
in the Military Services 04011-4 2.95
in NASA 02255-8 2.95
in Nursing Careers 03429-7 2.95
in Office Occupations 04434-9 2.95
in Optometry 02259-0 2.95
in Photography 02262-0 2.95
as a Physician 02263-9 2.95
as a Pilot 02260-4 2.95
in Publishing 03428-9 2.95
in Real Estate 02264-7 2.95
in Restaurants and Food Service 02229-9 2.95
in Salesmanship and Sales Mgmt. 03915-9 2.95
in Technical and Science Writing 03914-0 2.95
in Theater, Radio, Television
  or Filmmaking 04445-4 2.95
in Veterinary Medicine 03916-7 2.95
in Your Own Business 02236-1 2.95

S3693